tarot tales and magic spells

Demystifying Tarot Readings and Meanings One Card at a Time.

lorelai hamilton

also by lorelai hamilton

Lorelai Hamilton

Find Your Bliss

Teenage Witch's Grimoire

Tarot Reflection Journal

Tarot Refection Journal Coloring The Tarot

The Eclectic Witch's Grimoire

Dream Journal

Teenage Tarot

Tarot Tales and Magic Spells

Arcane In Verse

Unlock the secrets of the Tarot! Subscribe to Lorelai Hamilton's newsletter and get a free ebook. Whether you're a seasoned reader or just curious, this guide will enhance your journey. Plus, be the first to know about upcoming books, events, and more!

Additional Books by Rainbow Quartz Publishing

Jax Wilder

Tarot Fantasies Series

The Devil's Temptations

Strength of the Beast

Hanged Passions
Death's Embrace
3 of Swords
6 of Cups

Coral Cove Series

<u>Sleighed by Love</u>

<u>Harvesting Love</u>

<u>Dawning Desire</u>

Knead You Now

Love Rewound

Haunted by Her

Perfect Lover Spell

Miranda Levi

<u>From A Youth A Fountain Did Flow</u>

<u>The Sea Withdrew</u>

<u>A Tear In Time</u>

<u>Mo(ther) Na(ture)</u>

<u>In Orion's Hands</u>

Jackson Anhalt

<u>From The 911 Files</u>

Lorelai Hamilton

<u>Find Your Bliss</u>

<u>Teenage Witch's Grimoire</u>

<u>Tarot Reflection Journal</u>

<u>Tarot Refection Journal Coloring The Tarot</u>

<u>The Eclectic Witch's Grimoire</u>

<u>Dream Journal</u>

<u>Teenage Tarot</u>

<u>Tarot Tales and Magic Spells</u>

<u>Arcane In Verse</u>

Isla Watts

<u>A Fairy Bad Day</u>

[Surprise! You're a Vampire](#)

[Gorgeous, Gorgeous, Gorgons](#)

[Mork The Handsome Orc](#)

[Adopted By Werewolves](#)

[Bite Me If You Can](#)

That's The Spirit!

Rose Dawson's Book Journals

[My Time With The Fairies](#)

[Enchanted Escapades](#)

[Enchanted Escapades](#)

[Dewey Decimal Diaries](#)

[Siren's Songbook](#)

[Pride and Prejudice](#)

[Bibliophile's Bounty](#)

[Book of Books Journal](#)

[Pages & Passages Reading Journal](#)

[Bookworm's Companion Reading Journal & Tracker](#)

tarot tales and magic spells

Tarot Tales and
Magical Spells

Lorelai Hamilton

RAINBOW QUARTZ PUBLISHING

Tarot Spells and Magic Tales© 2024 by Lorelai Hamilton

All rights reserved. No part of this book may be reproduced, stored in a retrieval system, or transmitted in any form or by any means, electronic, mechanical, photocopying, recording, or otherwise, without the prior written permission of the publisher, except in the case of brief quotations embodied in critical articles and reviews.

Published by Rainbow Quartz Publishing

Edmonds, WA 98026

ISBN: 978-1-961714-37-3

First Edition: 2024

Cover design by Miranda Townsend

Interior design by Miranda Townsend

Library of Congress Cataloging-in-Publication Data has been applied for.

This book is a work of nonfiction. Names, characters, places, and incidents are either the product of the author's imagination or used fictitiously. Any resemblance to actual events, locales, or persons, living or dead, is entirely coincidental.

For permissions or inquiries, please contact:

RainbowQuartzPublishing@gmail.com or visit our website at

https://RQPublishing.com/

One person played a crucial role in my development as a reader, teacher, and tarot professional. This has been a labor of love, years in the making, and I'm privileged to know many talented readers. However, this one is for Ryan.

Lorelai Hamilton

introduction

When I was in seventh grade, a girlfriend named Kristin brought a tarot deck to lunch. I was in absolute awe. I couldn't explain why but everything in me knew this was something special. Something to be revered and something I would spend years of my life learning how to use. The problem was Kristin talked about tarot as if it was something to be feared. Not only feared, but only spoken of only in hushed tones when no one was looking. It was a secret club. Of all the secret clubs in the world, it was the one I most wanted to join.

It took me many years to learn that tarot, magic, and manifestation of any kind shouldn't be a secret club. I wish I could go back in time and tell that twelve-year-old version of myself to stay true to what I felt. Instead, I worried I'd get in trouble, or break some kind of unspoken code. I promise I will gatekeep nothing from you. Instead, I'm here to explain tarot, and even some magic, in digestible ways.

Nothing about reading tarot should be scary.

Nothing about playing with a tarot deck or picking out your first deck should feel wrong or forbidden. If it does, I'm so sorry you had that experience. I'm sending you a big cosmic hug right now.

The goal of this book is to be a comprehensive space for your tarot reading needs. By using this guidebook, you'll be able to select any deck that resonates with you and use these storytelling techniques to deliver exceptional readings—be it for yourself or someone else.

Many guidebooks accompanying tarot decks can be difficult to understand. The meaning of a card can seemingly differ from deck to deck, particularly for newcomers to tarot. Not to worry, there are universal

Introduction

meanings of the tarot cards. Those are the definitions you should always fall back on while learning tarot and navigating this new magical venture.

If you're an intuitive reader, different tarot decks can bring new perspectives and symbolism to the table. There are many reasons I love tarot and a lot of it is the art. The distinctiveness of each deck sets them apart, offering a range from traditional to comical. Universal meanings are at the core of every tarot card. Picking up any deck and confidently giving a reading is easy when you understand the thread of universal truth.

What you'll find in these pages are the universal meanings told through the lens of the cards. When I teach my students how to read tarot, I tell them about the cards as if the card itself was sharing their story. It's an incredibly valuable tool. I have faith that this book will boost your confidence in giving readings.

Inside these pages, you'll not only find the meanings of every card in the Rider-Waite-Smith deck, you'll learn how to read tarot, including how to craft tarot spreads. You're learn to harness your intuition, explore psychic symbols, and connect with spirit guides. I'm a firm believer that everyone should own the Rider-Waite-Smith deck, but if it's not for you, that's okay, too. It wasn't my first deck, and I'd be a hypocrite if I said it should be yours. But for the record, it makes an amazing first deck. Of my over two hundred decks .::Yes, 200::. this is the one I use the most.

More than anything, I hope this book helps you on your divination journey through the tarot.

Blessed be,

-Lorelai

how to read tarot cards
. . .

WHILE READING tarot may seem intimidating at first, it ultimately involves interpreting card narratives and trusting your intuition to apply their insights to your life. Mastering some fundamental techniques can enhance your readings, regardless of your level of experience.

Begin by selecting a tarot deck that speaks to you personally. With numerous decks on the market, each boasting its own distinctive artwork and symbolism, find one that resonates with your sensibilities. For this book, I'll be referring to the Rider-Waite Smith deck. Above all, approach the practice without trepidation.

the question

When I give a reading, my first question is always, "What would you like to know?" Even if you're just pulling cards for yourself, I recommend starting with a question until you get more confident. I would say that roughly half the time, my clients have a clear idea of what they want to ask, while the other half of the time I get a shrug. About seventy-five percent of the shrugs confess their question by the end of the reading. The shrugs are often out of fear of asking the hard questions. Getting a tarot reading is often driven by a deeper purpose and query.

Let me make this clear: general readings are normal and completely acceptable. That being said, when you're unclear about your question, it's common to pull cards on the things you are already aware of in life, instead of the unknown. Take caution when wording your questions. I usually tell my clients that this is a safe space, and they can be honest. By being honest about your true questions, your readings will become clearer as you learn.

I've been asked a wide range of questions by people hailing from twenty-five different nations. I can say definitively, there are universally human questions about love, careers, and family. And there are most definitely the odder questions. Like the time someone asked me to do a reading for their dog.

Sometimes I encounter unusual situations that make folks uncomfortable. Like, the multiple times when someone has inquired about the fate of their marriage or relationship and the cards pointed towards their secret lover. The cards speak the truth, however awkward it is.

the spread

Now that you have the question you're going to ask, decide what spread you're going to use in the reading. It truly doesn't matter which spread you pick. It could be a simple three card spread or a complex 25 card spread. The important part is that you believe the meaning of the card connects to the placement of the card. It's that simple. As you get more proficient in reading tarot, you'll be able to really develop your spreads or free form card pulling.

shuffle the cards

There's no wrong way to shuffle tarot cards, do so in whatever order you prefer. The important thing is that you shuffle, and you relax. Cut the deck if you like or not if you don't want to. Personally, this is the time where I think about the question at hand, rolling it over in my mind. It's a moment to relax before I lay the cards down. There's nothing overly complicated or scary about this process. I will say, it is absolute magic to watch the exact cards needed for the reading appear.

draw your cards & interpret

Whether you cut the deck and pull cards off the top or wait for them to fall out as you're shuffling—lay down your cards in your chosen spread. Now it's time to interpret the reading.

Use this book as your reference point while learning to weave the cards into a cohesive narrative. This is usually the part that most people are the most nervous about. The more you practice, the better you'll get.

card of the day

A fast way to become familiar with a tarot deck is by pulling one card a day. Go through the shuffle process and pull a single card. Ask something like, "What is the theme of the day?" This is considered a guided general reading. You're not asking a specific question about life, instead, you're asking what to be mindful of that day.

good & bad cards

People often ask me about the distinction between "good" and "bad" tarot cards. The truth is, there's no such thing as a "bad" card. Every single one of the 78 cards in the tarot is equally important. They represent real moments in life that we all experience. When you draw a card that seems less desirable, remember to take a moment and release your anxiety. Even though it may not be what you expected, there is still something valuable it can teach you.

the pictures & reversals

As you examine the reading, what emotions stir within you and emerge to the surface? Is there a person on the card you feel a connection to? Listen to your intuition and follow your gut on this. Take notes. Write your readings down so you can look back at them later.

When you look at the picture, is your initial reaction a positive feeling or a negative one? Your initial feeling when you look at the picture determines whether a card is read as upright or in reverse. You'll note that in this book, I don't provide specific reversal meanings. While there's some debate about this among readers, whether reading reversals is necessary, ultimately, it's up to you. What you will find with the breakdown of each card is a complete picture. You'll read about the positives and the negatives of the card as you come to understand each of their stories.

Listen to the feelings you get when you pull cards. Does it feel positive or negative? What part of the card do you feel most drawn to? The subtle meanings of each card can shift with every reading. While the theme might be similar, the exacts change a bit. Remember to relax and concentrate on your feelings.

For example, if you pulled the 9 of Swords during a love reading, ask yourself what your gut instinct is? Was it one of surprise or fear? It could be a warning of sleepless nights stressing about the relationship. But perhaps the card right before or right after you pulled the 9 of Swords was The Sun card. A feeling of warmth or relief suggests that your sleepless nights may turn into restful ones. Brighter days are coming and you'll soon move past the turmoil in your relationship.

Let's do one more example. Say you pulled the 5 of Cups, while doing a reading about career. Is the first thing you notice the three spilt cups? Or was it the castle, bridge, or two full cups? If it was the first choice, it could mean that there is a challenge in overcoming loss or recent circumstances. While if instead, you notice the positive symbolisms, it might indicate that you're moving on from recent loss or strife and your goals are in reach.

The greater your tarot reading skills become, the more elements you'll incorporate into your interpretations. There are the five elements, planets, zodiac, and even a simple yes or no answers (with the occasional maybe— use your intuition) for every card. Don't overwhelm yourself if you're new. Start with the meaning and go from there. You got this!

tarot journal

Tracking your daily spreads and personal experiences in a tarot journal will boost your mastery of the tarot. I have a book called the "Tarot Reflection Journal" available. You are under no obligation to buy mine, find whatever calls to you. But write them down. I also suggest reading books from multiple authors. Absorb the wisdom of the tarot and cultivate your personal insights about the cards. I encourage you to keep a record along the way.

crafting tarot spreads

. . .

TAROT SPREADS ARE a powerful tool for gaining insight, clarity, and guidance on various aspects of life, including relationships, personal growth, and decision-making. Here are some tarot spreads tailored to address common problems, along with instructions on how to read them effectively.

how to read tarot spreads

Start by shuffling the deck while focusing on the question or area of life you want insight into. Draw the cards and place them in the positions for the spread you've chosen. Interpret each card, while considering things like symbolism, imagery, and traditional meanings. Make sure you're paying attention to things like patterns, contrasts, or connections between the cards. Use your intuition and personal insights to weave together a cohesive narrative that offers guidance and clarity. Remember that tarot readings do not provide set outcomes, but rather offer insight into potential paths and outcomes based on current energies and influences. Most importantly, trust your intuition as you interpret the cards and apply their guidance in your life.

spreads

Past, Present, Future: The Past, Present, Future spread is a straightforward layout that offers insight into the querent's life journey across three distinct time frames. By exploring each position in the Past, Present, Future spread, the querent can gain clarity on their life journey, understand how past experiences have led to their current situation, and receive guidance on potential future outcomes. You can use this spread for self-reflection, decision-making, and planning for the road ahead.

1. **Past (Position 1):** This card reflects the influences and events that have shaped the querent's past. It offers insight into significant experiences, lessons learned, or patterns established that continue to impact the querent's present circumstances.
2. **Present (Position 2):** In this position, the card indicates the current circumstances and energies surrounding the querent. It provides a snapshot of the querent's current situation, including challenges, opportunities, and the overall atmosphere of the present moment.
3. **Future (Position 3):** This card offers insight into potential outcomes or the direction the querent's path may take. It provides a glimpse into what may unfold in the future based on the energies and influences present in the querent's life at the time of the reading.

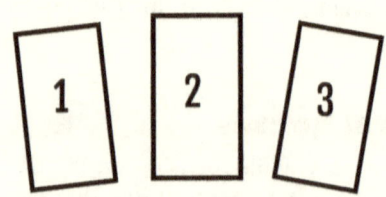

Celtic Cross Spread: The Celtic Cross Spread is a classic and comprehensive layout that provides insight into various aspects of a situation or question. By exploring each position in the Celtic Cross Spread, you'll gain a comprehensive understanding of the situation and receive guidance on how to navigate challenges, leverage opportunities, and achieve desired outcomes. Use this spread as a tool for introspection, decision-making, and personal growth.

1. **Present Situation:** This card represents the current circumstances or energies surrounding the querent. It provides a snapshot of the situation as it stands in the present moment.
2. **Challenges:** In this position, you'll uncover the obstacles or difficulties that the querent may be facing. This card offers

insights into the challenges that need to be addressed or overcome.

3. **Subconscious Influences:** Here, you'll explore the hidden or underlying influences at play in the situation. This card reveals subconscious motivations, fears, or desires that may be shaping the outcome.
4. **Recent Past:** This position delves into events or energies from the recent past that have led to the current situation. It offers insights into past experiences or decisions that are relevant to the querent's current circumstances.
5. **Higher Self:** In this position, you'll tap into the querent's intuition and inner wisdom. This card offers guidance from a higher perspective, encouraging the querent to trust their intuition and inner guidance.
6. **Near Future:** Here, you'll gain insights into the potential outcome or direction of the situation in the near future. This card offers a glimpse into what may unfold in the coming days, weeks, or months.
7. **Querent's Attitude:** This position reflects the querent's attitude or mindset toward the situation. It offers insights into the querent's thoughts, beliefs, or intentions and how they may be influencing the outcome.
8. **Others' Influence:** Similarly, this position explores the influence of others on the situation. This card represents the thoughts, actions, or intentions of people who may be involved or have an impact on the outcome.
9. **Hopes and Fears:** Here, you'll uncover the querent's hopes, desires, and fears related to the situation. This card offers insights into what the querent is hoping to achieve or avoid and how these emotions may be influencing their decisions.
10. **Outcome:** The final position reveals the potential outcome or resolution of the situation. It offers insights into the most likely outcome based on the energies and influences revealed in the spread.

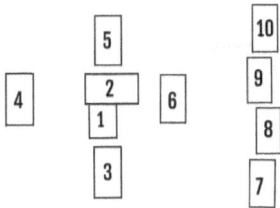

3. Relationship Spread: The Relationship Spread offers insights into various aspects of a romantic relationship, including individual perspectives, dynamics between partners, strengths, weaknesses, and guidance for growth. By exploring each position in the Relationship Spread, you'll gain valuable insights into your relationship dynamics, strengths, weaknesses, and opportunities for growth. Use this spread as a tool for communication, understanding, and building a strong foundation for your partnership.

1. **You:** This card represents your perspective, feelings, and thoughts within the relationship. It offers insights into your role, desires, and expectations.
2. **Your Partner:** In this position, you'll explore your partner's perspective, feelings, and thoughts within the relationship. It provides insights into their role, desires, and expectations.
3. **Relationship Dynamics:** Here, you'll delve into the dynamics between you and your partner. This card offers insights into how you interact, communicate, and relate to each other as a couple.
4. **Strengths:** In this position, you'll uncover the strengths and positive qualities of your relationship. This card highlights the aspects of your connection that support and enrich your bond.
5. **Weaknesses:** Similarly, this position reveals the weaknesses or challenges within your relationship. It offers insights into areas that may need attention, improvement, or resolution.
6. **Advice:** The final position provides guidance and advice for nurturing and enhancing your relationship. This card offers practical suggestions, wisdom, or insights to help you navigate challenges, capitalize on strengths, and cultivate a healthy, fulfilling partnership.

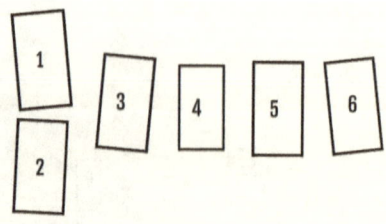

Decision-Making Spread: The Decision-Making Spread is structured to help you navigate through dilemmas and make informed choices. Use this spread as a guide to weigh your choices, evaluate the pros and cons, and choose the path that aligns best with your intentions and values.

1. **The Question:** This card represents the core question or dilemma you're facing. It sets the stage for the decision-making process and provides clarity on what you're seeking guidance for.
2. **Option 1:** In this position, you'll explore the first option or choice available to you. This card offers insights into the potential outcomes, benefits, or challenges associated with this option.
3. **Option 2:** Similarly, this position delves into the second option or choice. It provides insights into the potential outcomes, benefits, or challenges associated with this alternative.
4. **Factors to Consider:** Here, you'll uncover the key factors or considerations that should inform your decision-making process. This card offers insights into the various aspects, consequences, or implications of each option.
5. **Outcome of Option 1:** This position reveals the potential outcome or result if you were to choose Option 1. It offers insights into the likely consequences or effects of pursuing this course of action.
6. **Outcome of Option 2:** Similarly, this position reveals the potential outcome or result if you were to choose Option 2. It offers insights into the likely consequences or effects of pursuing this alternative.

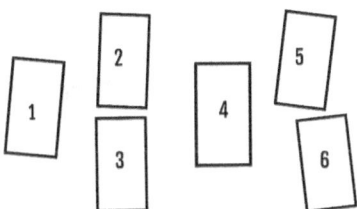

Horseshoe Spread: The Horseshoe Spread is for gaining insight into past, present, and future influences, as well as potential obstacles, unconscious influences, and advice for navigating your path. Use this spread as a tool for self-reflection, decision-making, and personal growth, allowing it to illuminate your path and empower you to create the life you desire.

1. **Past Influences:** This card represents the influences from your past that have shaped your current situation. It offers insights into past experiences, decisions, or events that may still be impacting your life today.
2. **Present Influences:** In this position, you'll uncover the current influences at play in your life. This card provides insight into the people, circumstances, or energies that are currently shaping your reality.
3. **Future Influences:** Here, you'll explore the potential future influences that may come into play. This card offers glimpses into the possible outcomes or trajectories of your current path, allowing you to make informed decisions and take proactive steps.
4. **Obstacles:** This position focuses on the obstacles or challenges that you may encounter on your path. It offers insights into potential hurdles, setbacks, or limitations that may require your attention and effort to overcome.
5. **Unconscious Influences:** In this position, you'll uncover the unconscious or hidden influences that may be affecting your situation. This card brings to light any underlying patterns, beliefs, or motivations that may be operating beneath the surface of your awareness.
6. **Advice:** The final position provides guidance and advice for navigating your path forward. This card offers practical suggestions, wisdom, or insights that can help you overcome obstacles, align with positive influences, and make the most of your opportunities.

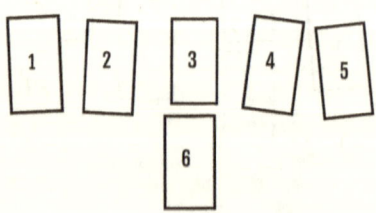

Health Spread: The Health Spread provides insight into various aspects of your well-being, including physical, emotional, mental, and spiritual health. By exploring each position in the Health Spread, you'll gain valuable insights into your physical, emotional, mental, and spiritual health. Use this spread as a tool for self-reflection, healing, and personal growth, and consider integrating the advice provided to enhance your overall well-being.

1. **Physical Health:** This card represents your current state of physical health. It offers insights into any physical ailments, imbalances, or areas of concern that may need attention or improvement.
2. **Emotional Health:** In this position, you'll explore your emotional well-being. This card offers insights into your emotional state, any unresolved emotions, or areas where you may need to focus on self-care and emotional healing.
3. **Mental Health:** Here, you'll uncover insights into your mental well-being. This card may reveal any mental challenges, stressors, or thought patterns that may be affecting your mental health and overall well-being.
4. **Spiritual Health:** This position focuses on your spiritual well-being and connection to your higher self or spiritual beliefs. It offers insights into your spiritual practices, sense of purpose, and alignment with your spiritual path.
5. **Advice:** The final position provides guidance and advice on how to improve and maintain your overall health and well-being. This card offers practical steps, self-care practices, or areas of focus to support your journey toward greater health and vitality.

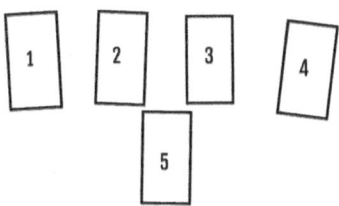

Career Spread: The Career Spread is a comprehensive tool designed to provide insight into your current career path, strengths, weaknesses, opportunities, and potential outcomes. By exploring each position in the Career Spread, you'll gain valuable insights. Use this spread as a guide to make informed decisions, maximize your potential, and achieve success in your career journey.

1. **Current Career Path:** This card represents your current position in your career journey. It offers insight into your role, responsibilities, and overall satisfaction with your career path at the present moment.
2. **Strengths:** In this position, you'll uncover your strengths and assets in relation to your career. These could include skills, talents, qualities, or experiences that set you apart and contribute to your success in your chosen field.
3. **Weaknesses:** Here, you'll identify your weaknesses or areas for improvement in your career. These could be skill gaps, limiting beliefs, personality traits, or obstacles that hinder your professional growth and advancement.
4. **Opportunities:** This card sheds light on potential opportunities for growth, advancement, or change in your career. It could represent new job prospects, networking opportunities, career development programs, or ways to leverage your skills and talents in new ways.
5. **Potential Outcome:** The final position reveals the potential outcome or direction of your career path based on the current trajectory and the opportunities available to you. It offers insights into where your career may be headed and what steps you can take to achieve your professional goals.

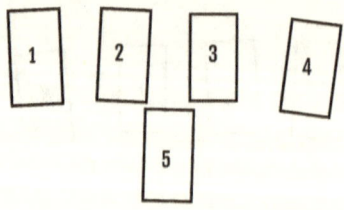

Spiritual Growth Spread: The Spiritual Growth Spread is for deepening your connection to your spiritual path, uncovering your inner strengths and obstacles, and gaining insight into external influences that may be affecting your journey. With five positions, each corresponding to a specific aspect of your spiritual growth, this spread offers guidance and clarity on your path of spiritual evolution.

1. **Current Spiritual Path:** The first position provides insight into your current spiritual journey and where you stand on your path of growth and self-discovery. This card offers clarity on the lessons, challenges, and experiences that are shaping your spiritual evolution at this time.
2. **Inner Strengths:** The second position focuses on your inner strengths and qualities that support your spiritual growth. This card reveals the inherent gifts, talents, and virtues that empower you on your journey, encouraging you to cultivate and nurture these qualities.
3. **Inner Obstacles:** The third position addresses the inner obstacles or challenges that may be hindering your spiritual growth. This card sheds light on the fears, doubts, and limitations that may be holding you back from fully embracing your spiritual path, offering guidance on how to overcome these obstacles.
4. **External Influences:** The fourth position explores the external influences of the outside world that are shaping your spiritual journey. This card reveals the people, environments, or circumstances that are impacting your spiritual growth, helping you navigate these influences with awareness and discernment.
5. **Potential Growth:** The fifth position highlights the potential for growth and transformation on your spiritual path. This card offers insights into the opportunities and possibilities that lie ahead, encouraging you to embrace new experiences, learn from challenges, and continue evolving on your journey of spiritual awakening.

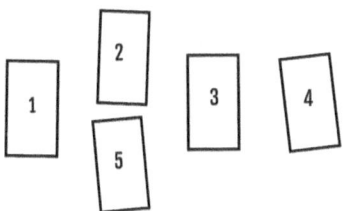

New Moon Spread: The New Moon Spread is a potent tool for harnessing the energy of the new moon to set intentions, release what no longer serves you, and embrace new opportunities for growth. With five positions, each corresponding to a specific aspect of your life, this spread offers guidance on navigating the energies of the new moon cycle.

1. **New Beginnings:** The first position provides insight into the new beginnings and fresh starts that are available to you during this new moon cycle. This card illuminates areas of your life where you can initiate change, set intentions, and plant the seeds for future growth.
2. **What to Release:** The second position focuses on what you need to release or let go of during this new moon cycle. This card reveals any habits, beliefs, or situations that are holding you back or preventing you from fully embracing new opportunities for growth.
3. **What to Embrace:** The third position highlights what you should embrace or welcome into your life during this new moon cycle. This card represents the qualities, opportunities, or experiences that will support your growth and evolution, encouraging you to open yourself up to new possibilities.
4. **Opportunities:** The fourth position uncovers the opportunities and potential paths that are available to you during this new moon cycle. This card offers insights into areas of your life where you can take inspired action and seize opportunities for growth, expansion, and success.
5. **Potential Challenges:** The fifth position identifies potential challenges or obstacles that you may encounter as you navigate this new moon cycle. This card offers guidance on how to navigate these challenges with grace and resilience, empowering you to overcome obstacles and stay aligned with your intentions.

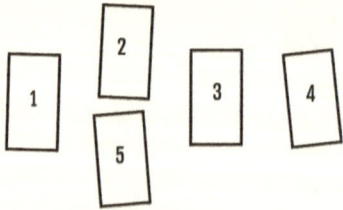

Full Moon Spread: The Full Moon Spread is for harnessing the energy of the full moon to gain insight, release what no longer serves you, and manifest your desires. With five positions, each corresponding to a specific aspect of your life, this spread offers guidance on navigating the energies of the full moon cycle.

1. **Current Situation:** The first position provides insight into your current circumstances and the energies surrounding you at the present moment. This card offers clarity on where you stand in your life and sets the foundation for the rest of the spread.
2. **What to Let Go:** The second position focuses on what you need to release or let go of during this full moon cycle. This card reveals any habits, beliefs, or situations that are holding you back or preventing you from moving forward on your path.
3. **What to Keep:** The third position highlights what you should hold onto or nurture during this full moon cycle. This card represents the aspects of your life that are supporting your growth and well-being, reminding you to cherish and cultivate them.
4. **Hidden Influences:** The fourth position uncovers any hidden influences or subconscious patterns that may be affecting your life during this full moon cycle. This card offers insights into underlying dynamics or unseen forces at play, helping you understand the deeper layers of your experience.
5. **Potential Outcome:** The final position provides a glimpse into the potential outcome or direction of your journey as you move through this full moon cycle. This card offers guidance on how to navigate the energies at play and suggests actions you can take to manifest your desires and intentions.

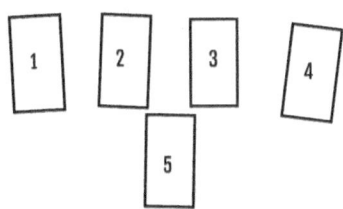

Elemental Spread: The Elemental Spread explores various aspects of your life through the lens of the four classical elements: Earth, Air, Fire, and Water. With five positions, each corresponding to an element, this spread offers insights into different facets of your being and provides guidance for achieving balance and integration.

1. **Earth (Physical Aspects):** The first position focuses on the element of Earth, which represents the physical realm, stability, and material concerns. This card reveals insights into your physical health, finances, and practical matters, offering

guidance on how to ground yourself and nurture your physical well-being.
2. Air (Mental Aspects): The second position addresses the element of Air, associated with intellect, communication, and mental clarity. This card explores your thoughts, beliefs, and communication style, offering insights into your mental processes and providing guidance on how to cultivate mental clarity and effective communication.
3. Fire (Spiritual Aspects): The third position centers on the element of Fire, which symbolizes passion, inspiration, and spiritual growth. This card delves into your inner spark, creativity, and spiritual aspirations, offering guidance on how to ignite your inner fire and pursue your spiritual path with enthusiasm and purpose.
4. Water (Emotional Aspects): The fourth position focuses on the element of Water, associated with emotions, intuition, and empathy. This card explores your feelings, relationships, and emotional well-being, offering insights into your emotional landscape and providing guidance on how to navigate your emotions with grace and compassion.
5. Integration and Advice: The final position serves as a synthesis of the four elements, offering guidance on how to integrate the insights gained from the previous positions and achieve overall balance and harmony in your life. This card provides practical advice and suggestions for integrating the lessons learned and moving forward with greater clarity and purpose.

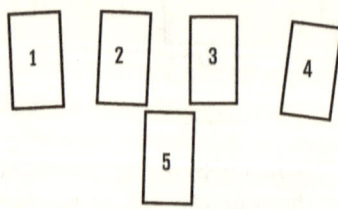

Chakra Spread: The Chakra Spread is a holistic tool for assessing and balancing the energy centers, or chakras, within the body. With seven positions, each corresponding to a different chakra, this spread provides insight into the state of your energetic body and offers guidance for achieving balance and harmony.

1. **Root Chakra (Security):** The first position focuses on the Root Chakra, which governs feelings of security, stability, and grounding. This card reveals any issues or imbalances related to your sense of safety and stability in the physical world.
2. **Sacral Chakra (Creativity):** The second position addresses the Sacral Chakra, associated with creativity, passion, and emotional expression. This card provides insight into your creative energy and emotional well-being, highlighting areas where you may need to nurture your creativity or address emotional blockages.
3. **Solar Plexus Chakra (Personal Power):** The third position centers on the Solar Plexus Chakra, which governs personal power, confidence, and self-esteem. This card sheds light on your sense of empowerment and self-worth, offering guidance on reclaiming your personal power and cultivating confidence.
4. **Heart Chakra (Love):** The fourth position focuses on the Heart Chakra, associated with love, compassion, and connection. This card explores the state of your relationships, both with yourself and others, and offers insights into how to cultivate greater love and compassion in your life.
5. **Throat Chakra (Communication):** The fifth position addresses the Throat Chakra, which governs communication, expression, and authenticity. This card examines how effectively you communicate your thoughts and feelings, as well as any blockages that may be hindering your ability to express yourself authentically.
6. **Third Eye Chakra (Intuition):** The sixth position centers on the Third Eye Chakra, associated with intuition, insight, and inner wisdom. This card offers guidance on connecting with your intuition and tapping into your inner guidance system to make decisions and navigate life's challenges.
7. **Crown Chakra (Spirituality):** The final position focuses on the Crown Chakra, which represents spirituality, higher consciousness, and connection to the divine. This card explores your spiritual beliefs and practices, as well as any blocks that may be preventing you from experiencing a deeper connection to the divine.

Lorelai Hamilton

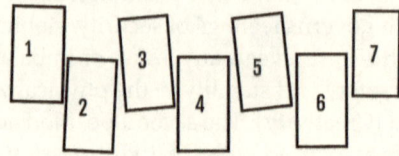

Dream Exploration Spread: Use the Dream Exploration Spread to delve into the deeper meanings of your dreams and gain insight into your subconscious mind. With five positions, this spread guides you through the process of understanding and integrating the messages from your dreams.

1. Dream Symbolism: In this position, you'll explore the symbolism present in your dream. This card reveals the hidden meanings behind the imagery, objects, or characters encountered in your dream, offering insights into your subconscious mind.
2. Underlying Emotions: The second position focuses on the underlying emotions evoked by your dream. This card uncovers the feelings and emotions that are at play beneath the surface, providing clarity on your innermost thoughts and desires.
3. Message from the Dream: In this position, you'll receive a message directly from your dream. This card offers guidance, wisdom, or advice based on the themes and events of your dream, helping you understand its deeper significance.
4. Guidance: The fourth position provides guidance on how to navigate the insights gained from your dream. This card offers practical advice or steps to take in order to address any issues or concerns raised by your dream, guiding you towards resolution and growth.
5. Integration: The final position focuses on integrating the lessons learned from your dream into your waking life. This card offers suggestions on how to apply the wisdom gained from your dream to your everyday experiences, promoting personal transformation and spiritual growth.

Tarot Tales and Magic Spells

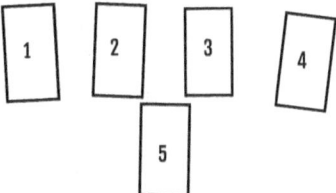

Love spread: The Love spread, will help with evaluating the dynamics of your relationship. Relationships, with their ebbs and flows, are complex webs of physical, emotional, mental, and spiritual connections. With this six-card spread, you can gain insights into the relevance, strength, and happiness of your relationship.

1. The first card reflects your current feelings towards the relationship, your approach, and your overall outlook.
2. The second card represents your partner's current emotions towards you, their attitude, and their expectations for the relationship.
3. The third card serves as a connection card, revealing common characteristics or shared traits between you and your partner.
4. The fourth card indicates the strength of your relationship, highlighting areas of resilience and stability.
5. The fifth card reveals the weaknesses or challenges present in your relationship, providing insight into areas that may need attention or improvement.
6. The final card is the True Love card, offering insight into the potential for long-term success in the relationship, based on the overall energy and dynamics revealed in the spread.

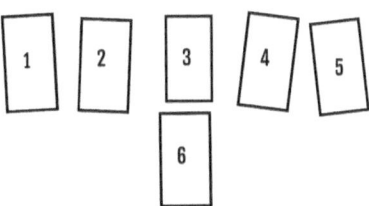

Success Spread: The Success Spread is used for uncovering the true nature of challenges you face and identifying the skills and resources needed to overcome them. With five cards, this spread provides clarity on your current situation and offers guidance on how to navigate towards success.

1. The first card sheds light on the true colors of the challenge ahead, helping you identify the necessary skill set and resources required not only to solve but also to overcome the obstacle.
2. The second card provides further clarification on your current problems and challenges, offering deeper insights into the nature of the obstacles you're facing.
3. The third card reveals hidden factors influencing your situation, offering crucial knowledge needed to overcome the obstacle. Understanding these factors is essential for devising effective solutions.
4. The fourth card represents new opportunities, connections, or resources that can aid in your growth. By embracing these new aspects, your perspective on the situation will shift, providing you with better solutions to your problems.
5. The final card outlines the requirements for success and warns against potential pitfalls that could lead to failure. A positive card indicates a path to success, while a negative card serves as a cautionary note, alerting you to potential disasters on the horizon. Use this insight to navigate towards success and avoid potential setbacks.

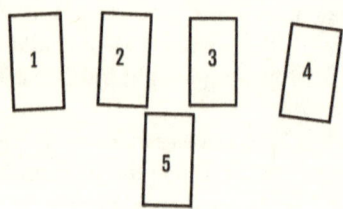

harnessing intuition
. . .

INTUITION IS the guiding force behind tarot reading, allowing you, the reader, to tap into your inner wisdom and connect with the deeper meanings behind the cards. It's the subtle voice that speaks from within, offering insight and guidance beyond the surface level of the cards.

Intuition is the innate ability to understand or know something with no conscious reasoning. It's the subtle sense of knowing that emerges from within. It's the gut feeling, also known as the inner voice or sixth sense. Intuition bypasses the limitations of logical thought and taps into the deeper realms of consciousness.

Intuition is like the bridge that connects the person getting the reading, the cards, and the reader, helping us understand the messages from the tarot better. While the cards themselves hold symbolic meanings, it's through intuition that you can discern the nuances and subtleties within each reading.

Use your instincts to interpret the cards based on the person's specific situation, feelings, and energy, giving them personalized guidance. It allows readers to perceive patterns, themes, and underlying messages that may not be immediately apparent from the cards alone.

So how is it done? How do you cultivate intuition in a tarot reading? We start by quieting the mind. Intuition thrives in moments of stillness and quietude. Before beginning a tarot reading, take a few moments to center yourself and create space for intuitive insights to arise.

Trust your gut and follow your intuition. Pay attention to subtle sensations, feelings, and impressions that arise during the reading.

Practice Mindfulness by cultivating presence during tarot readings.

Stay attuned to the energy of the cards, the querent's presence, and the intuitive guidance flowing through you.

Next, connect with the cards. Develop a personal connection with your tarot deck by spending time with it regularly. Doing a one card reading every day is a helpful method. Meditate on the cards, study their imagery and symbolism, take notes, and develop your own deeper interpretations based on your intuitive insights.

Tarot reading is a creative process that invites intuition to flow freely. Allow yourself to be innovative, trust your creative impulses, and explore new ways of interpreting the cards. Once you understand the basics, you'll see there's an entire world available to you.

Practice makes perfect. Like any skill, intuition grows stronger with practice. Dedicate time to regular tarot readings, journaling, and reflection to deepen your intuitive connection and refine your reading abilities.

Learn from experience. Work with a friend, accept readings from other tarot readers. All the while paying attention to your experiences and the outcomes of your readings. Notice how your intuitive insights align with the querent's experiences and the unfolding of events.

Stay receptive to the unexpected and embrace the mysteries of the tarot. Say the things that don't make sense. Trust that intuition will guide you toward deeper understanding and insight, even in the face of uncertainty.

I was doing a reading once, and I just had this feeling that my client should call her mom. But she came to the reading with questions of a romantic nature. The message I kept getting wasn't from her mom—it was about her mom. I let her know that there was a message about her mom and, as anticipated, she was dismissive. My client said she wasn't in a good place with her mom and she didn't want to talk about it. I took it in stride and tried to reframe the question. Tarot would not relent. My client's spirt guides came through in the reading and I kept hearing something like Loury, Lourey, Lorie. I let the client know that someone whose name sounds like that has a message for her and is trying to find her. She shrugged her shoulders. I encouraged her to take a mental note and let me know if anything comes of it before we moved on.

Fast forward to after our reading, my client asked if I'd have a cup of coffee with her. We were walking to a café when she runs into an old family friend. He tells her that her mom was in the hospital, and no one was sure how to contact her. After their visit was done, I asked what the gentleman's name was. She said, his last name is Lourey.

Sometimes your gut is right, even if it makes no sense at the moment. Say the thing anyway. Write it down, make the note. I'm often surprised by how often this happens to me.

Intuition is the lifeblood of tarot reading, infusing each reading with depth, insight, and meaning. By cultivating a deep connection with your intuition and trusting in its guidance, you can uncover profound truths that resonate with the querent's soul. Remember, the true magic of tarot lies not only in the cards themselves, but in the intuitive wisdom that flows through you as you embark on the journey of tarot reading.

exploring psychic symbols

. . .

PSYCHIC SYMBOLS SERVE as powerful messengers in tarot reading, conveying messages from spirit guides, higher consciousness, or the depths of the subconscious mind. These symbols often appear during readings to convey deeper insights, guidance, and wisdom to the querent.

Understanding psychic symbols is an important part of opening your intuition. Psychic symbols are vivid images or sensations that convey deep symbolic meaning. They may appear as images, colors, sensations, sounds, or intuitive impressions during a tarot reading.

Psychic symbols originate from the collective unconscious, spirit guides, or the higher self, serving as symbolic messages and guidance. This could be an image, a sound, words, or that knowing feeling. You will learn to cultivate your own meanings for the symbols you encounter. It is incredibly helpful to have a baseline to start with. Understanding psychic symbols demands not only intuition and sensitivity but also an open mind that can delve into their intricate meanings and implications.

When conducting readings, I tap into the querent's spirit guides, who communicate with me through visual and audible symbols. In my least favorite moments, I get physical ones too.

Once, I had the opportunity to do a reading for a woman who was curious about finding harmony between her work and personal life. Before I could even finish laying out the cards, a sharp ache shot through my back. As my kidneys throbbed with pain, my vision became speckled with dark spots. I was going to vomit—I got up and ran to the bathroom. Once I created some space between us, I felt instantly better.

That was the day I incorporated a spiritual shield for my physical well-being. Returning to the table, I wasted no time in sharing my experience, stressing the urgent message my intuition conveyed - she had to make a change, or face consequences that could be fatal. She shared with me the numerous hospital visits she had endured for her kidneys, all due to excessive stress. We continued the reading, and I saw a crossroads and key. As luck would have it, the two of swords was the next card drawn. I let her know that right then she was at a crossroads. With each passing moment of inaction, her fear grew stronger, paralyzing her. The woman depicted on the card has the ability to remove her blindfold and fully observe her surroundings. Just like in real life, there were no adversaries depicted on the card. She had an uncomfortable choice to make—leave her career and face the unknown or stay somewhere that was causing her physical pain.

We continued the reading, and I saw a child's onesie and dollar signs. I didn't have a clue what that meant, but I let her know and we finished up the reading. She came back to me a few days later. Turns out she quit her job after our reading, applied for a handful of jobs and had an interview scheduled for the following week at a children's clothing company in their advertising department. She was glowing and, best yet, no more back pain.

When interpreting psychic symbols during a tarot reading, prioritize trusting your intuition and inner guidance. Pay attention to the feelings, impressions, and sensations that arise in your body when encountering these symbols. Consider the context of the reading and the querent's current circumstances to discern the relevance and significance of each symbol.

Keep an open mind and be receptive to the multiple layers of meaning and symbolism that may emerge. Journaling and reflection can help deepen your understanding of psychic symbols and their implications.

Psychic symbols serve as gateways to deeper understanding, insight, and spiritual connection during tarot readings. By attuning to these symbols and embracing their messages with an open heart and mind, you can unlock profound wisdom, guidance, and illumination on your journey to self-discovery and spiritual growth. Trust in the power of intuition and the language of symbols to lead you towards greater clarity, alignment, and purpose in your tarot practice and spiritual path.

You never know what symbols might come to you, but they all have a meaning. Below, I've listed some common psychic symbols and their meanings. This is good a place to start.

common psychic symbols and their meanings

- Ankh: Represents eternal life, vitality, and the connection between the physical and spiritual realms.

- Anchor: Signifies stability, security, and staying grounded amidst life's challenges.
- Anvil: Signifies strength, resilience, and the power of creation.
- Arrow: Represents focus, determination, and aiming towards goals or aspirations.
- Beehive: Signifies community, cooperation, and the power of collective effort.
- Bell: Symbolizes awakening, awareness, and calling attention to important insights or messages.
- Book: Represents knowledge, wisdom, and the pursuit of learning and understanding.
- Bonsai Tree: Symbolizes patience, balance, and the beauty of simplicity.
- Bridge: Signifies connection, overcoming obstacles, and transitioning to new phases.
- Broom: Symbolizes cleansing, purification, and sweeping away negativity or obstacles.
- Bull: Signifies strength, resilience, and determination in the face of challenges.
- Butterfly: Represents transformation, growth, and the emergence of new beginnings.
- Chalice: Represents receptivity, intuition, and spiritual nourishment. Symbolizes spiritual communion, divine connection, and the vessel of the soul.
- Chessboard: Signifies strategy, planning, and navigating through life's challenges.
- Circle: Represents wholeness, unity, and the cyclical nature of existence.
- Colors:
- Black: Symbolizes mystery, the unknown, darkness, protection, and the subconscious mind. In psychic readings, black can represent hidden potential, transformation, and rebirth. It may also indicate protection from negative energies or spiritual awakening through facing one's fears.
- Blue: Represents calmness, tranquility, serenity, spirituality, communication, and intuition. In psychic symbolism, blue may indicate clarity, truth, healing, and inner peace. It can also signify depth, wisdom, and connection to the subconscious.
- Brown: Represents stability, grounding, practicality, and connection to the earth. In psychic symbolism, brown can symbolize reliability, security, and a sense of belonging. It may also indicate growth, endurance, and strength in challenging situations.

- Green: Symbolizes growth, renewal, fertility, abundance, prosperity, and harmony with nature. In psychic readings, green can represent balance, healing, and nurturing energy. It is also associated with money, wealth, and financial stability.
- Orange: Signifies creativity, enthusiasm, vitality, and optimism. In psychic readings, orange can represent joy, energy, and excitement. It may also indicate passion, adventure, and enthusiasm for life.
- Pink: Reflects love, compassion, nurturing, kindness, and emotional healing. In psychic symbolism, pink can symbolize unconditional love, gentleness, and compassion. It is often associated with romance, friendship, and emotional well-being.
- Purple: Signifies spirituality, wisdom, intuition, magic, mystery, and higher consciousness. In psychic readings, purple can represent psychic abilities, spiritual enlightenment, and connection to the divine. It may also indicate transformation, psychic protection, and inner strength.
- Red: Often associated with passion, vitality, energy, action, courage, and strength. In psychic readings, red can signify strong emotions, love, power, and determination. It can also symbolize anger, intensity, or warning.
- White: Represents purity, innocence, spirituality, divine light, and clarity. In psychic symbolism, white can symbolize truth, enlightenment, and spiritual awakening. It is often associated with healing, cleansing, and purification of the mind, body, and spirit.
- Yellow: Reflects joy, optimism, intellect, clarity, and creativity. In psychic symbolism, yellow can symbolize enlightenment, mental agility, and communication. It may also indicate confidence, positivity, and spiritual awakening.
- Compass: Represents guidance, direction, and finding one's true north.
- Crescent Moon: Represents intuition, feminine energy, and the cyclical nature of life.
- Crossroads: Signifies decision-making, choices, and the intersection of paths.
- Crown: Represents authority, achievement, and divine guidance.
- Dove: Represents peace, harmony, and spiritual enlightenment.
- Dragonfly: Signifies adaptability, transformation, and the power of illusion.
- Dreamcatcher: Signifies protection, purification, and filtering out negative energy.
- Elements:
- Air: Symbolizes intellect, communication, and mental clarity.

- Earth: Signifies stability, grounding, and material manifestation.
- Fire: Symbolizes passion, creativity, and transformational energy.
- Water: Represents emotions, intuition, and the ebb and flow of life.
- Feather: Symbolize spiritual guidance, protection, and messages from the divine.
- Fish: Symbolizes abundance, fertility, and the flow of life.
- Flower of Life: Represents sacred geometry, creation, and the interconnectedness of all living things.
- Globe: Represents global awareness, interconnectedness, and embracing diversity.
- Hamsa Hand: Signifies protection, blessings, and warding off evil.
- Harmony Symbol: Symbolizes balance, unity, and the integration of opposites.
- Heart: Signifies love, compassion, and emotional connection.
- Hourglass: Represents the passage of time, cycles, and the inevitability of change.
- Horseshoe: Represents luck, protection, and blessings.
- Infinity Symbol: Represents eternity, interconnectedness, and infinite possibilities.
- Key: Symbolizes unlocking hidden truths, opportunities, and solutions.
- Labyrinth: Represents the journey of self-discovery, inner exploration, and finding one's way.
- Ladder: Symbolizes progress, growth, and ascending to higher levels of consciousness.
- Lantern: Signifies illumination, guidance, and shining light in dark times.
- Lightening Bolt: Symbolizes sudden change, inspiration, and moments of enlightenment.
- Lotus Flower: Symbolizes spiritual enlightenment, purity, and the unfolding of divine consciousness.
- Magnifying Glass: Symbolizes clarity, insight, and the ability to see things more clearly.
- Mandala: Represents wholeness, unity, and the interconnectedness of all things.
- Map: Represents guidance, exploration, and charting one's course.
- Mirror: Represents self-reflection, introspection, and gaining insight into one's true self.
- Moon: Represents intuition, the subconscious mind, and cycles of growth and transformation.

Tarot Tales and Magic Spells

- Nature:
- Mountains: Signify challenges, obstacles, and the journey towards spiritual elevation.
- Trees: Symbolize strength, resilience, and the interconnectedness of all living beings.
- Waterfall: Represents emotional release, purification, and the flow of life energy.
- Numbers:
- 111: Indicates alignment with divine purpose and manifestation of intentions.
- 333: Symbolizes spiritual growth, ascended masters' presence, and divine protection.
- 888: Represents abundance, prosperity, and financial blessings.
- Owl: Signifies wisdom, intuition, and the ability to see beyond illusion.
- Ouroboros: Symbolizes infinity, cyclicality, and the eternal cycle of life and death.
- Pen: Represents communication, expression, and the power of written words.
- Pentagram: Represents balance, protection, and the five elements.
- Phoenix: Symbolizes renewal, rebirth, and rising from the ashes of adversity.
- Puzzle Pieces: Signify problem-solving, finding solutions, and piecing things together.
- Quill Pen: Represents communication, expression, and the power of written words.
- Rain: Represents cleansing, purification, and emotional release.
- Rainbows: Symbolize hope, promise, and the beauty of diversity.
- Rope: Symbolizes strength, unity, and the ability to overcome obstacles together.
- Scroll: Represents ancient wisdom, sacred teachings, and hidden knowledge.
- Scales: Signify balance, justice, and the weighing of decisions or actions.
- Scales of Justice: Signify balance, fairness, and the importance of ethical decision-making.
- Shield: Signifies protection, defense, and guarding against negativity or harm.
- Ship: Represents journey, exploration, and navigating through life's challenges.
- Snake: Symbolizes transformation, regeneration, and healing.

- Sphinx: Symbolizes mystery, riddles, and the quest for hidden knowledge.
- Spiral: Symbolizes growth, evolution, and the journey of self-discovery.
- Starfish: Represents regeneration, renewal, and the ability to overcome challenges.
- Stars: Symbolize guidance, inspiration, and the interconnectedness of the universe.
- Sun: Signifies vitality, enlightenment, and the light of divine consciousness.
- Sunflower: Symbolizes vitality, growth, and the pursuit of happiness.
- Sword: Symbolizes clarity, truth, and the power of discernment.
- Torch: Symbolizes enlightenment, illumination, and the pursuit of truth.
- Trinity Knot: Signifies unity, interconnectedness, and the threefold nature of existence.
- Trident: Represents power, authority, and mastery over the elements.
- Tree of Life: Represents interconnectedness, growth, and the cycle of creation.
- Trees: Symbolize strength, resilience, and the interconnectedness of all living beings.
- Triangle: Signifies balance, harmony, and the union of mind, body, and spirit.
- Wreath: Represents victory, achievement, and the celebration of success.
- Wolf: Symbolizes intuition, instinct, and the pathfinder on the spiritual journey.
- Yin-Yang: Signifies balance, harmony, and the interplay of opposing forces.

connecting with spirit guides
. . .

THE QUESTION that I am frequently asked is, "What exactly is a spirit guide?" Occasionally, I'm timidly asked, "Do I have a Spirit guide?"

Spirit guides are benevolent beings who offer guidance, support, and protection on our spiritual journey. They serve as wise and compassionate allies, helping us navigate life's challenges, discover our purpose, and fulfill our highest potential. Understanding who spirit guides are, how to communicate with them, and recognizing their presence can deepen our spiritual connection and enrich our lives in profound ways.

Spirit guides are non-physical entities that reside in the spiritual realm and are dedicated to our personal growth, well-being, and spiritual development. They can take various forms, including ancestors, angels, ascended masters, animal spirits, and departed loved ones just to name a few. Each spirit guide possesses unique wisdom, gifts, and insights tailored to our individual needs and spiritual path.

While spirit guides can do a number of things, here are a few of their core jobs. The role of spirit guides is to offer us wisdom and guidance as we face life's challenges, make decisions, and align ourselves with our soul's purpose. They provide protection and support, shielding us from negative energies, and guiding us towards paths of light and positivity. Spirit guides inspire us to explore our creativity, pursue our passions, and embrace our unique gifts and talents. They assist in emotional, physical, and spiritual healing, offering comfort, solace, and unconditional love during times of struggle and pain. Even In the darkest hours, you are never alone.

It is important to note that negative entities are not classified as spirit guides. Spirit guides are beings of love and light and do not seek to harm or manipulate us in any way. Spirit guides do not force their guidance upon us, but respect our free will and sovereignty to make our own choices. Unlike negative entities or deceptive energies, spirit guides always communicate with honesty, integrity, and compassion.

But how do I communicate with my spirit guides? Easy! There are lots of ways to communicate with your guides. Meditation is a powerful practice that can help calm the mind, elevate your energy, and establish a sacred environment for connecting with spiritual guides. I recommend setting clear intentions and offering prayers to invite your spirit guides to communicate with you and provide guidance. Keep a journal to record your thoughts, feelings, and intuitive impressions received during meditation or quiet reflection. Remember that your spirit guides hear you when you talk and when you don't.

In my opinion, one of the most fascinating methods of communication with them is through requesting a particular sign to obtain an answer to a question. For example, whenever I'm feeling stuck between two choices, I ask my guides to send me a specific sign. "To indicate that I should choose option A, kindly send me a purple unicorn. Alternatively, if option B is the better option, please send me a bowl of oranges." Inevitably, within a day, I see one of these obscure things and I know my guides are not just listening, they're communicating.

Using automatic writing can be a fun and enjoyable tool for communicating with your spirit guides. Enable the free movement of the pen while practicing automatic writing, allowing your spirit guides to communicate and share their messages. It's comparable to writing without consciously selecting the words beforehand. What shows up on paper may not make any sense at first, but the more you do it, the better you'll become.

Last, I encourage you to pay attention to dreams, visions, and symbols that may contain messages or guidance from your spirit guides. I have a dream journal available called "Dream Journal: Capturing Your Dreams From the In Between." Be it mine or someone else's, I highly recommend writing your dreams down. Especially if you go to sleep, asking your spirit guides a question like I do.

So, how do you recognize your spirit guides? First, consider your intuitive insights. Trust your intuition and inner guidance when sensing spirit guides or receiving intuitive messages. Notice synchronicities, meaningful coincidences, and signs that align with your intentions or prayers. Be aware of physical sensations, like tingling, chills, or warmth that may indicate the presence of spirit guides. Heck, even animals may appear as spirit guides, offering messages, protection, and guidance through their symbolism and behavior.

When communicating with your spirit guides, it's essential to approach the interaction with reverence, openness, and trust. Here's how you can engage in conversations with your spirit guide.

Start by setting your intentions. Clearly state your intention to connect with your spirit guide and invite them to communicate with you. Pose specific questions or seek guidance on areas of your life where you need clarity or support. The next is the hard part, listening. Listen closely. Pay attention to any thoughts, feelings, images, or words that come to you during the communication process. These may be messages from your spirit guide. Trust the guidance and insights you receive, even if they seem subtle or unexpected. Last, remember to thank your spirit guides for their guidance and presence, acknowledging the support they offer you on your journey.

Spirit guides are loving companions on our journey of self-discovery, healing, and spiritual growth. By cultivating awareness, trust, and openness to their guidance, we can deepen our connection with our spirit guides and receive the wisdom, love, and support they offer. Through honest and vulnerable communication, recognition, and honoring the signs they provide, we can embrace their presence as a source of inspiration, guidance, and divine grace in our lives.

major arcana

major arcana

...

IN THE QUIET spaces of our thoughts, we can hear the whispers of the universe. Tarot is an ancient tool for divination and self-reflection. Tarot isn't just mere symbols on paper, but living stories waiting to be told.

The Major Arcana is distinguished from the Minor Arcana by their significance and scope. It's a collection of 22 cards which hold profound symbolism and archetypal imagery. The cards portray the protagonist, The Fool, on a transformative and spiritually enlightening journey of self-discovery. You'll notice that The Fool is card 0, because The Fool is not part of the Major Arcana, he travels through it.

Each card in the Major Arcana carries unique lessons and insights that guide the reader through various stages of life and the human experience. Remember, it's easy to forget, we are all spiritual beings, living a human experience.

While the Minor Arcana focuses more on the day-to-day events and experiences, the Major Arcana covers deeper themes that shape the reader's life and journey in this world.

Each card in the Major Arcana represents an influential archetype and universal principle. This offers an insightful understanding into the human experience, psyche, and spiritual evolution.

So, what does all that mean? The Major Arcana can be compared to selecting a city to reside in, whereas the Minor Arcana resembles deciding on the activities you'll engage in locally.

Interpreting the Major Arcana means understanding the symbolism, archetypal meanings, and the story's narrative progression. Every single card tells a story. I hope to teach you what the story is and how it represents a specific stage or aspect of The Fool's journey. From innocence and wonder, we watch The Fool grow to wisdom and enlightenment.

There are other considerations when interpreting the Major Arcana cards, including the intuitive impressions it evokes inside of you, the position within the spread, and its relationship to the question or circumstances being asked.

The heart of the Major Arcana lies in The Fool's Journey. This narrative follows The Fool's passage through life's triumphs and trials. It can offer you insights, guidance, and illumination on your life and other's lives. The Major's should feel like a beacon of light that guides you to empowerment.

Choosing to attend college, travel the world, getting your new job, starting a family, or buying a home—should all feel like huge empowering moments in your life. When you embrace the lessons and messages, you can truly embark on self growth, healing, and even enlightenment. Unlocking the mysteries of the human soul and the universe itself are right around the corner!

0. the fool
...
"We were always free," The Fool.

Element: Air
Planet: Uranus

Key Words & Phrases:
Take a risk
Risk looking like a fool
Fresh start
A new hope
Spontaneity
Trust
Adventure awaits
Faith
New beginnings
Innocence
Clear conscience
Vanity
Foolishness

SYMBOLS:

- The sun in this card represents the tree of life. In history, the tree of life is the start of everything. So, the sun is the start of EVERYTHIG. The sun is always a good omen in tarot.
- The mountains in the background represent life's peaks and trials. As Miley says, "it's the climb." The mountains represent the journey we take climbing through life. All our ups and downs. The good and the bad.
- The young person on this card is The Fool. We call them the seeker. They are the soul in search of experience and guidance. This person also recognizes they're the main character in their own life. They're not a side character, or the best friend, they're the main hero and adventurer. So are you.
- The Fool has a feather in their hat. Feathers are a symbol of air, the element of this card.
- The white dog is a reminder to follow your instincts. To trust what you know to be true, even if others tell you different. Listen to your gut, and it will never lead you astray.

The Fool dances through the tarot instead of being part of it. He glides through each card, learning lessons and growing along the way. His journey in the tarot is one of self-actualization and evolution. When The Fool gets to the final card in the Major Arcana called The World, he starts his journey over again.

Like many glorious adventures we read about in novels, The Fool goes on the hero's journey, always starting a new quest. Life's worries don't weigh The Fool down. Instead, they are free to explore the world and follow the singular beat of their heart.

Without ego or pride, The Fool carries unlikely wisdom. Believing they're worthy of everything in life, just the way the way they are. They talk to themselves like a trusted friend and don't get down on themselves or care if people laugh at them.

Life is hard. No one is going to sit here and deny that. Try seeing the path ahead of you through the eyes of The Fool. They remain unstressed about potential hazards, like walking off a cliff. The universe has their back. The Fool doesn't walk off the cliff because the dog lets them know it's there. When The Fool takes a leap of faith, they will always land on their feet, unscathed. Trusting in yourself is the hardest and best thing you'll learn how to do.

When you draw The Fool, it presents itself to challenge your perspective. Are you more concerned with the things that others want, feel, or think? Or are you putting your own desires first? Don't be afraid of what the world might say. Let go of your fears, enjoy that warm sun, and laugh away your worries. You only live this life one time. Don't waste it.

Approach situations with humor and optimism. The Fool challenges you to release your fear of failing. Remember to breathe. When you are caught up in your worries, fear can take over. Anxiety can take control before trying something new and even when you think about being humiliated or dying. You're no longer living when you fall into these patterns.

The Fool should resonate with the exhilaration of uncertainty. It speaks to the excitement of exploring new horizons, making bold choices, and embracing independence.

You might see this card come up during big transitions, while pursuing passion or embracing on a journey of self-discovery. Remember to mirror The Fool's journey.

magic spell: the fool's leap:

With courage bold
and heart alight,
I take the leap,
embrace the flight.
Like The Fool,
I fear no fall,
With every step,
I heed the call.

materials needed:

- A small feather
- A piece of paper
- A green candle

instructions:

- Find a quiet space where you can focus without distractions.
- Light the green candle, representing The Fool's spirit of adventure and growth.
- Write down one thing you wish to pursue or manifest in your life on the piece of paper.
- Hold the feather in your hand and visualize yourself taking a bold leap towards your goal, just like The Fool.
- Repeat the following incantation:

"With courage bold and heart alight, I take the leap, embrace the flight. Like The Fool, I fear no fall, with every step, I heed the call."

- Allow the candle to burn while you meditate on your aspirations, feeling the energy of The Fool infuse you with bravery and optimism.
- Carry the feather with you as a talisman of your courage and willingness to embrace new beginnings.

As you journey through the realm of The Fool, may you embrace the spirit of adventure and possibility that lies within. Let go of fear, trust your instincts, and take that leap of faith into the unknown. With every step, you'll discover the magic of new beginnings and the boundless potential that awaits you on your path.

questions to ask yourself

1. What new opportunities am I being called to explore at this moment?
2. Am I allowing fear or uncertainty to hold me back from embracing this new chapter?
3. What lessons can I learn from past experiences as I embark on this journey?
4. How can I approach this situation with a sense of adventure and openness?
5. What aspects of myself do I need to let go of to fully embrace this fresh start?
6. What risks am I willing to take in pursuit of my dreams and aspirations?

7. Am I staying true to my authentic self as I navigate unfamiliar territory?
8. How can I cultivate trust in myself and the universe as I step into the unknown?
9. What support systems do I have in place to guide me through this transition?
10. What small steps can I take today to move forward with courage and optimism?

1. the magician

. . .

"Thoughts are like spells, they are powerful and have the power to mold your reality," The Magician.

Element: Air or Earth
Planet: Mercury
Answer: Maybe

Key Words & Phrases:
Conscious Awareness
Concentration
Belief in self power
Honest self-talk
Unity
Willpower
Manifestation
Creativity
Resourcefulness
Action

SYMBOLS:

- The Magician holds a wand high and points to the sky. As above, so below. This should be a reminder that you can manifest ANYTHING you desire into being through your vulnerability. Vulnerability is power magic and being humble enough to own your true desires and to be who you are without fear is the key.
- The infinity symbol is like a Mobius strip, forever folding back in on itself. You have the power to break cycles, the power to see the future and change it, the power to heal the past, and the power to be your best self in the here and now.
- The cup, sword, pentacle, and wand represent water, air, earth, and fire, respectively. Every obstacle The Magician can face requires a tool. He has all the tools necessary to be successful sitting at his fingertips. Everything you'll need to navigate not only tarot, but this situation successfully is already in your arsenal. You've got this, it's going to be okay.

Imagine for a minute that The Fool has left to travel the world. Along the way, he finds himself in a bustling marketplace amidst the scent of spices and the chatter of merchants, he encounters The Magician. The Magician easily channels the elements to manifest his deepest desires. He reveals the power of your will, intention, and resourcefulness.

The Magician card is a reminder that your thoughts are like magic spells. Your thoughts manifest the life you're experiencing. Do you want to change something in your life? Do you need or want something? It all begins with a thought.

By changing the fixation of your mind, you can start to change your environment. For example, do your thoughts control you, or do you control your thoughts? Does your mind harbor thoughts of positivity, or is it always lingering in the negativity?

Sitting on his altar, The Magician has every tool at his beck and call. When you pull the Magician, it's a reminder that you too have all the tools you need to be successful.

On the table, there's a cup representing the element of water. In the tarot, water is the representation of emotions. The water is inside of a cup, and it's calm, sitting before the Magician on the table. This tells us he's in control of his own emotions. They do not control him.

In the tarot, a pentacle represents the element of earth and the parts of life with monetary needs. The pentacle rests before him, therefore, representing that the Magician has everything needed to ground himself when life pushes back. He can feel comfortable in a world that requires money to thrive.

Swords represent the element of air as well as our minds and thoughts. Swords move fast as can thoughts. The Swords can express anxiety. However, they can also be a reminder that you can shift your fears and mindset to a safe place. Removing the cause of stress can present a calm place where you control your thoughts and can more easily put your fears in perspective and push them away.

Last, on the table sits a wand. Wands represent the element of fire, passion, and your ambitions in life. It is all the things that get you excited to get out of bed, the people who light you up inside and make your soul sing.

The Magician can manipulate the tools at his disposal to better his life. When you use the tools at your disposal, you can channel your Higher Self and reach the limitless part of you. You can manifest anything and everything into your life. When you pull the Magician, it should be a reminder of your abilities. You are magic.

Never let social norms or a societal voice tell you that you are lacking or that you don't measure up. You are worthy. Full stop. You are capable. Full stop. Your body is perfect just the way it is. Full stop. You are not a fraud. Full stop. You can, and you will succeed. Full stop. You are enough.

Hold on to courage in the darkest and scariest moments. Hold on to hope when you feel unsure about life and what lies ahead. Remember the true essence of who you are and your capabilities. The Magician will challenge you to take responsibility for your life. Don't let your mind dwell on things it cannot change. If you can make a change, do so. Don't let negative thoughts go unchallenged. The phrase, as above, so below, is about how your inner beliefs about yourself can shape your outer self.

Thoughts are like spells; they are powerful and can morph your reality. So let go of cluttering negative thoughts and manifest the reality you're craving.

magical spell: empowerment:

By the power of the elements,
I am the Magician of my destiny,
With fire, air, water, and earth,
I manifest my reality.
As this candle flame burns bright,
so too shall my dreams take flight,
Empowered by my will and guided by my light.

materials needed:

- A small piece of paper
- A pen or marker
- A candle (any color)
- Matches or a lighter

instructions:

- Light the candle and sit in a comfortable position.
- Take the piece of paper and write down a goal or desire that you wish to manifest. Be specific and clear about what you want to achieve.
- Hold the paper in your hands and visualize yourself achieving your goal with confidence and determination.
- Recite the following incantation aloud:

"By the power of the elements, I am the Magician of my destiny, With fire, air, water, and earth, I manifest my reality. As this candle flame burns bright, so too shall my dreams take flight, Empowered by my will and guided by my light."

- Fold the paper and hold it over the flame of the candle, allowing it to catch fire safely. As it burns, visualize your intentions being released into the universe.
- Once the paper has turned to ash, extinguish the flame and bury the ashes in the earth as a symbol of your commitment to your goal.

The Magician card serves as a potent reminder that you possess the power to shape your own destiny and manifest your desires. By harnessing the elements of creation and tapping into your inner wisdom, you can unlock the magic within and realize your fullest potential. Let The Magician be your guide as you embark on the journey of self-discovery and transformation.

questions to ask yourself

1. What new adventures or opportunities am I being called to explore in my life?
2. Am I feeling a sense of freedom and liberation, or am I hesitating due to fear or uncertainty?
3. What areas of my life could benefit from a fresh perspective or a willingness to take a leap of faith?
4. How can I cultivate a sense of childlike curiosity and wonder in my approach to life?
5. What limiting beliefs or self-imposed boundaries do I need to release in order to embrace new experiences?
6. Am I willing to trust in the journey and take risks, even if the outcome is uncertain?
7. How can I maintain a balance between being spontaneous and being mindful of potential consequences?
8. What lessons can I learn from past experiences that will guide me as I step into the unknown?
9. What support or resources do I need to navigate this new chapter of my life with confidence?
10. How can I stay grounded and centered amidst the excitement and uncertainty of new beginnings?

2. high priestess
...
"Trust your higher self and inner knowing," The High Priestess

Element: Water
Planet: Moon
Answer: Yes

Key Words & Phrases:
Intuition
Sacred Knowledge
Divine Feminine
Subconscious Mind
Intuition
Secrecy
Mystery
Subconscious
Reflection

SYMBOLS:

- The High Priestess's *headdress* is argued to have many meanings. The most common belief is that the headdress represents the phases of the moon: waxing, full, and waning. It also represents the triple goddess, Hecate. She's the goddess of magic, witchcraft, night, and the moon. She's represented by the maiden (waxing moon), the mother (full moon), and the crone (waning moon).
- The *Veil* behind The High Priestess is representing the thin veil between the conscious and unconscious realms. Inviting us to explore the depths of our psyche.
- The *pomegranates* are associated with Persephone, Hades, and the Underworld, specifically the death, life, and rebirth cycle.

As twilight falls, The Fool enters a sacred grove where the air hums with ancient wisdom. In the heart of the forest stands The High Priestess. She's the guardian of hidden knowledge and intuition. While veiled in mystery, The High Priestess invites you to explore the depths of your subconscious mind. She says trust that voice inside you. Embrace your intuition and the things you can't see.

The High Priestess is the personification of your intuition. When you trust your instincts, gut, and feelings, you embrace your inner High Priestess. That little voice or gut feeling that tells you a truth you can't deny, that's the High Priestess. She is the keeper of what lies beyond the veil.

The High Priestess is here as a reminder that you know more than you give yourself credit for. She has a deep knowing of the world and spirituality. She is modest in her wisdom and doesn't need to flaunt to the world when she is correct.

Life is not black and white, like the pliers. It's often complicated and messy. Life exists in the in-between. Sometimes it's hard to know where things in life are leading you. Embrace the known in equal measure with the unknown.

The High Priestess sees all of it. The High Priestess wears a crown adorned with the phases of the moon. She knows the beginning, middle, and end of everything. Behind the High Priestess hangs a tapestry with woven pomegranates. Pomegranates symbolize the underworld and the answers found beyond the fear of death and loss.

The High Priestess may arise when you feel lost and unsure about what to do. Consider her your guide back to your instincts. Look inward and know that you have all the answers within you—past, present, and future. Trust yourself and let go of the fears preventing you from finding comfort in that trust.

Your fears are not instincts. Fear will leave your body and muscles tight and anxious. Instincts should leave you feeling empowered to act. They are clear and will feel sharp.

Perhaps the High Priestess is presenting herself so that you will look at things from a different perspective. Do you get a lot of signs, reoccurring numbers, patterns, or symbolism? Fear for nothing. Instead, remember that the universe and your spirit guides are communicating with you. Ask yourself what it means to you and look inward for the answers.

If your answers don't leave you feeling empowered to act, then look again.

Lorelai Hamilton

magical spell: intuition awakening ritual:

I trust in the wisdom of my inner voice,
I embrace the mysteries that lie within,
With clarity and insight,
I am guided on my path.

materials needed:

- A quiet and comfortable space
- A white candle
- A small bowl of water
- A piece of amethyst or clear quartz crystal (optional)

instructions:

- Find a peaceful space where you can sit comfortably without distractions.
- Light the white candle and place it in front of you.
- Take a few deep breaths to center yourself and quiet your mind.
- Hold the bowl of water in your hands and visualize it filling with a soft, glowing light.
- Gaze into the water and allow yourself to connect with its gentle energy.
- Close your eyes and focus on the space between your eyebrows, known as the third eye.
- Repeat the following affirmation silently or aloud:

"I trust in the wisdom of my inner voice, I embrace the mysteries that lie within, With clarity and insight, I am guided on my path."

- Allow any thoughts or sensations to arise without judgment, trusting in the guidance of your intuition.
- If you have a crystal, hold it in your hands and feel its energy amplifying your intuitive abilities.
- When you feel ready, extinguish the candle and carry the energy of intuition with you throughout your day.

The High Priestess beckons you to explore the depths of your intuition and embrace the mysteries that lie within. By trusting in your inner wisdom and honoring the guidance of your subconscious mind, you can unlock a world of insight and illumination. Let The High Priestess be your beacon as you journey into the realms of intuition and self-discovery.

questions to ask yourself

1. How can I harness my personal power and potential to create the life I desire?
2. What skills, talents, or resources do I possess that I can leverage to achieve my goals?
3. Am I feeling empowered to take action and manifest my intentions, or do I need to cultivate a greater sense of confidence and self-belief?
4. What opportunities are available to me right now, and how can I seize them to move closer to my aspirations?

5. How can I align my thoughts, beliefs, and actions to support my vision for the future?
6. Am I taking responsibility for my own destiny, or am I waiting for circumstances to change before I take action?
7. What obstacles or challenges do I need to overcome in order to manifest my desires, and how can I approach them with creativity and determination?
8. What role does intention-setting and visualization play in my ability to manifest my desires?
9. How can I cultivate a mindset of abundance and possibility, rather than focusing on limitations or lack?
10. What steps can I take today to move closer to my goals and dreams, knowing that I have the power to create my own reality?

3. the empress

. . .

"You are safe," The Empress.

Element: Earth
Planet: Venus
Answer: Yes

Key Words & Phrases:
Nature
Growth
Fertility
Creativity
Feminine Devine
Abundance
Pure of Feeling
Fertility
Motherhood/Moms

SYMBOLS:

- The *scepter* is phallic in nature. It is, however, topped with an orb, a feminine symbol, showing the different energy The Empress brings to her rule. The scepter represents her rulership of the everyday world.
- The *pearl necklace* The Empress wears symbolizes her dominion over the oceans and emotions.
- *Waterfalls* and *Streams* are a life source. They purify, regenerate, and provide nourishment as the Empress does.
- The *wheat fields* represent fertility, sustenance, and the abundance of the harvest season.

Amidst fields of blooming flowers, orchards bearing ripe fruits, The Fool encounters The Empress. She offers warmth, comfort, and sustenance to all living beings. The Empress is the embodiment of nurturing abundance and fertility in your life.

The Empress is a beautiful woman resting upon a chaise. She represents the here and now, fertility and bearing life. The Empress is not a queen. She's the representation of all four queens. She controls her emotions with a passion for creativity and bringing new things into this world: life and energy.

The Empress is kind. She's the ultimate mother figure. So when the Empress presents herself, know you are safe to lay your worries at her feet and embrace the ever-loving nature of a mother who protects her children no matter what.

For those who have experienced childhood trauma, The Empress is enveloping you in her warm arms. She's here to tell you it's all going to be okay. Trust in yourself and trust in her.

The Empress encourages you to embrace your creative potential and cultivate a sense of abundance in your life. She's there to remind you to honor your creativity, trust in the natural rhythm of growth and renewal, and embrace the beauty of the world around you.

When you can see situations in the context of the eternal, there is no fear in the now. The Empress reminds us we all have a grand purpose, and while sometimes we get caught in fear of what is or isn't, she represents a knowing that all things happen at the right time.

Now is the time to unburden your heart and transcend fear with love. The Empress reminds you that love is all that matters in the grand scheme of things.

Everything will be okay. You are safe.

magical spell: creativity blossom ritual

materials needed:

- A quiet and comfortable space
- A small bowl of water
- A green candle
- Paper and colored markers or pencils

instructions:

- Find a peaceful space where you can sit comfortably without distractions.
- Light the green candle and place it in front of you.
- Take a few deep breaths to center yourself and connect with the energy of the earth.
- Hold the bowl of water in your hands and visualize it filling with vibrant, creative energy.
- Gaze into the water and allow yourself to connect with its nurturing and life-giving essence.
- Take the paper and markers or pencils and begin to draw or write down your creative aspirations and dreams.
- Allow your imagination to flow freely as you express yourself through art or words.
- Once you have finished, hold your creation close to your heart and infuse it with your intentions for growth, creativity, and abundance.
- Place the paper near the candle and allow the flame to imbue it with the energy of transformation.
- When you feel ready, extinguish the candle, and carry the energy of creativity with you throughout your day.

The Empress invites you to embrace your creative potential and cultivate a sense of abundance in your life. By honoring your inner creativity, nurturing your passions, and trusting in the natural cycles of growth and renewal, you can unlock a world of beauty and abundance. Let The Empress be your guide as you embark on a journey of self-discovery and creative expression.

questions to ask yourself

1. In what ways am I nurturing and caring for myself, and how can I deepen this self-care practice?
2. What areas of my life are experiencing abundance and growth, and how can I cultivate gratitude for these blessings?
3. How can I tap into my creativity and express myself more authentically in my daily life?
4. Am I feeling connected to nature and the cycles of life, or do I need to spend more time outdoors and reconnect with the natural world?
5. What projects or endeavors am I feeling inspired to nurture and bring to fruition at this time?
6. How can I cultivate a sense of balance and harmony in my relationships, both with myself and with others?
7. What aspects of my femininity or nurturing qualities am I embracing, and how are they serving me in my life?
8. What boundaries do I need to establish in order to protect my energy and maintain a healthy balance between giving and receiving?
9. How can I honor my intuition and trust my inner wisdom to guide me in making decisions?
10. What steps can I take to create a more fertile environment for growth and abundance to flourish in my life?

4. the emperor

. . .

"Reclaim your power," The Emperor.

Element: Fire
Planet: Mars
Answer: Yes

Key Words & Phrases
Abundance
Authority
Power
Execution
Realizations
Higher Thoughts
Pure of Thought
Structure
Stability
Leadership
Discipline

SYMBOLS:

- The *throne* is a symbol of The Emperor's rule. It sets a tone for The Emperor and represents his authority and power.
- The *ram's head* on the throne represents the astrological sign, Aries. It represents courage and the need to thrust forward, take immediate action, and push past obstacles.
- The king wears *armor* under his gown. The armor is made of iron and steel, thus connecting to the planet Mars—which governs such metals. The Emperor is ready to defend and fight for what is right and to protect his own.

In a grand hall decorated with symbols of authority, order, and leadership, The Fool meets The Emperor. He's the ruler of all realms. With a steady gaze and a firm hand, The Emperor guides his kingdoms with wisdom and strength, teaching leadership, discipline and the importance of boundaries through example.

The Emperor is all four kings of the tarot combined. Imagine for a moment what the responsibility of being a single king feels like. The Emperor is so much more. He doesn't have time for life's petty moments. He understands how temporary life is and how time-consuming things can be. In order to accomplish all the items on his plate, he must have firm boundaries.

The Emperor knows the most vital sense of security will come from strong boundaries. When you take control of your life, you demonstrate to others that they do not have permission to control you or influence your decisions. Doing so would be the equivalent of The Emperor giving his crown to a lesser king. It's easy to grapple with issues of autonomy, authority, and establishing boundaries.

The Emperor's personal honor code forbids victimization and requires him to speak up when things feel unjust. Do you feel like others aren't treating you with respect? Or that being nice somehow outweighs your personal needs? Do you find assertive people mean? Start by listening to your inner Emperor.

The Emperor sits on a throne ornamented with rams. Rams aren't afraid to charge forward to defend their territory and their mates. The Emperor himself wears armor, ready for battle at a moment's notice. He only acts when his empire needs stabilizing or protection.

In one hand, The Emperor wields an ankh, a symbol of masculinity, and in the other, an orb, a symbol of femininity. He knows they are equally indispensable and is comfortable with both. The spring flowing behind him connects him to his Empress and the element of water.

The Empress is pure of feeling, while The Emperor is pure of thought. Therefore, the Emperor protects the borders so his Empress can sit peacefully, bestowing love to the world.

You are both The Emperor and The Empress. You must protect your borders to be as loving as the Empress. It's important to remember that you must find the balance between these two within you.

magical spell: boundaries of strength:

With the strength of the Emperor,
I stand tall and firm,
I set boundaries of steel,
Protecting me from harm.
No negativity shall penetrate my sacred space,
I am the master of my destiny,
I hold my rightful place.

materials needed:

- A quiet and comfortable space
- A red candle
- A piece of paper
- A pen or marker

instructions:

- Find a peaceful space where you can sit comfortably without distractions.
- Light the red candle and place it in front of you.
- Take a few deep breaths to center yourself and connect with your inner strength.
- On the piece of paper, write down any negative influences or obstacles that you wish to overcome.
- Visualize a protective barrier forming around you, shielding you from harm and negativity.
- Hold the paper in your hands and recite the following incantation around:

"With the strength of the Emperor, I stand tall and firm, I set boundaries of steel, protecting me from harm. No negativity shall penetrate my sacred space, I am the master of my destiny, I hold my rightful place."

- Fold the paper and hold it over the flame of the candle, allowing it to safely burn.
- As the paper burns, visualize the flames transmuting the negativity into positive energy.
- Once the paper has turned to ash, extinguish the candle and release any remaining tension or fear.

- Carry the energy of strength and protection with you throughout your day, knowing that you are empowered to set healthy boundaries.

The Emperor reminds you to embrace your authority and establish healthy boundaries in your life. By cultivating self-discipline, asserting your authority, and setting clear boundaries, you can navigate life's challenges with strength and resilience. Let The Emperor be your guide as you step into your power and embrace your role as the master of your destiny.

questions to ask yourself

1. Where in my life do I need to establish more structure and order?
2. How can I take on a leadership role in my own life and take charge of my circumstances?
3. What areas of my life require a more disciplined approach, and how can I implement this discipline effectively?
4. Am I using my power and authority wisely, or am I being overly controlling or rigid?
5. What lessons can I learn from past experiences of authority or leadership, and how can I apply them moving forward?
6. How can I balance assertiveness with compassion and empathy in my interactions with others?
7. What aspects of my life require me to set boundaries and maintain healthy limits?
8. In what ways can I cultivate resilience and strength in the face of challenges or adversity?
9. How can I tap into my inner wisdom and intuition to make decisions with clarity and confidence?

10. What steps can I take to build a solid foundation for long-term success and stability in my life?

5. the hierophant
...
"Ask for what your heart and soul need," The Hierophant.

Lorelai Hamilton

Element: Earth
Planet: Venus
Answer: Maybe

Key Words & Phrases:
Marriage
Alliance
Tradition
Inspiration
Formal Education
Ethics
Spiritual Guidance
Revolution
Conventionalism
Institutionalism
Non-conformity
Unorthodox
Existentialist
Ceremony
Mentorship

SYMBOLS:

- The *three-tiered crown* the Hierophant wears symbolizes leveling up in life and the lessons we learn and move through.
- The *crossed keys* have been likened to Hades, who holds the key to the heavens, the higher consciousness, the underworld, and the unconscious and instinctual life.
- The right hand of the Hierophant is making a *blessing gesture*. This implies that sometimes during life, we need an outside perspective to bring attention to the things in plain sight. Perhaps the querent is denying the truth. The Hierophant means "reveal the sacred"—this refers to the need for someone in our lives to bring attention to something hidden from us.

In the sacred halls of tradition and ritual, The Fool finds the Hierophant and keeper of sacred wisdom and spiritual guidance. The Hierophant bridges the gap between the divine and earthly realms while reminding the Fool of the importance of tradition, community, and love.

The Hierophant symbolizes sacred knowledge. For all of human history, there have been spiritual beliefs. While a belief could be sacred to one person, in the same breath, it might mean absolutely nothing to another. The commonality, regardless of spiritualism, is how we pray, wish, and hope. It's universally human.

Spirit transcends identity and perceptions of religion, and that is beautiful. It's agreed among even atheists we evolved as humans to have instincts toward spiritual belief systems. Regardless of your beliefs, we can agree that humans have the instinct to commune with something bigger than ourselves.

In love and relationships, the Hierophant can point to a love match. It can also indicate that perhaps you pick traditional partners. Either way, the Hierophant's meaning concerning love can represent the more spiritual aspects of love. Partnerships should be loving, kind, and shared on a spiritual level. Sometimes in readings, this can indicate marriage.

The Hierophant can also represent deception, suppression, and even the alteration of truths. Are you being authentically you? Is someone else conforming at the expense of themselves—or even to deceive?

On the topic of deception, The Hierophant could be talking about a lie that's told to protect someone's feelings. This is your reminder that you should never assume to know better than someone else. If you're still withholding the truth when shielding someone or trying to protect them from specific knowledge. It will lead to hurting the other person; however well-meaning your intentions feel, it's still incredibly arrogant.

The Hierophant boils down to who defines right and wrong—whether it is someone in leadership or with authority defining right and wrong, versus someone defining right and wrong for themselves.

magical spell: wisdom invocation ritual:

Ancient spirits
guides of light,
Hear my prayer
On this sacred night.
Grant me wisdom,

Lorelai Hamilton

> Clarity, and grace,
> Illuminate my path
> In this sacred space.

materials needed:

- A quiet and comfortable space
- A white candle
- A piece of paper
- A pen or marker
- Ginger incense (optional)

instructions:

- Find a peaceful space where you can sit comfortably without distractions.
- Light the white candle, and optional incense and place them in front of you.
- Take a few deep breaths to center yourself and open your heart to wisdom.
- On the piece of paper, write down a question or issue that you seek guidance on.
- Hold the paper in your hands and visualize a beam of white light descending from above, filling you with clarity and insight.
- Recite the following invocation aloud:

"Ancient spirits, guides of light, Hear my prayer on this sacred night. Grant me wisdom, clarity, and grace, Illuminate my path in this sacred space."

- Allow any thoughts, feelings, or sensations to arise as you open yourself to receive guidance.
- Once you feel a sense of clarity or understanding, extinguish the candle and thank the spirits for their wisdom.
- Reflect on any insights or messages that came through during the ritual, trusting in the guidance of the divine.

The Hierophant invites you to seek spiritual guidance and connect with the wisdom of the ages. By honoring tradition, exploring your beliefs, and seeking guidance from higher sources, you can navigate life's challenges with clarity and grace. Let The Hierophant be your guide as you embark on a journey of spiritual discovery and self-transformation.

questions to ask yourself

1. In what ways do I seek guidance and wisdom from traditional institutions or belief systems?
2. How can I honor and respect the traditions and values passed down to me while still embracing my own individual beliefs and perspectives?
3. What role do mentors, teachers, or spiritual leaders play in my life, and how can I learn from their wisdom while maintaining my autonomy?
4. Am I adhering to societal norms and expectations out of a genuine sense of alignment, or am I conforming to avoid conflict or discomfort?
5. What spiritual practices or rituals resonate with me, and how can I incorporate them into my daily life for greater connection and alignment?
6. How can I balance the need for structure and order with my desire for personal growth and exploration?
7. What insights can I gain from exploring my own spirituality and beliefs, separate from external influences?
8. Am I open to receiving guidance and wisdom from sources beyond traditional authority figures, such as intuition or personal experience?
9. How can I cultivate a sense of inner knowing and trust in my own wisdom and intuition?
10. What steps can I take to deepen my spiritual journey and cultivate a deeper connection to the divine or higher consciousness?

6. the lovers
. . .
"Unconditional love comes from vulnerability that is free of self-consciousness," The Lovers.

Element: Air
Planet: Mercury
Answer: Yes/No

Key Words and Phrases:
Abundance
Passion
Union
Harmony
Love
Partnership
Ethics
Primordial Choice
Temptation
Interference
Discord
Moral Quandary

SYMBOLS:

- The *Tree of Knowledge* behind the couple represents wisdom, growth, and the choice that shape our lives.
- The serpent entwined around, and around the tree symbolizes temptation.
- Flames symbolize passion and transformation.
- The Angel represents divine intervein and the higher guidance that accompanies matters of the heart.

Underneath the branches of an ancient tree, The Fool comes across The Lovers entwined in a dance. This should be where the saying opposites attract originates. While so different, their union is harmonic.

Navigating the complexities of love and attraction, grappling with one's identity, and managing relationships are universally complicated tasks. The Lovers speak to the importance of making choices from the heart, embracing relationships that honor our true selves, and seeking harmony and balance in our connections with others. They remind you to trust your instincts, follow your heart, and embrace the power of love.

Their love transcends time and space and reflects the balance of opposites coming together as one. The Lovers remind us of the power of love, choice, and partnership along this journey called life.

The Lovers represent a lot of things, mostly about choice. They are an emblem of unity. Love isn't just romantic, but the love we have for anything. Love is always a choice. When we love something purely, be it work, hobbies, or a person, that love is what The Lovers card represents.

The Lovers stand beneath a radiant sky while the presence of divine energy looks down on them, illuminating the potential of love's transformative power.

The dual nature of human existence is reflected in the presence of two individuals, symbolizing not only romantic love but also the balance between opposing forces. The union of masculine and feminine energies transcends gender and physicality. It represents harmony and duality within oneself and in a relationship.

We all struggle with relationships and navigating the complexities of love and attraction. The Lovers speak to the importance of making choices from the heart, embracing relationships that honor our true selves, and seeking harmony and balance in our connections with others.

magical spell: heart's desire manifestation:

With love's light
I manifest my heart's desire
Guided by the angels
Fueled by passion's fire.
May my heart be open,
My spirit be free,

As I embrace love's journey,
So mote it be.

materials needed:

- A quiet and comfortable space
- A pink candle
- A piece of paper
- A pen or marker
- Pink Rose Quartz (optional)

instructions:

- Find a peaceful space where you can sit comfortably without distractions.
- Light the pink candle and place it in front of you next to the optional rose quartz.
- Take a few deep breaths to center yourself and connect with the energy of love.
- On the piece of paper, write down a specific desire or intention related to love or relationships.
- Hold the paper in your hands and visualize your desire coming to fruition, filling you with warmth and joy.
- Recite the following affirmation aloud:

"With love's light, I manifest my heart's desire, Guided by the angels, fueled by passion's fire. May my heart be open, my spirit be free, As I embrace love's journey, so mote it be."

- Allow the candle to burn as you focus on your intention, infusing it with your love and energy.
- Once the candle has burned down, fold the paper and place it under your pillow as you sleep.
- Trust in the power of love and the universe to manifest your heart's true desires.

The Lovers invite you to embrace the power of choice and the transformative energy of love. By honoring your true self, making choices from the heart, and seeking harmony in your relationships, you can create a life filled with joy, passion, and fulfillment. Let The Lovers be your guide as you navigate the journey of love and self-discovery.

questions to ask yourself

1. What important decisions or choices am I facing in my relationships or personal life?
2. How can I cultivate deeper connections and harmony in my relationships, both romantic and platonic?
3. What values and qualities do I seek in a partner, and how can I ensure that my relationships align with these values?
4. Am I being true to myself and my own needs in my relationships, or am I sacrificing my authenticity for the sake of harmony?
5. How can I communicate more openly and honestly with my partner(s) to strengthen our bond and resolve conflicts?
6. What lessons can I learn from past relationships or experiences of love, and how can I apply them in my current situation?
7. Am I willing to take responsibility for my role in the dynamics of my relationships, and what changes can I make to improve them?
8. How can I balance my own desires and needs with those of my partner(s) in a way that fosters mutual respect and understanding?
9. What fears or insecurities may be impacting my ability to fully engage in intimate relationships, and how can I work through them?
10. What steps can I take to cultivate self-love and self-acceptance, knowing that healthy relationships start with a strong foundation of self-awareness and self-care?

7. the chariot

...

"In the face of adversity, I am strong," The Chariot

Element: Water
Planet: Moon
Answer: Yes

Key Words and Phrases
Focus
Focused *action*
Self-belief
Confidence
Victory
Commitment
Drive and determination
Clear goals
Fighting for what you believe in
Overcoming obstacles
Hard, passionate work
Courage
Success
Positive movement forward

SYMBOLS:

- The Charioteer represents your willpower, determination, and ability to steer your life in the desired direction.
- Sphinxes or Horses symbolize opposing forces or energies, such as conscious and subconscious, light and shadow, or inner outer worlds.
- The Star Canopy represents guidance, inspiration, and divine protection on the journey to victory.
- The Crescent Moon symbolizes intuition, psychic abilities, and the cyclical nature of life's challenges and triumphs.
- The Chariot signifies movement, progress, and control over external circumstances despite challenges and obstacles.

Amidst the thunderous roar of battle, The Fool encounters The Chariot, a warrior charging forward with unwavering determination and focus. His chariot, pulled by opposing forces, symbolizes the triumph of will over adversary. They are union of light and shadow. The Chariot teaches us about perseverance, victory, and harnessing our inner drive.

The pressure to excel and make important decisions about the future can feel overwhelming. The Chariot encourages you to stay focused, with set goals, and persevere through challenges to achieve academic success.

You may face pressure to conform to social norms, experiment with risky behaviors, or compromise your values. The Chariot reminds you to stay true to yourselves, stand firm in your convictions, and assert your independence.

Now is a time of self-discovery and identity formation, which can shake your confidence and self-esteem. The Chariot teaches the importance of self-belief, resilience, and embracing personal power to overcome doubts and insecurities.

Conflict or tension within the family environment can create stress and uncertainty for anyone. The Chariot encourages you to maintain balance, assert healthy boundaries, and take charge of your own destiny despite familial challenges.

magical spell: harnessing the power of the chariot

I am the architect of my fate,
With unwavering courage, I navigate.
Through challenges I rise,
with strength untold,
My spirit resolute,
my destiny unfolds.
With determination as my guide,
I conquer obstacles, I do not hide.
Focused and clear, I journey on,

In the face of adversity, I am strong.
By the power within,
this spell I cast,
To manifest victory,
to hold steadfast.
With each step forward,
my path is clear,
I am the master of my destiny,
I persevere.

materials needed:

1. Red candle (for energy and courage)
2. White candle (for clarity and focus)
3. Pen and paper
4. Herbs: cinnamon (for success), basil (for protection), and rosemary (for mental clarity)

instructions:

- Set the Mood: Find a quiet, comfortable space where you can focus without distractions. Light the red and white candles to represent the dual energies of The Chariot.
- Center Yourself: Close your eyes, take several deep breaths, and visualize yourself sitting in the chariot, confidently holding the reins, and guiding your life's path.
- Write Your Intentions: On the piece of paper, write down specific goals or challenges you wish to overcome. Be clear and concise in your intentions.
- Anoint the Paper: Lightly sprinkle the paper with a pinch of cinnamon, basil, and rosemary to infuse it with magical energy for success, protection, and clarity.
- Affirmation: Hold the paper in your hands and recite the affirmation:

"I am the architect of my fate, With unwavering courage, I navigate. Through challenges I rise, with strength untold, My spirit resolute, my destiny unfolds.

With determination as my guide, I conquer obstacles, I do not hide. Focused and clear, I journey on, In the face of adversity, I am strong.

By the power within, this spell I cast, To manifest victory, to hold steadfast. With each step forward, my path is clear, I am the master of my destiny, I persevere."

- Visualize Success: Close your eyes and visualize yourself driving The Chariot forward, overcoming obstacles with ease, and reaching your desired destination.
- Burn the Paper: Safely light the paper with the flame of the red candle and let it burn in the fireproof container. As it burns, visualize releasing your intentions to the universe.
- Close the Spell: Express gratitude to The Chariot for its guidance and empowerment. Blow out the candles, and carry the energy of victory and determination with you as you go about your day.

By harnessing the energy of The Chariot, you can tap into your inner strength, overcome challenges, and navigate life's journey with confidence and determination.

questions to ask yourself

1. What goals or ambitions am I currently pursuing, and how can I stay focused and determined to achieve them?
2. What obstacles or challenges am I facing on my path, and how can I overcome them with resilience and perseverance?
3. Am I effectively harnessing my willpower and self-discipline to navigate through difficult situations?
4. What inner conflicts or opposing forces do I need to reconcile in order to move forward with clarity and purpose?
5. How can I maintain a sense of balance and control in my life, even amidst chaos or uncertainty?
6. What strategies or plans can I implement to stay on course and make progress towards my desired outcomes?

7. Am I allowing external circumstances to dictate my direction, or am I taking charge of my own destiny?
8. How can I integrate my intellect and emotions to make decisions that align with my highest good?
9. What lessons can I learn from past experiences of triumph and perseverance, and how can I apply them in my current situation?
10. What support or resources do I need to call upon in order to overcome obstacles and achieve my goals?

8. strength

. . .

"Courage is not the absence of fear. It's deciding that someone or something is more important than your fear, and doing it anyway," Strength.

Tarot Tales and Magic Spells

Element: Fire
Planet: Sun
Answer: Yes

Key Words and Phrases:
Inner strength
Fighting fear and hate with compassion
Dignified resistance
Emotional labor
Forgiveness
Love in the face of anger or fear
Accepting and loving the shadow self
Self-love
Compassionate

SYMBOLS:

- The infinity sign is about transcendence, magical powers, and tapping into something higher.
- The Lion Represents the *wild beast* within each of us. It's the primal instincts, raw emotions, and the untamed aspects of the human psyche.
- A woman taming a lion is courageous. She's filled with love despite her fear. Her gentle demeanor and calm expression symbolize the power of love and compassion to tame even the fiercest beasts.

In the heart of the wilderness, The Fool encounters Strength, a gentle soul embracing a fearsome lion with love and compassion. Through inner courage and resilience, she tames the wild beast, embodying the power of patience, compassion, and inner fortitude. Strength teaches us that true power arises from the depths of the heart.

The Strength card embodies courage, resilience, and the ability to overcome challenges through inner fortitude. Depicted as a woman gently taming a lion, she represents the power of compassion, patience, and self-control. The card symbolizes the triumph of the human spirit over adversity and the capacity to harness inner strength in the face of fear or uncertainty.

Self-esteem and self-doubt are turbulent waters. The Strength card speaks to the importance of recognizing and embracing one's inner power, resilience, and capacity for growth. You possess the strength and courage to face life's challenges with grace and determination.

Look at that woman with the lion. Imagine for a moment how courageous she is to put her hand/head inside of a lion's mouth. It's not that she isn't afraid. Instead, she knows that courage isn't the absence of fear. It's knowing that someone or something is more important than your fear and doing it, anyway.

The Strength card invites you to go on a journey of self-discovery and empowerment, urging you to embrace the depths of your inner strength and resilience. It's a timeless reminder of courage and fortitude that lives in each of us.

magical spell: courage infusion ritual:

Strength within,
Courage rise,
I face my fears,
I claim my prize.
With lion's heart
And steadfast grace,
I conquer all,

I claim my place."

materials needed:

- A quiet and comfortable space
- A yellow candle
- A piece of paper
- A pen or marker
- Lavender or rosemary essential oil (optional)

instructions:

- Find a peaceful space where you can sit comfortably without distractions.
- Light the yellow candle and place it in front of you.
- Take a few deep breaths to center yourself and connect with your inner strength.
- If you have essential oil, dab a drop on your wrists or pulse points to invoke a sense of calm and courage.
- On the piece of paper, write down a specific fear or challenge that you wish to overcome.
- Hold the paper in your hands and visualize yourself facing the fear with courage and determination.
- Recite the following affirmation aloud:

"Strength within, courage rise, I face my fears, I claim my prize. With lion's heart and steadfast grace, I conquer all, I claim my place."

- Allow any emotions or sensations to arise as you affirm your inner strength and resilience.
- Fold the paper and hold it over the flame of the candle, allowing it to safely burn.
- As the paper burns, visualize the flames transmuting your fear into courage and empowerment.
- Once the paper has turned to ash, extinguish the candle and carry the energy of strength and courage with you throughout your journey.

The Strength card reminds you to embrace your inner power and resilience in the face of adversity. By nurturing compassion, patience, and self-control, you can conquer your fears and overcome life's challenges with grace and courage. Let The Strength be your guiding light as you navigate the journey of self-discovery and personal growth.

questions to ask yourself

1. What challenges or obstacles am I currently facing, and how can I tap into my inner strength to overcome them?
2. How can I cultivate a greater sense of resilience and perseverance in the face of adversity?
3. Am I being compassionate and gentle with myself as I navigate difficult situations, or am I being overly critical?
4. What fears or insecurities do I need to confront in order to unleash my true strength and potential?
5. How can I cultivate a sense of inner peace and tranquility, even amidst chaos or uncertainty?
6. What areas of my life require courage and bold action, and how can I summon the bravery to move forward?
7. Am I using my strength and power responsibly and ethically, or am I exerting control in harmful ways?
8. How can I channel my passions and desires in constructive ways that align with my values and principles?
9. What lessons can I learn from past experiences of overcoming adversity, and how can I apply them in my current situation?
10. What practices or rituals can I incorporate into my daily life to nurture and strengthen my mind, body, and spirit?

8. the hermit

...

"Do not fear the quiet. Embrace it," The Hermit.

Element: Mercury
Planet: Saturn
Answer: No

Key Words and Phrases:
Solitude
Retreat
Peace and quiet
Tranquility
Working things through on your own
Claiming space and time for you
Mentoring
Reflection
Inner Wisdom
Finding a mentor
Guidance
Enlightenment

SYMBOLS:

- The lantern symbolizes the light of inner wisdom and spiritual guidance that illuminates the darkness of ignorance and uncertainty.
- The staff The Hermit carries represents serving as a steady guide and support along the path of self-discovery.
- The Mountains in the background symbolize the challenges and obstacles that must be overcome on the journey to enlightenment.

Upon a windswept mountain, The Fool finds The Hermit, a solitary figure illuminated by the light of his own inner wisdom. With lantern in hand, he journeys inward, seeking enlightenment in the silence of solitude.

The Hermit guides us on a path of introspection, reflection, and inner guidance.

The Hermit speaks to the periods of introspection and self-discovery we all go through. It's essential for personal growth and finding your true path in life. The Hermit is the guardian of inner wisdom and spiritual enlightenment.

Symbolically, the lantern the Hermit holds represents the illuminating power of inner wisdom and introspection. The light of the Hermit will help you move through shadow work, casting light upon those reassesses of your soul. It serves as a beacon of guidance in times of uncertainty and confusion, offering clarity and insight amidst the tumult of existence.

At its core, the Hermit card embodies the essence of introspection and contemplation. Whatever your struggle is, you must sit in it, then move through it. Ignoring it won't help you, it will only hinder you. There is a transformative power of inner wisdom and self-awareness guiding you to a deeper understanding of yourself and the world.

magical spell: inner wisdom invocation ritual:

In the silence of my soul,
I seek the truth,
Guide me, oh Hermit,
With wisdom and youth.
Illuminate my path,
Reveal what's unseen,
In the depths of my being,
Let knowledge convene.

materials needed:

- A quiet and comfortable space
- A white candle

- A piece of paper
- A pen or marker
- Lavender or sage incense (optional)

instructions:

- Find a peaceful space where you can sit comfortably without distractions.
- Light the white candle and place it in front of you.
- If you have incense, light it and allow the fragrant smoke to fill the air, creating a sacred atmosphere.
- Take a few deep breaths to center yourself and quiet your mind.
- On the piece of paper, write down a question or issue that you seek guidance on.
- Hold the paper in your hands and visualize the answer or insight unfolding before you, like a beam of light piercing the darkness.
- Recite the following invocation aloud:

"In the silence of my soul, I seek the truth, Guide me, oh Hermit, with wisdom and youth. Illuminate my path, reveal what's unseen, In the depths of my being, let knowledge convene."

- Allow any thoughts or feelings to arise as you open yourself to receive guidance.
- Fold the paper and hold it over the flame of the candle, allowing it to safely burn.
- As the paper burns, visualize the flames carrying your question to the realms of the divine, where answers await.
- Once the paper has turned to ash, extinguish the candle and trust in the wisdom that resides within you.

The Hermit invites you to embark on a journey of self-discovery and inner wisdom. By embracing solitude, reflection, and the quest for truth, you can illuminate the path toward enlightenment and find clarity amidst life's uncertainties. Let The Hermit be your guiding light as you navigate the depths of your soul and uncover the treasures that lie within.

questions to ask yourself

1. In what areas of my life am I seeking solitude or introspection, and why?
2. What insights or wisdom can I gain from spending time alone and reflecting on my thoughts and experiences?
3. Am I embracing the opportunity to connect with my inner self, or am I avoiding introspection out of fear or discomfort?
4. What truths or answers am I seeking within myself, and how can I access them through quiet contemplation?
5. How can I cultivate a deeper sense of self-awareness and understanding through introspective practices such as meditation or journaling?
6. What guidance or intuitive insights am I receiving from my inner wisdom, and how can I trust and follow them?
7. What lessons can I learn from past experiences of solitude or introspection, and how can I apply them in my current situation?
8. Am I using my time alone productively, or am I isolating myself in a way that leads to loneliness or disconnection?
9. How can I balance the need for solitude and introspection with the importance of maintaining connections with others?
10. What steps can I take to honor and nurture my inner wisdom and intuition, knowing that they are valuable sources of guidance and direction?

10. the wheel of fortune

. . .

"Recognize where you have control in your life and where you don't. Release what you have no control over and write your own destiny with the rest," Wheel of Fortune

Element: Earth / Air / Fire / Water
Planet: Jupiter

Lorelai Hamilton

Answer: Yes

Key Words and Phrases:
Change
Cycles
Fortune
Luck
Predictions
Prophesies
Destany
Fate
Controlling your destiny
Taking Control of your life
Letting go of what you can't control
Power dynamics
Responsibilities
Interconnectedness
Bigger picture

SYMBOLS:

- Four Elements are represented on the card, earth, air, fire, and water with the four fixed signs of the zodiac.
- Rotating wheel represents the ever-changing cycle of life.

    The Fool comes to the Wheel of Fortune, watching it turn. They witness the ever-changing cycle of life and destiny embodied by the Wheel. Rising and falling, spinning endlessly, it's there to remind you of the impermanence of all things. Change is inevitable. The Wheel of Fortune teaches us to surrender to the flow of life and embrace the mysteries of fate.
    Within the kaleidoscope of the tarot's imagery, the Wheel of Fortune emerges as a profound testament to the ebb and flow of existence.
    At the heart of the Wheel of Fortune lies the wheel. It's adorned with arcane symbols that speak to the intricacies of fate and fortune. As it turns,

so too does the fabric of reality, ushering in new beginnings and closing the chapters of the past. The figures that surround the wheel represent the diverse manifestations of destiny, from triumph and success to adversity and challenges.

Symbolically, the Wheel of Fortune embodies the ceaseless rhythm of life's fluctuations. It's reminding you of the impermanence of all things and the inevitability of change. In the darkest of times, the wheel continues to turn, offering a promise of opportunities and fresh beginnings.

Sometimes the Wheel of Fortune is the catalyst for transformation and renewal. Embrace fate, and the winds of change. It challenges you to actively participate in shaping your own fate through conscious intention and mindful action. What do you want? Where do you want your life to be? Now is the time to discover the power of choice.

Have courage and know that now is the time for you to change your reality and embrace the change you want.

magical spell: destiny manifestation ritual:

Wheel of Fortune,
Turn in my favor,
Manifest my destiny,
Grant me your flavor.
With courage and faith,
I embrace the unknown,
My dreams are realized,
My power is shown.

materials needed:

- A quiet and comfortable space
- A candle (any color)
- A small piece of paper

- A pen or marker
- Lavender or rose petals (optional)

instructions:

- Find a peaceful space where you can sit comfortably without distractions.
- Light the candle and place it in front of you.
- If you have lavender or rose petals, scatter them around the candle to create a sacred space.
- Take a few deep breaths to center yourself and connect with the energy of the universe.
- On the piece of paper, write down a specific goal or desire that you wish to manifest.
- Hold the paper in your hands and visualize your goal coming to fruition, feeling the excitement and joy as if it has already happened.
- Recite the following incantation aloud:

"Wheel of Fortune, turn in my favor, Manifest my destiny, grant me your flavor. With courage and faith, I embrace the unknown, My dreams are realized, my power is shown.

- Allow yourself to feel a sense of gratitude and empowerment as you affirm your intentions.
- Fold the paper and hold it over the flame of the candle, allowing it to safely burn.
- As the paper burns, visualize the flames carrying your desires into the universe, where they will be fulfilled.
- Once the paper has turned to ash, extinguish the candle and trust in the magic of the Wheel of Fortune to guide you on your journey.

The Wheel of Fortune reminds you to embrace the ebb and flow of life's journey, knowing that change is inevitable and that destiny is always in motion. By embracing change with an open heart and a spirit of adventure, you can navigate the wheel of fortune with grace and courage, knowing that every turn brings new opportunities for growth and transformation. Let The Wheel of Fortune be your guiding light as you navigate the twists and turns of your destiny.

questions to ask yourself

1. What cycles or patterns am I currently experiencing in my life, and how are they influencing my journey?
2. Am I open to embracing change and the opportunities it brings, or am I resisting it out of fear or uncertainty?
3. What aspects of my life are within my control, and what aspects are subject to the forces of fate or destiny?
4. How can I adapt to the ebbs and flows of life with grace and resilience?
5. What lessons can I learn from past experiences of change and transformation, and how can I apply them in my current situation?
6. What new opportunities or challenges are on the horizon, and how can I prepare myself to navigate them effectively?
7. Am I willing to trust in the universe and surrender to the natural rhythms of life, even when things seem unpredictable or chaotic?
8. How can I cultivate a sense of gratitude and acceptance for the blessings and lessons that come my way, regardless of their perceived positive or negative nature?
9. What role does my attitude and mindset play in shaping my experience of change and uncertainty?
10. What steps can I take to align myself with the flow of life and co-create my reality in harmony with the universe?

1. justice

. . .

"Decision should be based on truth and fairness,"
Justice.

Element: Air
Planet: Venus
Answer: Maybe

Key Words and Phrases:
Rational
Logical thought
Objectivity
Binary thinking (Right/Wrong)
Fairness
Balance
Accountability
Social justice principles
Intersectionality
Cause and effect
Legal affairs

SYMBOLS:

- The scales symbolize balance, impartiality, and the weighing of evidence to make fair and equitable judgments.
- The sword represents clarity of thought, discernment, and the ability to cut through deception to reveal truth.
- The placement of the figure, between the pillars, signifies the middle path and the need to find equilibrium between opposing forces.

The Fool encounters the embodiment of justice and balance as the Justice card. Justice stands as a steadfast guardian of truth and fairness, beckoning the seeker to embrace the principles of equity and integrity in their journey through life.

In the Hallowed halls of cosmic justice, with scales in hand and blindfolded, Justice symbolizes the quest for truth untainted by bias or prejudice. She's a beacon of moral clarity in this world fraught with ambiguity and uncertainty.

Symbolically, the scales held by Justice represent the delicate balance of cause and effect, action, and consequence. As she weighs the deeds of the past, Justice imparts wisdom on the importance of accountability and responsibility in shaping one's destiny. Her blindfold speaks to the impartiality of the law, reminding you that justice transcends personal biases and agendas.

At its core, the Justice card embodies the principles of integrity and accountability. It urges you to confront your actions and decisions with honesty and integrity. It serves as a potent reminder that every choice carries weight and consequence. True wisdom lies in embracing the repercussions of your choices with courage and humility.

With your personal growth and self-reflection, the Justice card invites you to examine your motivations and intentions with clarity and discernment. Confront your bias and prejudice and strive for fairness.

magical spell: balance and harmony ritual:

Justice guide me,
balance restore,
Harmony reigns,
peace evermore.
With clarity and fairness,
I seek the light,
In truth and integrity,
all wrongs set right.

materials needed:

- A quiet and comfortable space
- A blue or silver candle

- A small piece of paper
- A pen or marker
- Lavender or chamomile essential oil (optional)

instructions:

- Find a peaceful space where you can sit comfortably without distractions.
- Light the blue or silver candle and place it in front of you.
- If you have essential oil, dab a drop on your wrists or pulse points to invoke a sense of calm and balance.
- Take a few deep breaths to center yourself and connect with the energy of balance and harmony.
- On the piece of paper, write down a situation or relationship in your life that feels out of balance or unjust.
- Hold the paper in your hands and visualize the situation resolving peacefully and harmoniously, with all parties treated fairly and respectfully.
- Recite the following affirmation aloud:

"Justice guide me, balance restore, Harmony reigns, peace evermore. With clarity and fairness, I seek the light, In truth and integrity, all wrongs set right."

- Allow yourself to feel a sense of peace and tranquility as you affirm your intentions.
- Fold the paper and hold it over the flame of the candle, allowing it to safely burn.
- As the paper burns, visualize the flames carrying your intentions into the universe, where they will be manifested in perfect balance and harmony.
- Once the paper has turned to ash, extinguish the candle and trust in the power of Justice to bring balance and fairness to your life.

Justice reminds you to seek fairness, balance, and integrity in all your dealings. By making decisions based on truth and fairness, and treating others with respect and compassion, you can create a world where justice prevails and harmony reigns. Let Justice be your guiding light as you navigate the complexities of life and strive to create a more just and equitable world.

questions to ask yourself

1. Where in my life am I seeking fairness and justice, and how can I advocate for these principles?
2. Am I making decisions with integrity and honesty, or am I acting out of self-interest or bias?
3. What areas of my life require greater balance and equilibrium, and how can I restore harmony in those areas?
4. Am I taking responsibility for my actions and their consequences, or am I avoiding accountability?
5. How can I ensure that I am treating others with respect and dignity, regardless of their background or circumstances?
6. What truths or realities do I need to acknowledge and confront to achieve a sense of inner balance and peace?
7. Am I willing to face the consequences of my choices and actions, even if they are difficult or uncomfortable?
8. How can I cultivate a sense of fairness and justice in my interactions with others, both personally and professionally?
9. What values and principles guide my sense of right and wrong, and how can I uphold them in my daily life?
10. What steps can I take to seek resolution and reconciliation in conflicts or disputes, rather than perpetuating resentment or hostility?

12. the hanged man
. . .

"Embrace the power of stillness and non-action. Sometimes, the greatest progress is made in moments of quiet contemplation," The Hanged Man

Lorelai Hamilton

Element: Water
Planet: Neptune
Answer: No

Key Words and Phrases:
Passivity
Patience
Surrender
Perspective
Sacrifice
Release
Enlightenment
Meditation
Inner peace
Self-acceptance
Overcoming ego

SYMBOLS:

- Upside-Down figure symbolizes surrendering to circumstance beyond your control. Try looking at the world from a different perspective.
- The serene expression on the hanged man's face signifies acceptance and peace in the face of adversity.
- The halo around it his head represents enlightenment and spiritual awakening that was attained through surrender and sacrifice.

Suspended between earth and spirit, The Fool comes across the Hanged Man. He's a figure of surrender and sacrifice. Instead of resisting, he embraces his current situation and lets go of control and his own point of view. He gains enlightenment through his surrender. The Hanged Man invites you to embrace the wisdom of letting things go and surrendering to the ebb and flow of life.

The Hanged Man is reminding you to let go of your preconceived notions and expectations to gain a fresh perspective on life's challenges and opportunities.

Symbolically, the Hanged Man embodies the concept of sacrifice and selflessness. Surrender ego and desires in exchange for higher truth and spiritual growth. When you can release your ego, you'll find the liberating power of letting go.

True wisdom lies in the ability to view the world from a different perspective. It serves as a potent reminder that, in moments of hardship and adversity, surrendering to the flow of life can lead to unexpected revelations and newfound clarity.

Have patience when you're feeling uncertainty and doubt. The Hanged man is a beacon of hope and guidance.

magical spell: perspective shift ritual:

Hanged Man,
guide me,
grant me grace,
Surrendered to the unknown,
I find my place.
From new perspectives,
wisdom blooms,
Illuminating paths,
dispelling gloom.

materials needed:

- A quiet and comfortable space
- A purple or indigo candle
- A small piece of paper

- A pen or marker
- Lavender or frankincense incense (optional)

instructions:

- Find a peaceful space where you can sit comfortably without distractions.
- Light the purple or indigo candle and place it in front of you.
- If you have incense, light it and allow the fragrant smoke to fill the air, creating a sacred atmosphere.
- Take a few deep breaths to center yourself and quiet your mind.
- On the piece of paper, write down a situation or issue in your life where you feel stuck or uncertain.
- Hold the paper in your hands and visualize yourself letting go of control and surrendering to the flow of life.
- Recite the following affirmation aloud:

"Hanged Man, guide me, grant me grace, surrendered to the unknown, I find my place. From new perspectives, wisdom blooms, Illuminating paths, dispelling gloom."

- Allow yourself to feel a sense of peace and acceptance as you affirm your intentions.
- Fold the paper and hold it over the flame of the candle, allowing it to safely burn.
- As the paper burns, visualize the flames purifying your intentions and opening you to new perspectives and insights.
- Once the paper has turned to ash, extinguish the candle and trust in the power of surrender to bring clarity and wisdom to your life.

The Hanged Man invites you to embrace surrender and gain new perspectives on life's challenges. By letting go of control and viewing situations from different angles, you can gain valuable insights and find peace amidst uncertainty. Let The Hanged Man be your guide as you navigate the journey of self-discovery and spiritual awakening.

questions to ask yourself

1. In what areas of my life do I need to surrender and let go of control?
2. What attachments or beliefs am I holding onto that are hindering my personal growth and development?
3. How can I shift my perspective to see challenges or setbacks as opportunities for learning and growth?
4. What sacrifices am I willing to make in order to gain a deeper understanding of myself and my life's path?
5. Am I resisting change or transformation out of fear, and how can I embrace the process of letting go?
6. What insights or wisdom can I gain from embracing a state of suspension and allowing myself to be present in the moment?
7. How can I cultivate a sense of acceptance and trust in the universe, knowing that sometimes surrendering is the most empowering choice?
8. What new perspectives or insights can I gain by stepping back and observing my life from a different angle?
9. What patterns or habits do I need to release in order to create space for new opportunities and growth?
10. How can I use the experience of suspension to deepen my spiritual practice and connect more fully with my inner self?

13. death

. . .

"The caterpillar doesn't know the beautiful butterfly it will become. It is not the end, it's simply change," Death.

Element: Water
Planet: Pluto
Answer: No

Key Words and Phrases:
Personal transformation
Starting over
The ending of a cycle
Letting go
New cycle
Change
Transformation
Rebirth
Release
Renewal

SYMBOLS:

- The skeletal figure represents the universal aspect of death that touches all living beings.
- The scythe symbolizes the cutting away of old and the clearing of obstacles to make way for new growth.
- The sun rising in the background represents the promise of renewal and new beginnings after the darkness of night
- The different figures (a priest, a king, a young woman, and child) remind you that no one escapes the Death card. Everyone goes through changes and cycles.

In the shadow of an ancient oak tree, The Fool comes across Death, the harbinger of transformation and rebirth. With his scythe, he cuts away the old and outdated, making way for new beginnings and growth. Death reminds us that all things must pass, paving the way for renewal, regeneration, and transformation.

The Death card stands as a symbol of transition and renewal, urging the seeker to release the shackles of the past and embrace the boundless potential of the future. Amidst life, Death serves as a steadfast reminder that all things must come to an end for new beginnings to emerge.

Symbolically, the imagery of the Death card depicts a figure clocked in black, wielding a scythe to harvest the fruits of the past. As the old gives way to the new, Death invites you to confront their fears and insecurities, paving the way for personal growth and evolution.

The Death card challenges you to embrace change with courage and grace. It's a reminder that even when life throws you a curveball, and it feels like your life is in upheave, there is a promise of renewal and transformation on the horizon.

The Death card holds profound implications for your understanding of impermanence. Life is fleeting, transient, and now is the time to embrace the beauty of the present with gratitude.

As the Fool navigates the tarot, the Death card is a testament to the eternal cycle of life. Remember that the caterpillar doesn't know it's going to become a butterfly. That cocoon feels like death to the caterpillar. Remember that change can be lovely. Perhaps you're just growing your wings right now.

magical spell: renewal and transformation ritual:

Death, guide me through
The cycle of change,
Embracing endings,
New beginnings
I arrange.
From darkness to light,
From death to rebirth,
I embrace transformation,
Finding my worth.

materials needed:

- A quiet and comfortable space
- A black candle
- A small piece of paper
- A pen or marker
- Sage or rosemary (optional)

instructions:

- Find a peaceful space where you can sit comfortably without distractions.
- Light the black candle and place it in front of you.
- If you have sage or rosemary, burn it and allow the fragrant smoke to cleanse the space and your energy.
- Take a few deep breaths to center yourself and connect with the energy of transformation.
- On the piece of paper, write down something in your life that you are ready to release or transform.
- Hold the paper in your hands and visualize yourself letting go of the old and welcoming the new.
- Recite the following affirmation aloud:

"Death, guide me through the cycle of change, Embracing endings, new beginnings I arrange. From darkness to light, from death to rebirth, I embrace transformation, finding my worth."

- Allow yourself to feel a sense of liberation and empowerment as you affirm your intentions.
- Fold the paper and hold it over the flame of the candle, allowing it to safely burn.
- As the paper burns, visualize the flames consuming the old and making way for new growth and renewal.
- Once the paper has turned to ash, extinguish the candle and trust in the power of transformation to guide you on your journey.

Death reminds you that change is inevitable, and that transformation is a natural part of life's journey. By embracing endings and letting go of the old, you can make way for new opportunities, growth, and renewal. Let Death be your guide as you navigate the cycle of life and embrace the transformative power of change.

questions to ask yourself

1. What aspects of my life are ready for transformation or change?
2. Am I holding onto situations, relationships, or patterns that no longer serve my highest good?
3. What fears or attachments do I need to release in order to embrace the process of transformation?
4. How can I view endings as opportunities for new beginnings and growth?
5. What parts of myself am I willing to let go of in order to align more fully with my true purpose and potential?
6. Am I resisting change out of fear or uncertainty, and how can I cultivate trust in the process of transformation?
7. What lessons can I learn from past experiences of loss or transition, and how can I apply them in my current situation?
8. What support or resources do I need to navigate the changes occurring in my life with grace and resilience?
9. How can I honor the endings in my life while also embracing the potential for new beginnings and opportunities?
10. What steps can I take to actively participate in the process of transformation and co-create my reality in alignment with my deepest desires and intentions?

14. temperance
. . .

"Have patience. Powerful work is happening now, it's a magical process," Temperance.

Element: Fire
Planet: Jupiter
Answer: Yes

Key Words and Phrases:

Balance
Harmony
Duality
Alchemy
Nonbinary
Self-care
Grace
Gentleness
Integration
Moderation
Patience

SYMBOLS:

- The angel represents divine guidance and spiritual balance. While the wings symbolize freedom and transcendence.
- The cups represent the margining of opposing forces, such as fire and water, to create harmony and synergy.
- The flowing water between the cups, symbolizes the flow of energy and the need to find balance between extremes.

By the tranquil waters of a following stream, The fool encounters Temperance. The figure pours the elixir of balance and harmony between the two cups. With grace and poise, Temperance blends opposing forces, finding equilibrium and moderation in all things. Temperance teaches us the art of patience, moderation, and finding harmony within ourselves.

With one foot grounded in the material world, and the other immersed in the waters of the soul, Temperance serves as a bridge between the realms of earth and spirt.

Symbolically, the imagery of the Temperance card depicts an angelic figure pouring liquid from one vessel to another, symbolizing the alchemical process of transformation and renewal. As the waters of consciousness flow freely between the vessels, Temperance invites you to cultivate a sense of inner balance and harmony, the ebb and flow of life.

Temperance challenges you to embrace the virtues of patience and moderation. True fulfillment lies in the cultivation of balanced, harmonious existence. Through the practice of temperance, you can discover the beauty of alignment.

Along this journey called life, Temperance is a beacon of hope and guidance. In the tranquil waters of Temperance, you can find the boundless depths of the human soul.

magical spell: harmony invocation ritual:

Temperance,
Guide me,
Balance restore,
Harmony reigns,
Peace evermore.
With patience and grace,
I seek the light,
In balance and moderation,
All is right.

materials needed:

- A quiet and comfortable space
- A green or blue candle
- A small piece of paper

- A pen or marker
- Lavender or chamomile essential oil (optional)

instructions:

- Find a peaceful space where you can sit comfortably without distractions.
- Light the green or blue candle and place it in front of you.
- If you have essential oil, dab a drop on your wrists or pulse points to invoke a sense of calm and harmony.
- Take a few deep breaths to center yourself and connect with the energy of balance and harmony.
- On the piece of paper, write down areas of your life where you seek greater balance and harmony.
- Hold the paper in your hands and visualize yourself finding balance and harmony in those areas.
- Recite the following affirmation aloud:

"Temperance, guide me, balance restore, Harmony reigns, peace evermore. With patience and grace, I seek the light, In balance and moderation, all is right."

- Allow yourself to feel a sense of peace and tranquility as you affirm your intentions.
- Fold the paper and hold it over the flame of the candle, allowing it to safely burn.
- As the paper burns, visualize the flames purifying your intentions and bringing balance and harmony into your life.
- Once the paper has turned to ash, extinguish the candle and trust in the power of Temperance to guide you towards inner peace and harmony.

Temperance reminds you to find balance and harmony in all aspects of your life. By practicing moderation, patience, and self-control, you can cultivate inner peace and harmony amidst life's ups and downs. Let Temperance be your guide as you navigate the journey of self-discovery and personal growth.

questions to ask yourself

1. Where in my life do I need to find greater balance and equilibrium?
2. How can I integrate conflicting aspects of myself or my circumstances to create harmony?
3. Am I practicing moderation in my thoughts, behaviors, and actions, or am I being pulled to extremes?
4. What areas of my life could benefit from a more patient and temperate approach?
5. How can I blend different aspects of my life or personality to create a more cohesive and unified whole?
6. What practices or rituals can I incorporate into my daily routine to cultivate inner peace and balance?
7. Am I seeking fulfillment through external sources, or am I cultivating a sense of contentment and satisfaction from within?
8. What lessons can I learn from past experiences of imbalance or excess, and how can I apply them in my current situation?
9. How can I maintain a sense of perspective and avoid getting caught up in the chaos or drama of life?
10. What steps can I take to cultivate a more harmonious relationship with myself and others?

15. the devil
...
"Everything in moderation," The Devil.

Element: Earth
Planet: Saturn
Answer: No

Key Words and Phrases
Bondage
Addiction
Materialism
Destructive behaviors
Harmful cycles
Losing sight of what is important in life
Confronting fear
Accountability to yourself
Delusion…and self-awareness
Committing to your own freedom

SYMBOLS:

- The chains around the figures' necks represent the bondage of materialism, addition, and any negative habits, and temptations that imprison you.
- The figures represent the shadow aspects of our psyche and the illusions that keep us trapped in patterns of self-destruction.

In the depths of the underworld, they confront The Devil, a figure of bondage and temptation. Chains bind those who succumb to material desires and illusions, trapping them in a cycle of fear and attachment. The Devil reminds us of the importance of breaking free from self-imposed limitations, embracing liberation, and reclaiming our personal power.

The Devil beckons you to confront your deepest fears and desires. Within the intricate web of the tarot, The Devil serves as a mirror reflecting the primal urges and untamed instincts that dwell within.

The Devil can symbolize darker aspects of human nature, but it can also just be referring to indulging in too much of a good thing. Remember, everything in moderation.

Symbolically, the imagery of The Devil card depicts a figure adorned with horns and wings, standing atop a pedestal adorned with symbols of material wealth and excess. With chains wrapped around the necks of two figures, The Devil symbolizes the bondage of the ego.

At its core, The Devil card challenges you to confront the shadows that lurk within your own heart. Life is full of pressure, societal expectations, and the allure of instant gratification. The Devil card speaks of negative influences in your life. If you have lingering shadow work to do, this is your sign. Otherwise, this is your reminder to indulge in moderation.

magical spell: liberation from bondage ritual:

In the depths of night
where shadows dwell,
I conjure forth the light unseen,
To break the chains and set me free.
I call upon the power within,
To break the bonds, release, begin.
From the darkness, I now rise,
With fire inside I claim the skies,
Shadows fade, and light prevails,
As I chart anew, my destined trails,
By the power of the Devil's decree,
I break free now, so mote it be!

materials needed:

- A quiet and comfortable space
- A black candle
- A small piece of paper

- A pen or marker
- Lavender or sage incense (optional)

instructions:

1. Find a peaceful space where you can sit comfortably without distractions.
2. Light the black candle and place it in front of you.
3. If you have incense, light it, and allow the fragrant smoke to cleanse the space and your energy.
4. Take a few deep breaths to center yourself and connect with the energy of liberation and transformation.
5. On the piece of paper, write down a negative habit, fear, or limitation that you wish to release.
6. Hold the paper in your hands and visualize yourself breaking free from the chains of bondage and stepping into the light of liberation.
7. Recite the following affirmation aloud:

"In the depths of night where shadows dwell, I conjure forth the light unseen. To break the chains and set me free. I call upon the power within. To break the bonds, release, begin. From the darkness, I now rise. With fire inside I claim the skies, Shadows fade, and light prevails, As I chart anew, my destined trails, By the power of the Devil's decree, I break free now, so mote it be!"

1. Allow yourself to feel a sense of empowerment and liberation as you affirm your intentions.
2. Fold the paper and hold it over the flame of the candle, allowing it to safely burn.
3. As the paper burns, visualize the flames consuming the chains of bondage and setting you free from your limitations.
4. Once the paper has turned to ash, extinguish the candle and trust in the power of liberation to guide you on your journey towards freedom.

The Devil card reminds you to confront your fears, limitations, and attachments to attain liberation and spiritual growth. By acknowledging and releasing the negative patterns that hold you captive, you can break free from bondage and step into the light of your true essence. Confront temptation and embrace the path of liberation and self-discovery.

questions to ask yourself

1. What unhealthy patterns or habits am I currently indulging in that are holding me back from reaching my full potential?
2. In what areas of my life do I feel trapped or enslaved by my desires or fears?
3. How can I recognize and release the negative influences or toxic relationships that are keeping me bound?
4. What attachments or dependencies do I need to let go of in order to experience true freedom and liberation?
5. Am I allowing external circumstances or influences to control my actions and decisions, or am I taking responsibility for my own choices?
6. What fears or insecurities are driving me to seek comfort or security in material possessions or superficial pleasures?
7. How can I break free from limiting beliefs or societal expectations that are keeping me stuck in a cycle of dissatisfaction or self-sabotage?
8. What steps can I take to reclaim my power and autonomy in situations where I feel powerless or helpless?
9. Am I willing to confront the darker aspects of myself and acknowledge my shadow side to facilitate healing and growth?
10. How can I cultivate a sense of self-awareness and mindfulness to resist temptation and make choices that align with my highest good?

16. the tower

. . .

"Transformation is inevitable, but your reaction to it is within your control," The Tower.

Element: Fire
Planet: Mars
Answer: No

Key Words and Phrases:
Revolution
Disaster
Shock
Mourning
Demolition
Toppling power
Potential
New Cycles
Rebuilding
A blessing in disguise as a disaster
Rehabilitation
Regeneration

SYMBOLS:

- The lightning bolt represents a sudden and disruptive force disrupting the status quo.
- The flames symbolize chaos, destruction, and the breaking down of old standards.
- The crown at the top of the tower symbolizes the false sense of security and ego driven pride.
- One of the figures was pushed out of the tower, while the other jumped. This symbolizes what happens when you refuse to leave a bad situation. The universe has your back and will force change on you if you're not prepared to take steps on your own.

Amidst a lightning storm with thunder clapping, The Fool witnesses The Tower. A structure crumbling in the face of divine intervention and upheaval. Flames engulf the tower, symbolizing destruction and chaos, clearing the path for new growth and transformation. The Tower teaches us the importance of embracing change and releasing attachments. While The Tower can be a catalyst, it's always with good intent. Sometimes wonderful transformation is a painful process.

The Tower symbolizes the destruction of illusions and the collapse of false beliefs. The lightning bolt of truth strikes with relentless force. Look at the two figures falling: one person appears to have been pushed out of the tower, unwilling to change, grow, and break free from negative influences. This resistance has resulted in a forceful expulsion from their comfort zone. They ignored the call to change when it arrived.

The second figure jumped out of the window. They anticipated change and embraced it instead of resisting. They let go of the burdens in their life and welcomed transformation. The Tower's strike doesn't necessarily signify a negative process. Transformation is inevitable, but your reaction to it is within your control.

magical spell: transformation and renewal ritual:

Tower, guide me,
old I shed,
Transformation comes,
from chaos led.
In destruction's wake,
renewal blooms,
From ashes to phoenix,
new life resumes.

materials needed:

- A quiet and comfortable space
- A white candle

- A small piece of paper
- A pen or marker
- Lavender or rosemary essential oil (optional)

instructions:

- Find a peaceful space where you can sit comfortably without distractions.
- Light the white candle and place it in front of you.
- If you have essential oil, dab a drop on your wrists or pulse points to invoke a sense of calm and renewal.
- Take a few deep breaths to center yourself and connect with the energy of transformation and renewal.
- On the piece of paper, write down something in your life that you wish to release or transform.
- Hold the paper in your hands and visualize yourself breaking free from the old and embracing the new.
- Recite the following affirmation aloud:

"Tower, guide me, old I shed, Transformation comes, from chaos led. In destruction's wake, renewal blooms, From ashes to phoenix, new life resumes."

- Allow yourself to feel a sense of liberation and empowerment as you affirm your intentions.
- Fold the paper and hold it over the flame of the candle, allowing it to safely burn.
- As the paper burns, visualize the flames purifying your intentions and paving the way for new beginnings and growth.
- Once the paper has turned to ash, extinguish the candle and trust in the power of transformation to guide you on your journey towards renewal.

The Tower reminds you that change and upheaval are natural parts of life's journey. By embracing the destruction of old paradigms and structures, you can pave the way for new growth, renewal, and transformation. Let The Tower be your guide as you navigate the chaos of life and embrace the potential for profound change and renewal.

questions to ask yourself

1. What areas of my life are experiencing sudden disruption or upheaval?
2. What structures or beliefs have I built my life upon that may no longer serve me?
3. Am I resisting necessary change, and if so, why?
4. What can I learn from this sudden shift or crisis?
5. How can I embrace change and see it as an opportunity for growth?
6. What illusions have I been holding onto that need to be shattered?
7. What aspects of my life need to be rebuilt or reevaluated after this upheaval?
8. How can I better prepare myself emotionally and spiritually for unexpected events?
9. Am I avoiding confronting a difficult truth or situation in my life?
10. What support systems do I have in place to help me navigate this turbulent period?

17. the star
. . .
"Embrace hope and Inspiration," The Star

Element: Air
Planet: Uranus
Answer: Yes

Key Words and Phrases
Hope
Love
Support
Self-care
Healing
Intuition
Integrity
Honesty
Luck
Wishes

SYMBOLS:

- The woman represents our connection to the divine and the intuitive guidance that flows from within you.
- The water symbolizes emotions, renewal, and the subconscious mind.
- The stars represent hope, inspiration, and the infinite possibilities that await us in the universe.

In the tranquil hours of twilight, a lone figure stood at the edge of a serene lake, where the sky mirrored its depths, reflecting a canvas of stars. This figure, draped in a flowing robe adorned with celestial patterns, gazed up at the heavens, seeking guidance in the shimmering tapestry above. She was the embodiment of The Star, a beacon of hope and inspiration amidst the darkness.

With a gentle sigh, she raised her arms to the sky, as if conducting a symphony of celestial bodies. Above her, the stars seemed to twinkle with newfound brilliance, casting a soft glow upon her face. In that moment, she felt a profound connection to the universe, as if each twinkling light held the secrets of the cosmos within its luminous embrace.

The Star spoke to her of dreams and aspirations, of infinite possibilities waiting to be discovered. It whispered of the boundless potential that lay dormant within her, urging her to reach for the stars and manifest her deepest desires.

As she stood there, bathed in the soft glow of moonlight, she felt a sense of peace wash over her. The anxieties and uncertainties that had plagued her mind seemed to melt away, replaced by a profound sense of clarity and purpose.

The Star symbolized faith and renewal, reminding you that even in the darkest of nights, there was always a glimmer of hope to guide your way. It encouraged you to trust in the universe and believe in the power of your own inner light.

And so, with renewed determination, The Fool set forth on its journey, guided by the light of The Star and fueled by the unwavering belief that their dreams were within reach. For they knew that as long as they remained true to themselves and followed the path illuminated by the stars, they would always find their way home.

magical spell: manifesting dreams ritual:

Bathed in the guiding light of stars,
I beckon dreams from realms afar,
Manifesting, let it be done,
Through the veils of night, my visions unfold,
As the universe listens, my story is told,
In the tapestry of fate, my dreams weave
A symphony of wishes, I now believe,
With every breath, I embrace the night,
As dreams take flight, in the star's soft light.

Starlight guide me, dreams I see,
Manifesting, as it's meant to be.

materials needed:

- A quiet and comfortable space
- A yellow or gold candle
- A small piece of paper
- A pen or marker
- Lavender or jasmine essential oil (optional)

instructions:

1. Find a peaceful space where you can sit comfortably without distractions.
2. Light the yellow or gold candle and place it in front of you.
3. If you have essential oil, dab a drop on your wrists or pulse points to invoke a sense of peace and inspiration.
4. Take a few deep breaths to center yourself and connect with the energy of hope and inspiration.
5. On the piece of paper, write down a dream or goal that you wish to manifest.
6. Hold the paper in your hands and visualize yourself achieving your dream with clarity and confidence.
7. Recite the following affirmation aloud:

"Bathed in the guiding light of stars, I beckon dreams from realms afar, Manifesting, let it be done, Through the veils of night, my visions unfold, As the universe listens, my story is told, In the tapestry of fate, my dreams weave. A symphony of wishes, I now believe, With every breath, I embrace the night, As dreams take flight, in the star's soft light. Starlight guide me, dreams I see, Manifesting, as it's meant to be."

1. Allow yourself to feel a sense of excitement and anticipation as you affirm your intentions.
2. Fold the paper and hold it over the flame of the candle, allowing it to safely burn.
3. As the paper burns, visualize the flames carrying your intentions out into the universe, where they will be manifested in divine timing.
4. Once the paper has turned to ash, extinguish the candle and trust in the power of the Star to guide you towards the fulfillment of your dreams.

The Star reminds you to have faith in the universe and to trust in the guidance of your intuition and higher self. By embracing hope and inspiration, you can manifest your dreams and create a life filled with joy, fulfillment, and abundance. Let The Star be your guiding light as you navigate the journey of self-discovery and personal growth.

questions to ask yourself

1. What brings me a sense of hope and inspiration in my life right now?
2. In what ways am I aligning with my true purpose and calling?
3. How can I better connect with my intuition and inner guidance?
4. What dreams and aspirations am I currently pursuing or wishing to manifest?
5. Am I nurturing myself emotionally and spiritually, or do I need to prioritize self-care?
6. What areas of my life need healing or renewal, and how can I facilitate this process?
7. What signs or synchronicities am I noticing that could be guiding me towards my highest good?
8. How can I cultivate a greater sense of trust and faith in the universe and its plan for me?
9. What steps can I take to bring more positivity and optimism into my life and the lives of others?
10. What opportunities for growth and expansion are presenting themselves to me, and how can I embrace them fully?

18. the moon
...

"You are both the dog and the wolf, the sun and the moon," The Moon.

Element: Water
Planet: Neptune
Answer: No

Key Words and Phrases:
Shadow work
Intuition
Hope
Inspiration
Renewal
Guidance
Aspiration
Secret messages
Signs and symbols
Witchcraft
Magic
Wearing a mask
Deceiving yourself

SYMBOLS:

- The moon represents the realm of the subconscious and the mysteries that lie beyond conscious awareness.
- The dog and the wolf symbolize the domesticated and wild aspects of our nature.
- The winding path leading into the distance represents the journey to the unknown and the need to trust your inner guidance.

In the stillness of the night, they wander beneath the pale glow of The Moon. She's a symbol of intuition and subconscious wisdom. Shadows dance amidst the moonlit landscape, revealing hidden truths and mysteries lurking beneath the surface. The Moon teaches us to trust our instincts, navigate the realms of the unknown, and embrace the cycles of our inner world.

The Moon symbolizes illusion, intuition, and the subconscious mind. Depicted as a scene with a moon, a dog, and a wolf, it represents the mysteries of the subconscious, hidden truths, and the ebb and flow of emotions. The card encourages us to trust our intuition, explore the depths of our psyche, and navigate through uncertainty with courage and wisdom.

Sometimes this card speaks to unseen truths or things hidden from view. If The Moon comes out during a love reading, pause and recognize there's likely something about the relationship you don't know yet.

The Moon speaks to the common uncertainty, confusion, and the exploration of subconscious that everyone faces. It's natural to express periods of darkness and uncertainty, but trust your intuition and inner wisdom. They will help you find your way thorough the shadows and emerge stronger and wiser.

magical spell: unveiling truth ritual:

Moonlight guide me
Shadows reveal,
Truth and wisdom,
I now feel.
In darkness' embrace,
Clarity, I find,
Unveiling secrets,
Expanding my mind."

materials needed:

- A quiet and comfortable space
- A silver or white candle

- A small piece of paper
- A pen or marker
- Lavender or sandalwood essential oil (optional)

instructions:

- Find a peaceful space where you can sit comfortably without distractions.
- Light the silver or white candle and place it in front of you.
- If you have essential oil, dab a drop on your wrists or pulse points to invoke a sense of clarity and intuition.
- Take a few deep breaths to center yourself and connect with the energy of intuition and insight.
- On the piece of paper, write down a question or issue that you wish to gain clarity on.
- Hold the paper in your hands and visualize a beam of silver light illuminating the shadows and revealing the truth.
- Recite the following affirmation aloud:

"Moonlight guide me, shadows reveal, Truth and wisdom, I now feel. In darkness' embrace, clarity I find, Unveiling secrets, expanding my mind."

- Allow yourself to feel a sense of openness and receptivity as you affirm your intentions.
- Fold the paper and hold it over the flame of the candle, allowing it to safely burn.
- As the paper burns, visualize the flames transmuting your question into insights and understanding.
- Once the paper has turned to ash, extinguish the candle and trust in the power of the Moon to illuminate your path and reveal the truth.

The Moon reminds you to trust in your intuition and explore the depths of your subconscious mind. By embracing uncertainty and navigating through the shadows with courage and wisdom, you can uncover hidden truths and emerge stronger and wiser than before. Let The Moon be your guide as you journey into the mysteries of the soul and discover the power of your inner wisdom.

questions to ask yourself

1. What fears or anxieties are currently lurking beneath the surface of my consciousness?
2. Am I deceiving myself or ignoring certain truths in my life?
3. What illusions or illusions am I currently experiencing that may be clouding my judgment?
4. How can I better connect with and understand my subconscious mind?
5. What hidden aspects of myself, or my situation do I need to acknowledge and address?
6. What role is intuition playing in my decision-making process, and am I trusting it enough?
7. What recurring dreams or symbols am I experiencing, and what messages might they hold for me?
8. Am I avoiding confronting difficult emotions or situations, and if so, why?
9. How can I bring more clarity and illumination into areas of my life that feel uncertain or murky?
10. What steps can I take to navigate through this period of confusion or uncertainty with courage and resilience?

19. the sun

. . .

"Embrace your power. Reclaim it if it's slipped from your grasp. If it's eluded you, let the warmth of a tender kiss on your cheeks guide you back to its source," The Sun.

Element: Fire
Planet: Sun
Answer: Yes

Key Words and Phrases:
Positivity
Saying yes
Joy
Gratitude
Success
Simple pleasures
New Projects
Birth
Children
Vitality
Enlightenment
Celebration
Optimism

SYMBOLS:

- The Sun represents vitality, enlightenment, and the source of life and energy.
- The joyful scene with the child ridding a white horse symbolizes innocence, freedom, and the pure expression of joy.
- The sunflower symbolizes growth, abundance, and the radiant energy of the sun.

As dawn breaks upon the horizon, The Fool basks in the radiant warmth of The Sun. Joy, vitality, and enlightenment radiate from The Sun. With laughter and exuberance, children dance beneath its golden rays, celebrating the beauty of life and the promise of a new day. The Sun reminds you to embrace the fullness of your being. Shine brightly and cultivate a sense of joy and gratitude in every moment.

Arguably the best card in the tarot (equal to the Ten of pentacles in levels of joy), The Sun serves to illuminate joy and reasons to celebrate. Enveloped in the golden embrace of dawn, The Sun symbolizes the dawning of a new day, heralding a time of clarity, vitality, and inner radiance. It serves as a reminder that even amidst the darkest of nights, the light of hope and possibility shines eternally, guiding the way toward a brighter tomorrow.

In matters of the heart, The Sun radiates with the warmth of love and connection, illuminating the path toward deep emotionally fulfilling relationships. It symbolizes the blossoming of romantic bonds, friendships, and familial ties. The Sun infuses these relationships with joy, warmth, and camaraderie. Nurture the relationships that bring light and laughter into your life.

You are ready to embrace your highest potential and pursue your dreams with unwavering enthusiasm and determination. The Sun cards encourages you to embrace the fullness of life with open arms and an open heart. As The Fool continues their journey through the tarot, The Sun is a symbol of hope and enlightenment. Don't be afraid to say YES.

magical spell: radiant confidence ritual:

Sunlight guide me,
Confidence ignite,
Radiant energy,
Shining bright.
With joy in my heart,
I embrace the day,
In the sun's warm embrace,
I find my way."

materials needed:

- A quiet and comfortable space
- A yellow or gold candle
- A small piece of paper
- A pen or marker
- Citrine or sunstone crystal (optional)

instructions:

- Find a peaceful space where you can sit comfortably without distractions.
- Light the yellow or gold candle and place it in front of you.
- If you have a citrine or sunstone crystal, hold it in your hands to amplify the energy of the sun.
- Take a few deep breaths to center yourself and connect with the warmth and vitality of the sun.
- On the piece of paper, write down a quality or attribute that you wish to cultivate within yourself, such as confidence, joy, or optimism.
- Hold the paper in your hands and visualize yourself basking in the radiant energy of the sun, feeling confident and empowered.
- Recite the following affirmation aloud:

"Sunlight guide me, confidence ignite, Radiant energy, shining bright. With joy in my heart, I embrace the day, In the sun's warm embrace, I find my way."

- Allow yourself to feel a sense of warmth and vitality as you affirm your intentions.
- Fold the paper and hold it over the flame of the candle, allowing it to safely burn.
- As the paper burns, visualize the flames transforming your intention into reality, filling you with confidence and joy.
- Once the paper has turned to ash, extinguish the candle and carry the energy of the sun with you throughout your day, knowing that you shine brightly from within.

The Sun reminds you to embrace joy, vitality, and the radiant energy of your true self. By cultivating optimism, confidence, and a sense of inner light, you can illuminate the world around you and inspire others with your positivity and warmth. Let The Sun be your guiding light as you journey forward with joy and radiance in your heart.

questions to ask yourself

1. What brings me the most joy and fulfillment in my life right now?
2. In what areas of my life am I experiencing success and abundance?
3. How can I embrace and celebrate my achievements and victories?
4. What aspects of myself or my life could benefit from more positivity and optimism?
5. Am I living in alignment with my true self and values, or are there areas where I need to make adjustments?
6. What opportunities for growth and expansion are currently available to me?
7. How can I bring more light and clarity into areas of my life that feel cloudy or uncertain?
8. What steps can I take to cultivate a greater sense of vitality and energy?
9. Am I expressing gratitude for the blessings and abundance in my life?
10. How can I share my warmth, light, and positivity with others?

20. judgement
. . .

"Own your actions, your thoughts, your words.
Then let it all go," Judgement.

Lorelai Hamilton

Element: Fire
Planet: Pluto
Answer: Yes

Key Words and Phrases:
Liberation
Freedom
Casting off shackles
Putting to rest old baggage
Self-acceptance
Accountability
Integrity
Honesty
Forgiveness
Forgiveness
Self-love
Letting go
Forward movement
Growing Up
Transformation

SYMBOLS:

- The figures rising from their graves symbolize liberation from past mistakes, awakening to hire truths, and embracing a new sense of purpose and identity.
- The Angel sounding the trumpet represents divine guidance, spiritual awakening and the call to self-discovery and transformation.
- The ocean in the background represents the vast depths of the subconscious and the endless possibilities for growth and renewal.

In the echoes of existence, The Fool encounters the Judgment card. It's a herald of transformation and spiritual awakening. It's a symbol of rebirth, renewal, and awakening to hire consciousness. The judgement card asks you to reflect on your past actions and embrace self-discovery.

Rich with symbolism, the Judgment card speaks of the liberation from self-imposed limitations and the shackles that hold you to the past. In the background, graves symbolize the past, while figures rising from them signify rebirth and renewal.

The Judgment card asks you to heed your inner voice, make amends, and embark on the journey of spiritual evolution. Like the phoenix rising from the ashes, it symbolizes the opportunity for renewal and redemption.

This card can be a powerful reminder of the importance of self-reflection and accountability. It urges you to confront past mistakes, learn from them, and strive for personal growth. Listen to your inner wisdom.

In relationships, the Judgment card may signify the need for forgiveness, reconciliation, and healing. Let go of old resentments and embrace a new beginning based on honesty and mutual respect.

The Judgment card also carries a message of liberation from societal expectations and conformity. Break free from the chains of peer pressure and societal norms. Live authentically and embrace your true self. Every choice you make has a consequence. You have the power to shape your own destiny.

magical spell: rebirth and renewal ritual:

Judgment guide me,
Past I release,
Rebirth and renewal,
I find my peace.
From darkness to light,
From pain to grace,
I embrace my journey,

Lorelai Hamilton

I claim my place.

materials needed:

- A quiet and comfortable space
- A white candle
- A small piece of paper
- A pen or marker
- Lavender or rosemary essential oil (optional)

instructions:

- Find a peaceful space where you can sit comfortably without distractions.
- Light the white candle and place it in front of you.
- If you have essential oil, dab a drop on your wrists or pulse points to invoke a sense of peace and renewal.
- Take a few deep breaths to center yourself and connect with the energy of rebirth and transformation.
- On the piece of paper, write down something from the past that you wish to release or forgive yourself for.
- Hold the paper in your hands and visualize yourself letting go of the past and embracing a new beginning.
- Recite the following affirmation aloud:

"Judgment guide me, past I release, Rebirth and renewal, I find my peace. From darkness to light, from pain to grace, I embrace my journey, I claim my place."

- Allow yourself to feel a sense of liberation and empowerment as you affirm your intentions.
- Fold the paper and hold it over the flame of the candle, allowing it to safely burn.
- As the paper burns, visualize the flames purifying your intentions and clearing the path for new beginnings and growth.
- Once the paper has turned to ash, extinguish the candle and trust in the power of Judgment to guide you on your journey towards self-discovery and transformation.

Judgment reminds you to embrace self-discovery, forgiveness, and the opportunity for renewal and transformation. By releasing yourself from the burdens of the past and awakening to your true potential, you can embrace a new beginning filled with hope, purpose, and possibility. Let

Judgment be your guiding light as you journey forward on the path of self-discovery and spiritual growth.

questions to ask yourself

1. In what areas of my life am I being called to make significant changes or decisions?
2. What aspects of myself or my life need to be reassessed or reconsidered at this time?
3. Am I listening to my inner voice and following my true calling?
4. What past experiences or patterns am I ready to release or let go of to move forward?
5. How can I embrace forgiveness and compassion towards myself and others?
6. What opportunities for growth and evolution are presenting themselves to me now?
7. What old beliefs or behaviors are holding me back from stepping into my highest potential?
8. Am I living authentically and in alignment with my soul's purpose?
9. How can I embrace the process of transformation with courage and openness?
10. What actions can I take to fully integrate the lessons of the past and step into a new chapter of my life with clarity and conviction?

21. the world

. . .

"Align your actions with your deepest desires,"
The World.

Element: Fire
Planet: Pluto
Answer: Yes

Key Words and Phrases:
Completion
Wholeness
Knowing yourself
Connected
Goals
Completion
Celebration
Integration
Fulfillment
Unity

SYMBOLS:

- The naked woman represents the essence of truth in its purest form.
- The four elements (earth, air, fire, water) are depicted in the corners of the card through astrology signs and the seasons of life.
- The wreath serves as a frame, symbolizing protection, success, and the framework of existence. Its circular shape also signifies the cyclical nature of life and the interconnectedness of all things.

At the crossroads of time and space, The Fool encounters The World, dancing amidst the cosmic symphony of creation and completion. Surrounded by the four elements, The World embodies wholeness, integration, and fulfillment. Now is the time to recognize your interconnectedness with all of existence and embracing the infinite possibilities of the universe.

The World beckons The Fool to embrace the totality of their journey, acknowledging the wisdom gained and the lessons learned along the way. It serves as an example to the transformative power of experience, urging you to celebrate their achievements and embrace the infinite possibilities that lie ahead.

At its essence, The World card symbolizes a sense of fulfillment and accomplishment, signifying the attainment of your goals and the realization of your true potential. It represents the culmination of a long and arduous journey, marking the beginning of a new cycle filled with promise, opportunity, and infinite potential.

In matters of the heart, The World radiates with the warmth of love, compassion, and unity, reminding the seeker of the profound connections that bind us all together. It symbolizes the harmonious union of hearts and souls, inviting you to cultivate deeper connections with others and foster a sense of community, understanding, and empathy.

Now is the time to transcend perceived limitations and embrace the boundless possibilities that await you. Step boldly into the fullness of your being. Trust the wisdom of the universe will guide your path.

The World card invites you to celebrate the completion of one chapter in your life and begin another. Within each ending is a new beginning, with adventures waiting to reveal themselves to you.

The World stands a symbol of wholeness, integration, and the infinite potential of the human spirit.

magical spell: manifesting wholeness ritual:

World, guide me,
Goals I see,
Wholeness and fulfillment,
Set me free.
With balance and harmony,

Lorelai Hamilton

> I embrace my fate,
> In the world's embrace,
> I find my state."

materials needed:

- A quiet and comfortable space
- A green candle
- A small piece of paper
- A pen or marker
- Rosemary or cinnamon essential oil (optional)

instructions:

- Find a peaceful space where you can sit comfortably without distractions.
- Light the green candle and place it in front of you.
- If you have essential oil, dab a drop on your wrists or pulse points to invoke a sense of abundance and harmony.
- Take a few deep breaths to center yourself and connect with the energy of wholeness and fulfillment.
- On the piece of paper, write down a goal or intention that represents fulfillment and integration in your life.
- Hold the paper in your hands and visualize yourself achieving your goal with confidence and joy.
- Recite the following affirmation aloud:

"World, guide me, goals I see, Wholeness and fulfillment, set me free. With balance and harmony, I embrace my fate, In the world's embrace, I find my state."

- Allow yourself to feel a sense of empowerment and excitement as you affirm your intentions.
- Fold the paper and hold it over the flame of the candle, allowing it to safely burn.
- As the paper burns, visualize the flames igniting your passion and determination to achieve your goal.
- Once the paper has turned to ash, extinguish the candle and trust in the power of The World to guide you towards fulfillment and integration in your life.

The World reminds you to embrace wholeness, fulfillment, and the realization of your potential. By aligning your actions with your deepest desires and embracing all aspects of yourself, you can achieve a sense of harmony and unity that transcends limitations. Let The World be your guiding light as you journey forward on the path of self-discovery and fulfillment.

questions to ask yourself

1. What major accomplishments or milestones have I recently achieved in my life?
2. In what ways do I feel a sense of completion or fulfillment in my current endeavors or projects?
3. How can I integrate the lessons and experiences from my past into my present moment?
4. What areas of my life need closure or resolution, and how can I bring about this closure?
5. Am I feeling connected to a sense of wholeness and balance within myself and my life?
6. What new opportunities or adventures await me as I step into this new phase of completion?
7. How can I expand my horizons and embrace a broader perspective on life and its possibilities?
8. What aspects of myself or my journey am I ready to celebrate and honor?
9. How can I share my wisdom and experiences with others to support their growth and evolution?
10. What steps can I take to continue evolving and growing, even as I reach this moment of completion and fulfillment?

minor arcana

Minor Arcana

introduction to the minor arcana

. . .

THE MINOR ARCANA consists of a collection of 56 cards that offer insights into your everyday experiences, challenges, and the triumphs of life. Unlike the Major Arcana, which delves into universal themes and archetypal energies, the Minor Arcana explores the nuances of daily existence, reflecting the querent's journey through emotions, actions, intellect, and material concerns.

The Minor Arcana is divided into four suits: Wands, Cups, Swords, and Pentacles, each representing a distinct aspect of human experience:

- Swords: Represent thoughts, communication, and the realm of the intellect. It's the fastest moving suite—think days.
- Wands: Symbolize creativity, passion, and inspired action. They are the second fastest moving suite—think weeks.
- Cups: Reflect emotions, relationships, and the realm of the heart. This moves at a slower pace—think months.
- Pentacles: Embody material abundance, practical concerns, and the realm of the physical. This moves at the slowest pace—think years.

Each suit comprises 14 cards, including numbered cards from Ace to Ten and four court cards: Page, Knight, Queen, and King. Together, the Minor Arcana cards paint a detailed portrait of your daily life, offering insights into their relationships, challenges, opportunities, and aspirations.

In a tarot reading, the Minor Arcana cards provide practical guidance, clarity, and insight into your current circumstances and potential outcomes. While the Major Arcana offers overarching themes and spiritual insights, the Minor Arcana delve into the specifics of your situation, highlighting key areas of focus and potential courses of action.

Each card is a mirror reflecting the depths of human experience, offering guidance, insight, and wisdom along the path of self-discovery. May the conversations with the cards continue, illuminating the path of the seeker and inspiring the unfolding of infinite possibilities. By harnessing the wisdom and symbolism of the Minor Arcana, you can gain clarity, perspective, and empowerment in navigating life's challenges, deciding, and embracing the opportunities for growth and transformation that lie ahead.

ace of swords

...

"You will overcome the mountains, with clear thinking and decisive action," Ace of Swords.

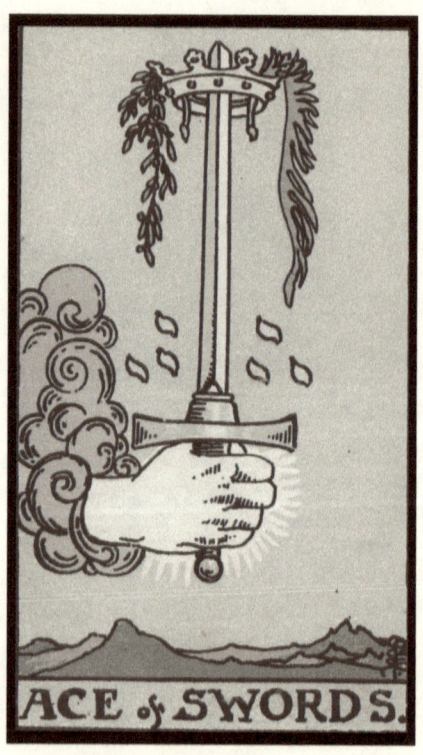

Answer: Yes

Key Words and Phrases:
Success
Strength
Intellect
Determination
New Ideas
New beginnings
New projects
Mental Clarity
Breakthroughs
Thinking
Overcoming obstacles
Rationalizing

SYMBOLS:

- The hand emerging from the clouds suggest divine inspiration and insight, guiding you toward truth and enlightenment.
- The sword represents the power of intellect, truth, and mental clarity. It's a symbol of strength, determination, and the ability to overcome obstacles through clear thinking and decisive action.

In the quiet recesses of the mystical forest, where the ancient trees whisper secrets to the wind, The Fool stumbles upon a glade bathed in ethereal light. Here, amidst the dappled shadows and shimmering leaves, stands a solitary figure, cloaked in robes of deepest blue. The figure beckons to The Fool with a steady gaze, offering a gleaming sword adorned with intricate symbols and a single, radiant gemstone.

This figure is the Ace of Swords, a harbinger of clarity, truth, and intellectual insight. As The Fool approaches, the Ace of Swords weaves a tale of its own, revealing the profound symbolism and meaning that lie within its blade.

The sword represents the power of the intellect, a weapon of thought and reason that cuts through the fog of confusion and illusion. It symbolizes the quest for truth and the pursuit of knowledge, urging The Fool to seek answers and unravel the mysteries of the universe.

In the story told by the Ace of Swords, there once lived a young knight named Aric, whose village was besieged by darkness and despair. Faced with insurmountable odds, Aric embarked on a perilous journey to seek the legendary Sword of Clarity, said to possess the power to vanquish even the darkest of shadows.

Through trials and tribulations, Aric faced his fears and overcame countless obstacles, guided by the unwavering light of the sword. Along the way, he encountered wise mentors and benevolent spirits who imparted upon him the wisdom of the ages.

Finally, after a long and arduous quest, Aric stood before the Sword of Clarity, its blade shimmering with otherworldly brilliance. With a steady hand and a resolute heart, he grasped the hilt of the sword and felt its power coursing through his veins.

In that moment, Aric understood the true meaning of clarity and insight. In that moment, Aric realized people fight the greatest battles not with steel and stone, but with courage and conviction. Armed with the Sword of Clarity, he returned to his village, bringing hope and light to all who dwelled within its walls.

As The Fool listens to the tale of Aric and the Sword of Clarity, they begin to understand the profound significance of the Ace of Swords in their own journey. Like Aric, they are called to embrace the power of intellect and reason, to seek truth in a world shrouded in shadow.

With the Ace of Swords as their guide, The Fool embarks on a quest for knowledge and understanding, ready to face whatever challenges lie ahead. For in the gleaming blade of the Ace of Swords, they find not only the strength to conquer adversity, but the wisdom to illuminate the path forward.

magical spell: clarity and mental focus:

> Ace of Swords,
> Grant me clarity and insight,
> Guide my mind,
> Illuminate my path bright.
> With wisdom and truth,
> I cut through the haze,
> Clearing my thoughts,
> Guiding my ways."

materials needed:

- White candle
- Clear quartz crystal or any clarity-enhancing crystal
- Lavender essential oil or dried lavender
- Journal and pen

instructions:

- Find a quiet and comfortable space where you can focus on your mental well-being.
- Light the white candle, symbolizing purity, clarity, and new beginnings.
- Hold the clear quartz crystal or clarity-enhancing crystal in your hand, connecting with its cleansing and clarifying energy.
- Inhale the calming scent of lavender essential oil or dried lavender to promote mental focus and clarity.
- Take a few deep breaths to center yourself and quiet your mind.
- Close your eyes and visualize a bright, shining light surrounding you, illuminating your path with clarity and insight.
- Open your journal and write down any thoughts, questions, or concerns you have regarding a particular situation or decision.
- Reflect on the information you have gathered and consider the different perspectives and possibilities available to you.
- Repeat the following affirmation aloud or silently to yourself:

"Ace of Swords, grant me clarity and insight, Guide my mind, illuminate my path bright. With wisdom and truth, I cut through the haze, Clearing my thoughts, guiding my ways."

- Allow the candle to burn down safely as you continue to journal and reflect on your thoughts and insights, knowing that you possess the wisdom and clarity to navigate life's challenges with confidence and purpose.

The Ace of Swords encourages you to trust in your intellect, seek truth, and embrace mental clarity as you navigate the journey of adolescence. By harnessing the power of your mind, seeking truth, and making decisions that align with your authentic self, you can overcome obstacles, gain insight, and embark on new beginnings with confidence and determination. Let the Ace of Swords be your guide on your quest for clarity, wisdom, and understanding, empowering you to cut through confusion and embrace the truth that lies within.

questions to ask yourself

1. What new ideas or intellectual breakthroughs am I experiencing?
2. How can I harness the power of clarity and mental focus in my life?
3. What truth or insight am I ready to confront or embrace?
4. How can I communicate my thoughts and ideas more effectively?
5. What new perspectives or understandings are emerging within me?
6. Am I facing any mental obstacles or challenges, and how can I overcome them?
7. How can I use my intellect and reasoning to solve current problems or conflicts?

8. What opportunities for mental growth and expansion are presenting themselves to me?
9. How can I cultivate a sense of mental discipline and discernment?
10. In what ways can I channel my mental energy towards positive outcomes and achievements?

two of swords

...

"Sometimes any decision is better than no decision," Two of Swords

Answer: Maybe
Key Words and Phrases

Indecision
Options
Indecisive
Waiting
Balance
Stalemate
Impasse
Inner Conflict
Overwhelmed
Feeling stuck
Lack of action
Avoidance
Confusion
Decisions made
Moving forward
Change
Release
Hard decisions

SYMBOLS:

- The crossed swords represent opposing choices or conflating viewpoints, indicating a stalemate or impasse in decision making.
- The blindfold symbolizes the inability to see clearly suggesting the need to rely on inner guidance and intuition. Or the need to remove the blinders in your life.
- Her hands are not tied. There is nothing preventing her from taking off her blindfold and defending herself properly or making a decision.
- The calm waters in the background represent emotional tranquility and inner peace. Remind to approach decisions with a sense of serenity and balance.

In the stillness of twilight, where the sky meets the sea in a seamless dance of colors, The Fool encounters a young woman seated upon a rocky cliff, her blindfold adorned with two gleaming swords crossed over her heart. The air is heavy with anticipation as The Fool approaches, drawn by the mysterious presence of the Two of Swords.

This card, with its symbolism of indecision and inner conflict, speaks to the turmoil that often clouds the human mind. The woman before The Fool embodies the struggle to make a choice, to reconcile opposing forces within herself, and to find clarity amidst uncertainty.

As The Fool draws closer, the woman shares her story—a tale of a solitary journey across a vast and treacherous desert. In her quest for truth and understanding, she encountered myriad challenges and obstacles, each one testing the limits of her resolve.

At the heart of the desert, she came upon a crossroads, where two divergent paths stretched out before her, each shrouded in mystery and possibility. Uncertain of which path to follow, she paused, grappling with the weight of her decision.

In that moment of hesitation, the woman realized the significance of the Two of Swords—the delicate balance between reason and intuition, logic and emotion. With her senses heightened and her mind sharpened, she sought solace in the stillness, allowing the gentle whispers of the wind to guide her.

With a steady hand and a courageous heart, the woman made her choice, embracing the uncertainty of the unknown and trusting in the wisdom of her inner voice. In that act of surrender, she found liberation. Making a choice is better than sitting in indecision, unmoving.

As The Fool listens to the woman's story, they too begin to confront their own inner conflicts and uncertainties. The Two of Swords urges them to confront the choices that lie before them, to acknowledge the fears and doubts that hold them back, and to embrace the transformative power of decision.

In the gentle embrace of the Two of Swords, The Fool discovers the profound beauty of vulnerability—the courage to confront the darkness within and emerge stronger, wiser, and more resolute than before. With each passing moment, they inch closer to the light, guided by the unwavering strength of their own heart.

magical spell: clarity and decision-making:

Oh spirit of the two of cards,
Guide me through these uncertain times.
Grant me clarity and insight,
To see the path that truly shines.
Within myself,
The answers lie,
I trust my intuition,
Soaring high.

materials needed:

- White candle
- Lavender essential oil or dried lavender
- Pen and paper
- Blindfold or scarf (optional)

instructions:

1. Find a quiet and comfortable space where you can focus on your thoughts and emotions.
2. Light the white candle, symbolizing clarity, guidance, and illumination.
3. Inhale the soothing scent of lavender essential oil or dried lavender to promote relaxation and clarity of mind.
4. Take a few deep breaths to center yourself and quiet your thoughts.
5. Hold the pen and paper in your hand, preparing to journal your thoughts and feelings about the decision you are facing.

6. If you have a blindfold or scarf, you may choose to gently cover your eyes to symbolize the need to rely on intuition and inner guidance.
7. Close your eyes and visualize yourself surrounded by a sphere of white light, representing clarity, protection, and divine guidance.
8. Reflect on the decision you need to make and consider the different options available to you.
9. Write down your thoughts, feelings, and concerns about each choice, allowing yourself to explore your emotions and desires without judgment.
10. Take a moment to connect with your intuition and inner wisdom, trusting that the answers you seek lie within you.
11. Repeat the following affirmation aloud or silently to yourself:

"Oh spirit of the two of cards, Guide me through these uncertain times. Grant me clarity and insight, To see the path that truly shines. Within myself, the answers lie, I trust my intuition, soaring high."

1. Allow yourself to sit with your thoughts and feelings, knowing that you possess the wisdom and strength to make decisions that honor your values and aspirations.
2. Blow out the candle, symbolizing the end of the ritual, and carry the sense of clarity and balance with you as you navigate the decision-making process.

The Two of Swords invites you to confront your inner conflicts, embrace your intuition, and find balance amidst uncertainty. By trusting your instincts, listening to your inner voice, and seeking clarity of mind, you can navigate life's challenges with confidence and grace. Let the Two of Swords be your guide as you face difficult decisions, knowing that you possess the wisdom and strength to choose the path that aligns with your highest good.

questions to ask yourself

1. What decisions or choices am I currently struggling with?
2. What inner conflicts or dilemmas am I experiencing?
3. How can I find balance and harmony amidst conflicting interests or opinions?
4. Am I avoiding making a necessary decision out of fear or uncertainty?
5. What blind spots or biases might be influencing my decision-making process?
6. How can I gain clarity and insight into my options?
7. What compromises or middle ground can I explore to resolve conflicts?
8. What insights can I gain from considering the perspectives of others?
9. How can I trust my intuition and inner wisdom when facing tough choices?
10. What steps can I take to move forward with confidence and conviction?

three of swords

. . .

"This too shall pass," Three of Swords.

Answer: No

Key Words and Phrases
Loss
Irritable
Conflict
Misunderstandings
Hurt feelings
Heartbroken
Stress
Sorrow
Painful situations
Grief
Stressful change
Loss
Pain
Deep emotions
Pain ending
Recovering
Stuck in the past
Regret
Optimistic
Negative self talk
Releasing pain
Forgiving

SYMBOLS:

- The pierced heart represents emotional pain, sorrow, and heartbreak.
- The stormy clouds in the background signifies turbulent emotions and inner turmoil.
- The raindrops symbolize tears shed during times of sorrow and grief.

In the quiet depths of the forest, where shadows dance among the trees and whispers linger on the breeze, The Fool stumbles upon a clearing bathed in moonlight. There, amidst a bed of delicate wildflowers, lies a solemn figure—the Three of Swords.

The air is heavy with sorrow as The Fool approaches, drawn by the weight of the figure's grief. The Three of Swords, with its symbolism of heartache and emotional pain, speaks to the profound depths of human suffering and the scars that linger long after the wounds have healed.

As The Fool draws closer, the figure shares their story—a tale of love lost and betrayal endured. They speak of a time when their heart was whole, filled with boundless joy and endless possibility. But as fate would have it, their world came crashing down with the sting of a thousand swords, shattering their dreams and leaving them broken and alone.

In the aftermath of their pain, the figure sought solace in the wilderness, seeking refuge among the trees and the stars. In the stillness of the forest, they learned to embrace their sorrow, allowing it to wash over them like a gentle rain, cleansing their spirit and renewing their strength.

With each passing day, the figure found healing in the simple beauty of the natural world—the warmth of the sun on their skin, the melody of birdsong in the air, and the quiet rhythm of the earth beneath their feet. And though the pain of their past still lingers, they have emerged from the darkness, resilient and unbroken, ready to face whatever challenges lie ahead.

As The Fool listens to the figure's tale, they too begin to confront their own pain and suffering. The Three of Swords urges them to acknowledge the wounds that dwell within their own heart, to embrace their vulnerability, and to find strength in the power of forgiveness and healing.

In the gentle embrace of the Three of Swords, The Fool discovers the profound beauty of resilience—the courage to confront adversity and emerge stronger, wiser, and more compassionate than before. With each step they take, they move ever closer to the light, guided by the enduring power of hope and the boundless capacity of the human heart.

magical spell: healing heart ritual:

> I release the pain that weighs heavy on my heart,
> I embrace healing and allow love to restart.
> Like a phoenix rising from ashes anew,
> I reclaim my joy, my light shining true.

materials needed:

- Pink candle
- Rose quartz crystal or any heart-shaped stone
- Pen and paper
- Lavender essential oil or dried lavender
- Healing herbs such as chamomile, rose petals, or lavender

instructions:

- Find a quiet and comfortable space where you can perform the ritual without distractions.
- Light the pink candle, symbolizing love, healing, and compassion.
- Hold the rose quartz crystal or heart-shaped stone in your hand, connecting with its soothing and healing energy.
- Anoint the candle with a few drops of lavender essential oil or sprinkle dried lavender around it to invoke calming and healing vibrations.
- Take a few deep breaths to center yourself and focus your intention on healing your heart and releasing emotional pain.
- Write down your feelings of heartache, sadness, or grief on the piece of paper, allowing yourself to express and acknowledge your emotions without judgment.
- Hold the paper over the flame of the candle and visualize the fire transmuting your pain into healing energy.
- Place the paper in a fire-safe container and allow it to burn completely, symbolizing the release of emotional baggage and the purification of your heart.
- Hold the rose quartz crystal or heart-shaped stone to your heart and repeat the following affirmation aloud or silently:

"I release the pain that weighs heavy on my heart, I embrace healing and allow love to restart. Like a phoenix rising from ashes anew, I reclaim my joy, my light shining true."

- Spend a few moments meditating on the warmth and comfort of the candle flame, allowing its gentle glow to envelop you in love and healing energy.
- When you feel ready, extinguish the candle and thank the universe for the healing and transformation that is taking place within you.
- Carry the rose quartz crystal or heart-shaped stone with you as a talisman of love and healing, reminding you to nurture and cherish your heart as you journey toward wholeness.

The Three of Swords teaches us that while heartache and pain are inevitable aspects of the human experience, they also offer opportunities for growth, healing, and transformation. By acknowledging and processing our emotions with compassion and self-care, we can begin the journey toward healing and emotional well-being. Let the Three of Swords be a guiding light during times of darkness, reminding you that even in the midst of sorrow, there is hope, healing, and the promise of brighter days ahead.

questions to ask yourself

1. What emotional pain or heartache am I currently experiencing?
2. How can I heal from past hurts or disappointments?
3. What unhealthy patterns or beliefs may be contributing to my suffering?
4. Am I allowing myself to grieve and process my emotions fully?
5. What lessons can I learn from my experiences of loss or betrayal?
6. How can I cultivate self-compassion and forgiveness towards myself and others?

7. What support systems or resources can I turn to for healing?
8. How can I release resentment and find closure in difficult situations?
9. What opportunities for growth and transformation are hidden within my pain?
10. How can I nurture my heart and cultivate resilience in the face of adversity?

four of swords

...

"Now is the time for rest and relaxation," Four of Swords.

Answer: No
Key Words and Phrases

Rest
Recharge
Relaxation
Renew
Retreat
A break
Regroup
Meditation
Withdrawal
Pray
Contemplate
Healing
Thinking
Slow down
Getting away
Waiting
Patience

SYMBOLS:

- The figure on the bier represents a state of rest, stillness, and contemplation. It symbolizes the need to withdraw from the busyness of life to find inner peace and tranquility.
- Three swards above the figure symbolize the challenges, conflicts and mental stress that have been endured. The suggest the need to pause and reflect on past experiences to find closure and healing.
- Fourth sword below the figure represents the power of the mind to overcome adversity and find inner peace. It suggests that by confronting our inner demons and fears, we can achieve mental clarity and emotional balance.

In the hushed corridors of the ancient monastery, The Fool stumbles upon a solitary figure kneeling in quiet contemplation—a figure that embodies the essence of the Four of Swords.

The Fool approaches, drawn by the tranquil energy that envelops the chamber. The Four of Swords, with its symbolism of rest, reflection, and recuperation, speaks to the profound importance of finding inner peace amidst life's tumultuous journey.

As The Fool draws closer, the figure's presence seems to radiate a sense of calm, as if they have found solace in the stillness of their own mind. With closed eyes and hands folded in prayer, they appear to be in a state of deep meditation, seeking refuge from the chaos of the world outside.

In the gentle glow of candlelight, the figure shares their story—a tale of battles fought, and victories won, of wounds endured and scars healed. They speak of a time when the relentless demands of duty and honor consumed them, and their spirit grew weary from the weight of the world upon their shoulders.

But in the wake of their struggles, they made a choice—a choice to lie down their sword, to surrender to the embrace of silence, and to seek sanctuary within the sanctuary of their own soul. And in that sacred space, they discovered a profound truth—that strength lies not in the might of one's arm, but in the peace that resides within.

With each passing moment, the figure found renewal in the restorative power of solitude—the opportunity to rest, to recharge, and to replenish their spirit for the journey ahead. And though the world outside may be filled with chaos and strife, they have learned to seek sanctuary within themselves, guided by the wisdom of their own heart.

As The Fool listens to the figure's tale, they too felt the gentle tug of inner peace—the invitation to quiet the noise of the world and to listen to the whispers of their own soul. The Four of Swords urges them to embrace the power of stillness, to honor the rhythms of rest, and to trust in the healing journey that lies ahead.

In the tranquil embrace of the Four of Swords, The Fool discovers the profound beauty of inner peace—the courage to surrender to the silence and to find solace in the sanctuary of their own soul. With each breath they take, they move ever closer to the heart of their truest self, guided by the timeless wisdom that lives within.

magical spell: self-care and inner peace:

Four of Swords,
grant me rest and peace,
In quiet reflection,
my mind finds release.
I honor my needs,
I nurture my soul,
Embracing stillness,
I am whole."

materials needed:

- White candle
- Lavender essential oil or dried lavender
- Pen and paper
- Comfortable space for meditation

instructions:

- Find a quiet and comfortable space where you can relax without distractions.
- Light the white candle, symbolizing clarity, purity, and renewal.
- Inhale the calming scent of lavender essential oil or dried lavender to promote relaxation and tranquility.
- Close your eyes and take several deep breaths, allowing yourself to sink into a state of deep relaxation.
- Visualize a healing light surrounding you, enveloping you in a cocoon of peace and serenity.
- Reflect on any stress, worries, or burdens you have been

carrying. Acknowledge them without judgment and release them into the light.
- Take the pen and paper and jot down any thoughts, feelings, or insights that arise during this meditation. Allow your intuition to guide your writing.
- Repeat the following affirmation aloud or silently to yourself:

"Four of Swords, grant me rest and peace, In quiet reflection, my mind finds release. I honor my needs, I nurture my soul, Embracing stillness, I am whole."

- Sit in silence for a few moments, basking in the gentle glow of the candle and the warmth of your own presence.
- When you feel ready, gently open your eyes and extinguish the candle, carrying the sense of calm and tranquility with you as you return to your daily activities.

The Four of Swords reminds us of the importance of self-care, rest, and introspection. By taking time to retreat from the demands of everyday life, we can nurture our minds, bodies, and spirits, and emerge stronger and more resilient than before. Let the Four of Swords be your guide as you prioritize your well-being and embrace moments of peace and stillness on your journey of self-discovery.

questions to ask yourself

1. In what areas of my life do I need to rest and recharge?
2. How can I create more peace and tranquility in my surroundings?

3. What mental or physical burdens am I carrying that I need to release?
4. Am I allowing myself to take a break and recuperate from stress or exhaustion?
5. How can I incorporate mindfulness and meditation into my daily routine?
6. What inner guidance or insights am I receiving during periods of quiet reflection?
7. How can I set healthy boundaries to protect my energy and well-being?
8. What habits or routines can I establish to promote relaxation and rejuvenation?
9. How can I cultivate a sense of inner peace and serenity amidst external chaos?
10. What steps can I take to restore balance and harmony in my life?

five of swords

. . .

"Winning at all costs, isn't winning at all," Five of Swords.

Answer: No
Key Words and Phrases

Negative thoughts
Competition
Conflict
Selfish
Winning at a cost
Betrayal
Insecure
Discord
Manipulation
Arguments
Consequences
Picking up the pieces
Ego

SYMBOLS:

- The figure holding the swards symbolizes the desire for dominance, power, and triumph over others at all costs. It represents the aggressive pursuit of personal gain without regard for the well-being of others.
- The figures walking away in the distance represent defeat, resignation, and the choice to disengage from conflict rather than perpetuate it. They acknowledge the wisdom in choosing peace over continued confrontation.
- The swords symbolize the realm of intellect, communication, and conflict resolution. The crossed swords suggest the clash of opposing ideas and the potential for resolution through negotiation and compromise.

In the dimly lit clearing of a forgotten battlefield, The Fool stumbles upon a scene of conflict—a scene that embodies the essence of the Five of Swords.

The air is heavy with tension as The Fool approaches, drawn by the clash of steel and the echo of harsh words exchanged between bitter rivals.

The Five of Swords, with its symbolism of discord, defeat, and dishonor, speaks to the perils of pride and the consequences of unchecked aggression.

As The Fool draws closer, they witness a confrontation unfolding between two adversaries locked in a bitter struggle for supremacy. Swords gleam in the fading light as tempers flare and egos collide, each combatant driven by the relentless pursuit of victory at any cost.

In the heat of battle, soldiers draw lines, test alliances, and fill the air with the clash of steel, the sting of defeat, and the bitter taste of resentment. Pride and ambition fueled each sword stroke, each victory celebrated with a hollow sense of triumph.

But as the dust settles and the echoes of conflict fade into silence, The Fool sees the toll that the battle has taken—the shattered bonds of friendship, the scars of betrayal, and the lingering shadow of regret that hangs heavy in the air.

Amidst the wreckage of broken promises and shattered dreams, The Fool hears the whisper of a timeless truth—that victory gained through deceit and manipulation is a hollow triumph, a fleeting illusion that crumbles beneath the weight of its own deception.

In the aftermath of the battle, The Fool sees the folly of unchecked ambition and the destructive power of pride—the realization that true strength lies not in the conquest of others, but in the courage to stand with integrity and honor, even in the face of defeat.

With each passing moment, The Fool learns the profound lesson of the Five of Swords—that victory gained at the expense of others is a hollow prize, a fleeting mirage that fades into obscurity, leaving only the bitter taste of regret in its wake.

In the sobering embrace of the Five of Swords, The Fool discovers the wisdom of humility and the importance of empathy—the understanding that true victory lies not in the defeat of others, but in the triumph of the human spirit, united in compassion and grace.

magical spell: harmony and conflict resolution:

> Five of Swords,
> I call upon thee,
> Guide me to resolve
> Conflict peacefully.
> With words of kindness,
> Let harmony reign,
> May understanding
> And empathy remain.

materials needed:

- White candle
- Peaceful music or nature sounds
- Pen and paper
- Chamomile tea or dried chamomile flowers

instructions:

- Find a quiet and peaceful space where you can perform your spell without interruptions.
- Light the white candle, symbolizing purity, clarity, and harmony.
- Play soothing music or nature sounds to create a calming atmosphere conducive to reflection and inner peace.
- Take a few moments to center yourself and ground your energy, focusing on your intention to promote harmony and resolve conflicts.
- Brew a cup of chamomile tea or create a sachet of dried chamomile flowers to harness the herb's calming and soothing properties.
- Write down any conflicts or disagreements you have been experiencing, being honest and specific about the issues at hand.
- Hold the paper in your hands and visualize the conflicts dissolving away, replaced by a sense of understanding, empathy, and mutual respect.
- Repeat the following incantation aloud or silently to yourself:

Five of Swords, I call upon thee, Guide me to resolve conflict peacefully. With words of kindness, let harmony reign, May understanding and empathy remain.

- Take a sip of chamomile tea or hold the sachet close to your heart, allowing its calming energy to wash over you.
- Sit in quiet contemplation, allowing the peaceful energy to envelop you and infuse your being with a sense of tranquility and serenity.
- When you feel ready, extinguish the candle and carry the sense of inner peace and harmony with you as you navigate your relationships and interactions with others.

The Five of Swords reminds us of the importance of addressing conflicts with compassion, empathy, and understanding. Through open communication, active listening, and a willingness to seek common ground, we can overcome differences and foster harmonious relationships built on mutual respect and cooperation. Let the Five of Swords serve as a reminder to choose peace over conflict and to strive for understanding and reconciliation in all areas of your life.

questions to ask yourself

1. What conflicts or power struggles am I currently involved in?
2. How can I assert myself without resorting to aggression or manipulation?
3. What underlying fears or insecurities may be fueling my need to win at all costs?
4. Am I willing to consider the perspectives and needs of others, even in conflict?
5. How can I find resolution and closure in situations of disagreement or rivalry?
6. What lessons can I learn from experiencing defeat or setbacks?

7. How can I rebuild trust and repair damaged relationships after conflict?
8. What compromises or concessions am I willing to make for the greater good?
9. How can I cultivate empathy and understanding towards those I perceive as opponents?
10. What healthy boundaries can I establish to protect myself from toxic dynamics?

six of swords

...

"Now's the time to move on to calmer waters,"
Sixth of Swords.

Answer: Maybe

Tarot Tales and Magic Spells

Key Words and Phrases
Change
Releasing
Solace
Letting go
Transition
Better ahead
Leaving a painful past
Go with the flow
Traveling
Moving on
Healing Guidance
Endings
Relief

SYMBOLS:

- The boat represents the journey of transition and movement from one phase of life to another. It symbolizes the willingness to leave behind the past and embark on a new path, even if it means stepping into the unknown.
- The calm waters signify a sense of peace, tranquility, and emotional stability. They suggest that despite the challenges faced, smoother times are ahead, offering respite and relief from previous struggles.
- The figure and child symbolize guidance, protection, and support during times of transition. The figure may represent a mentor, a trusted friend, or one's own inner wisdom guiding the way forward.

In the twilight hours, under a sky painted with hues of violet and indigo, The Fool embarks on a journey across the tranquil waters of the river. In the distance, a figure waits—a solitary boatman poised at the helm of a vessel adorned with six gleaming swords.

As The Fool approaches, they recognize the figure as the embodiment of the Six of Swords—a symbol of transition, healing, and moving forward from troubled waters. The boatman's steady gaze reflects wisdom earned through the trials of the past, offering a beacon of hope amidst the shadows of uncertainty.

With a gentle nod, the boatman invites The Fool to embark on a voyage of introspection and renewal—a journey that will carry them beyond the turbulent currents of the past and into the calm waters of a brighter tomorrow.

As the boat glides across the tranquil surface, The Fool feels the weight of their burdens lift, replaced by a sense of peace and clarity that permeates the air like a soothing balm.

Along the journey, The Fool reflects on the challenges they have faced —the tumultuous storms that once raged within their heart, threatening to consume them in their depths. Yet, with each passing wave, they find strength knowing that even the fiercest tempest must eventually give way to the serenity of a new dawn.

As the boatman guides them onward, The Fool witnesses the dawning of a new day—a horizon tinged with the soft hues of sunrise, signaling the promise of a fresh beginning and the hope of brighter tomorrows.

In the quietude of the river's embrace, The Fool comes to understand the profound wisdom of the Six of Swords—that while the journey may be fraught with challenges and uncertainties; it is through perseverance and resilience that we find the strength to navigate the waters of change.

With each stroke of the oar, The Fool embraces the transformative power of healing and renewal, knowing that even in the darkest of nights, the light of hope will guide them home.

As they draw nearer to the distant shore, The Fool realizes that the journey itself is a testament to the resilience of the human spirit—a reminder that even in the face of adversity, we possess the strength to rise above the storm and sail toward a brighter tomorrow.

With a grateful heart, The Fool steps ashore, ready to embrace the possibilities that lie ahead—to embrace the journey of the Six of Swords, knowing that with each passing moment, they move ever closer to the promise of a new beginning.

magical spell: journey of healing:

Swords of strife,
I leave behind,
On tranquil waters,
My spirit finds.
Guided by light,
I journey on,
Towards healing, peace,
And the dawn.

materials needed:

- Blue candle
- Lavender essential oil or dried lavender
- Paper and pen
- Small bowl of water

instructions:

- Begin by lighting the blue candle, representing peace, healing, and emotional clarity.
- Place a few drops of lavender essential oil or a pinch of dried lavender into the palm of your hand and inhale deeply, allowing the calming scent to soothe your senses.
- Sit in a comfortable position and close your eyes. Take several deep breaths, allowing yourself to relax and let go of any tension or worries.
- Visualize yourself standing at the edge of a serene lake, with a small boat waiting to carry you across the water.

- As you step into the boat, feel a sense of relief and release wash over you, knowing that you are leaving behind any emotional baggage or turmoil.
- With each stroke of the oar, imagine yourself moving further away from the challenges and struggles of the past, towards a brighter and more peaceful future.
- Take the paper and pen and write down any thoughts, feelings, or intentions related to your journey of healing and transition.
- Fold the paper and hold it over the small bowl of water, allowing any negative energy or emotions to be released and purified by the water.
- Repeat the following incantation aloud or silently:

"Swords of strife, I leave behind, On tranquil waters, my spirit finds. Guided by light, I journey on, Towards healing, peace, and the dawn.

- Place the paper in a safe place where it can remain undisturbed, symbolizing your commitment to your journey of healing.
- Sit in quiet reflection for a few moments, feeling the soothing energy of the candle and the water enveloping you in a cocoon of peace and serenity.
- When you feel ready, extinguish the candle, knowing that the journey towards healing and renewal has begun.

The Six of Swords reminds us that even in times of difficulty and transition, there is always hope for a brighter future. By embracing change, releasing the past, and staying open to new possibilities, we can navigate through life's challenges with courage and grace. Let the Six of Swords be your guide as you embark on your journey towards healing, peace, and emotional renewal.

questions to ask yourself

1. What transitions or changes am I currently navigating in my life?
2. How can I find stability and security amidst uncertainty?
3. What old habits or patterns am I leaving behind as I move forward?
4. Am I open to seeking guidance and support during times of transition?
5. How can I trust the journey and embrace the unknown with courage?
6. What insights or wisdom can I gain from past experiences that will guide me forward?
7. How can I let go of attachments and embrace new opportunities for growth?
8. What challenges or obstacles am I leaving behind as I embark on this journey?
9. How can I maintain a sense of optimism and resilience in the face of change?
10. What resources or skills do I possess that will help me navigate this transition successfully?

seven of swords

. . .

"Be cautious, for not all that glitters is gold. Sometimes, the greatest victories come from strategic retreats." Seven of Swords

Answer: Maybe

Key Words and Phrases:
Deception
Lies
Lying to yourself
Do something covertly
Cut your loses
Things happening beneath the surface
Something behind your back
Secrecy
Betrayal
Learning secrets about yourself
Secrets being revealed
Truths coming to light
Tricky
Dishonesty
Moving somewhere new
Avoidance
Escaping
Stealth
Appreciation
Advice
Getting something back
Indecision
Missed opportunities
Looking at the past

SYMBOLS:

- The figure in the card represents someone who is sly and strategic. They are depicted in a sneaky posture, suggesting secrecy and deceit.
- The swords symbolize thoughts, intellect, and communication. The figure leaving behind two swords may imply the act of making choices and leaving something behind while taking what is deemed valuable or necessary.
- The landscape is barren and in the background. This suggests desolation or the feeling of being alone in one's actions or decisions.

In the quiet shadows of dusk, The Fool stumbles upon a figure lurking in the depths of a dimly lit alleyway. A sense of secrecy lingers in the air, and the figure's eyes shine with mischief while tightly clutching a handful of gleaming swords.

With a wary gaze, The Fool recognizes the embodiment of the Seven of Swords—a symbol of cunning, deception, and the art of subtlety. The figure's movements are swift and deliberate, weaving through the darkness like a shadowy specter, leaving behind a trail of half-truths and whispered secrets.

As The Fool draws closer, they glimpse the figure's hidden agenda—a tangle of lies and deceit, carefully concealed beneath a veil of false promises and empty assurances.

With a sly grin, the figure beckons The Fool closer, tempting them with the allure of forbidden knowledge and hidden truths. But as The Fool reaches out to grasp the swords, they feel a chill run down their spine—a warning of the dangers that lurk beneath the surface of deceit.

The Seven of Swords is a card of caution, a reminder that not all that glitters is gold, and not all secrets are meant to be unearthed. It is a warning to tread carefully, to trust in one's instincts, and to remain vigilant against the whispers of deception that threaten to lead astray.

Observing the fading figure, The Fool reflects on the Seven of Swords' lessons, emphasizing the need to discern truth from falsehood, navigate deceit with clarity, and safeguard their heart from cunning deceivers.

With a renewed sense of purpose, The Fool continues their journey, mindful of the dangers that lie in wait, yet steadfast in their resolve to walk the path of truth and integrity. For in the darkness of deception, the light of honesty shines brightest, illuminating the way forward with unwavering clarity and grace.

magical spell - veil of protection:

materials needed:

- White candle
- Piece of paper
- Black pen
- Sage or lavender herbs

instructions:

- Light the white candle and focus on its flame, envisioning a shield of protection surrounding you.
- On the piece of paper, write down any fears or anxieties you wish to protect yourself from.
- Fold the paper and hold it over the candle flame (be cautious with fire).
- As the paper burns, visualize the negative energies dissipating into the flame.
- Sprinkle the sage or lavender herbs around your living space, imagining a veil of protection enveloping you.

Like the figure in the Seven of Swords, you can navigate tricky situations with clarity and confidence. Know you are protected by your own inner strength and intuition. While the Seven of Swords can signify deception, trickery, and strategizing, it can also mean the need to ask for help. The figure can't carry everything by himself, leaving two swords behind.

questions to ask yourself

1. What deceptions or dishonesty am I currently facing or engaging in?
2. How can I confront deceit or betrayal with integrity and honesty?
3. What hidden motives or agendas might be at play in my interactions?
4. Am I being true to myself and my values, or am I compromising them for personal gain?
5. How can I discern between truth and illusion in challenging situations?
6. What boundaries do I need to set to protect myself from manipulation or exploitation?
7. How can I take responsibility for my actions and their consequences?
8. What lessons can I learn from experiences of deception or betrayal?
9. How can I rebuild trust and repair relationships damaged by dishonesty?
10. What steps can I take to cultivate authenticity and transparency in my interactions?

eight of swords

. . .

"Break free from the binds of your mind. Liberation awaits beyond the veil of fear." Eight of Swords.

Answer: No

Lorelai Hamilton

Key Words and Phrases:
Negative thinking
Feeling trapped
Fear
Victim
Limiting beliefs
Disempowered
Confinement
Stuck
Isolated
Limiting yourself
Liberation
Lack of confidence
Worry
Unhappy
Perception
Confused
Critical
Restriction

SYMBOLS:

- The blindfold symbolizes ignorance or a lack of awareness of one's own abilities and options. It suggests that the woman may not see way out of her current situation due to fear or self-doubt.
- The swords surrounding the woman represent mental anguish, negative thoughts, and the feeling of being surrounded by obstacles. However, the way the swords are positioned leaves gaps for her to escape, indicating that the barriers may not be insurmountable at all, but merely in her head.
- The water at the woman's feet symbolizes emotions and the intuition. Despite feeling trapped, she is still connected to her emotional depth and intuition, which can guide her toward liberation.

In the stillness of the night, The Fool wanders into a dense thicket, surrounded by towering trees that seem to close in around them. The air is heavy with a sense of confinement, and The Fool feels a knot of fear tighten in their chest as they struggle to find their way through the labyrinth of tangled branches.

In the heart of the forest, The Fool encounters the figure of the Eight of Swords—a symbol of entrapment, fear, and the limitations we place upon ourselves. The figure stands amidst a circle of towering swords, blindfolded and bound, unable to see the path that lies before them.

As The Fool draws closer, they feel the weight of the figure's despair, a palpable sense of helplessness that hangs heavy in the air like a shroud. The figure's hands tremble as they reach out, seeking guidance and solace in the darkness that surrounds them.

With a gentle touch, The Fool removes the blindfold from the figure's eyes, revealing the truth that lies hidden beneath the veil of fear and uncertainty. In that moment of clarity, the figure sees that the swords that once bound them were nothing more than illusions, shadows cast by their own doubts and insecurities.

As the realization dawns upon them, the figure's spirit is set free, liberated from the confines of their own mind and empowered to forge a new path forward. With each step they take, the swords that once threatened to ensnare them fall away, shattered by the strength of their newfound courage and determination.

The Fool watches as the figure disappears into the darkness, a beacon of hope amidst the shadows, a testament to the transformative power of liberation and self-discovery.

The Eight of Swords is a card of liberation, a reminder that even in our darkest moments, we possess the strength and resilience to break free from the chains that bind us and embrace the boundless potential that lies within.

As The Fool continues on their journey, they carry with them the wisdom of the Eight of Swords—the knowledge that true freedom comes not from the outside, but from within, and that the only limits we face are those we impose upon ourselves.

Lorelai Hamilton

magical spell - breaking barriers:

>Swords of doubt,
>Chains of fear,
>I release you now,
>I draw near.
>With clarity of mind
>And spirit bright,
>I break free
>from this endless night.
>Eight of Swords,
>No more to bind,
>Liberation of the soul,
>I now find."

ingredients:

- Eight small white candles
- A length of black ribbon or cord
- A blindfold (optional)
- A quiet, secluded space

instructions:

- Set up the eight white candles in a circle, evenly spaced apart, forming a sacred space for the spell.
- Take a moment to center yourself and clear your mind of distractions. Breathe deeply and focus on the intention of freeing yourself from mental constraints and limitations.
- If you have a blindfold, consider placing it nearby as a symbolic representation of the restrictions you seek to overcome.

- Stand or sit in the center of the circle of candles, feeling the energy and warmth they emit.
- Close your eyes and visualize the Eight of Swords card in your mind. Imagine the feeling of being bound or restricted by limiting beliefs, doubts, or fears.
- With determination and resolve, reach for the black ribbon or cord. As you hold it in your hands, affirm your intention to break free from the shackles of self-imposed limitations.
- Begin to weave the ribbon or cord around your hands, symbolizing the entanglement of thoughts and beliefs that hinder your freedom.
- As you weave, recite the following incantation:

"Swords of doubt, chains of fear, I release you now, I draw near. With clarity of mind and spirit bright, I break free from this endless night. Eight of Swords, no more to bind, Liberation of the soul, I now find."

- With each repetition of the incantation, feel the grip of limitations loosening, allowing space for clarity and liberation to enter your mind and spirit.
- Once you have completed the weaving, hold the bound ribbon or cord high above your head, visualizing yourself breaking free from the confines of your own mind.
- Light each of the white candles one by one, symbolizing the illumination of truth and clarity in your life.
- Take a moment to reflect on the newfound sense of freedom and empowerment coursing through you. Embrace the liberation of your mind and spirit.
- If you have the blindfold, consider placing it aside or removing it, symbolizing your willingness to see things with fresh eyes and embrace new perspectives.
- Close the ritual with gratitude for the insights gained and the courage to confront and overcome limitations. Blow out the candles, knowing that you hold the power to navigate your journey with clarity and freedom.
- Carry the energy of this spell with you, trusting in your ability to break free from mental constraints and embrace the boundless potential that awaits you.

questions to ask yourself

1. In what ways do I feel trapped or restricted in my life right now?
2. How can I break free from self-imposed limitations or negative thought patterns?
3. What fears or doubts are holding me back from pursuing my goals?
4. Am I allowing external circumstances to dictate my sense of freedom and agency?
5. How can I shift my perspective to see opportunities for growth and change?
6. What support or resources do I need to overcome feelings of helplessness or confinement?
7. How can I reclaim my power and autonomy in challenging situations?
8. What small steps can I take to move towards liberation and self-expression?
9. What lessons can I learn from experiences of feeling restricted or trapped?
10. How can I cultivate courage and resilience in the face of adversity?

nine of swords

...

"Face your fears, for in the darkness lies the seed of your resilience. Illuminate your path with courage and find solace in the dawn." The Nine of Swords.

Answer: No

Lorelai Hamilton

Key Words and Phrases:
Worry
Anxiety
Fear
Sad
Stressed
Depressed
Nightmares
Lack of confidence
Hopeless
Feeling unloved
Feeling not good enough
Insomnia

SYMBOLS:

- The person in bed represents the individual experiencing emotional distress and mental anguish. They may feel overwhelmed by their thoughts and unable to find peace of mind.
- The swords symbolize the thoughts, worries, and fears that plague the person's mind. The swords hanging on the wall behind them represent the weight of anxieties and the feeling of being surrounded by mental anguish.
- The darkness symbolizes the depths of despair and the feeling of being trapped in your mind, unable to find relief from distressing thoughts.

In the dead of night, under a moonless sky, The Fool stumbles upon a desolate landscape shrouded in darkness. The weight of sorrow hangs heavy, and a sense of foreboding fills the silence as The Fool cautiously treads through the murky abyss.

Amidst the shadows, The Fool encounters the haunting figure of the Nine of Swords—a symbol of anguish, anxiety, and the relentless torment of the mind. The figure sits hunched over, consumed by despair, surrounded by a halo of piercing swords that pierce through the veil of night like jagged shards of broken dreams.

As The Fool approaches, they feel the suffocating grip of the figure's torment, a sense of dread that threatens to swallow them whole. Tears fill the figure's eyes as they are haunted by the specter of fear and uncertainty that looms over them like a specter in the night.

With a trembling voice, the figure reaches out to The Fool, their words choked with sorrow and regret. They speak of sleepless nights and restless days, of a mind consumed by shadows and a heart weighed down by the burden of unspoken fears.

During that moment, The Fool is overwhelmed by the figure's pain, a weighty burden that could potentially crush them. Yet, even in the depths of despair, there is a flicker of hope—a glimmer of light that pierces through the darkness and illuminates the path ahead.

With a gentle touch, The Fool offers solace to the figure, a beacon of light amidst the shadows, a reminder that even in our darkest moments, we are never truly alone. Together, they stand against the tide of despair, united in their shared struggle to find peace amidst the chaos that surrounds them.

The Fool watches as the figure rises from the depths of despair, their spirit renewed by the promise of a new dawn. With each step they take, the swords that once threatened to consume them fade into the darkness, scattered by the gentle touch of hope and the promise of a brighter tomorrow.

The Nine of Swords is a card of resilience, a testament to the strength of the human spirit in the face of adversity. It reminds us that even in our darkest moments, we possess the power to rise above our fears and embrace the light that lies within us all.

magical spell - banishing anxiety:

I release these fears and anxieties.
I am safe, protected, and at peace.

materials needed:

- White candle
- Piece of paper
- Lavender or chamomile herbs
- Pen

instructions:

- Light the white candle and place it in a quiet, comfortable space.
- Sit in front of the candle and take several deep breaths to center yourself.
- On the piece of paper, write down any worries, fears, or anxieties that are weighing heavily on your mind.
- Fold the paper and hold it in your hands, visualizing a bright light surrounding you and filling you with peace and calm.
- As you hold the paper, repeat the affirmation until you feel it in your bones:

"I release these fears and anxieties. I am safe, protected, and at peace."

- Place the paper in the flame of the candle (be careful with fire) and let it burn, visualizing the worries being transformed into smoke and dissipating into the air.
- Sprinkle the lavender or chamomile herbs around the candle, inviting relaxation and tranquility into your space.

The nine of swords depicts a person sitting up in bed, head in hands, surrounded by nine swords hanging on the wall behind them. This card often represents anxiety, fear, and worry, especially when it comes to mental anguish and overwhelming thoughts that keep one awake at night. It suggests the burden of inner turmoil and the need to confront and address the root causes of distress.

questions to ask yourself

1. What anxieties or worries are keeping me up at night?
2. How can I release my fears and find peace of mind amidst uncertainty?
3. What negative thought patterns or beliefs are contributing to my distress?
4. Am I seeking support from others or suffering in silence?
5. How can I practice self-compassion and kindness towards myself during times of struggle?
6. What healthy coping mechanisms can I employ to manage stress and anxiety?
7. How can I challenge irrational fears and cultivate a sense of perspective?
8. What lessons can I learn from my experiences of worry and sleepless nights?
9. How can I prioritize self-care and prioritize my mental health?
10. What steps can I take to address the root causes of my anxieties and fears?

ten of swords

. . .

"Embrace the end, for with closure comes new beginnings. Release the burdens of the past and welcome the dawn of transformation," Ten of Swords

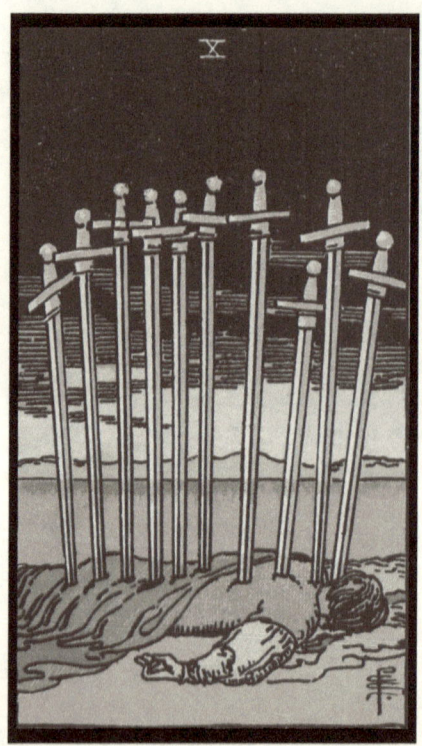

Answer: No

Key Words and Phrases:
Repeating patterns
Stuck in old patterns
Endings
Cycles ending
Feeling defeated
Change
Time to let go
Negative thinking
Loss
Betrayal
Wounds
Pain
The worst is done
Resisting change
Surrender
Healing
Recovery
Release
Improvement
Learn from the past

SYMBOLS:

- The figure represents a person who faced betrayal, defeat, or overwhelming challenges. They may feel powerless and defeated by the circumstances they are facing.
- The swords symbolize the culmination of mental anguish, painful endings, and betrayal. The ten swords piercing the figure's back suggest the depth of suffering and the feeling of being completely overwhelmed by adversity.
- The dark ominous sky in the background reflects the sense of despair and hopelessness that accompanies the card. It represents the darkness before the dawn, signifying that even in the darkest moments, there is the potential for new beginnings and growth.

In the depths of despair and darkness, The Fool encounters the chilling presence of the Ten of Swords. Here, amidst the desolate landscape, lies a figure sprawled upon the cold, unforgiving ground, pierced through by ten sharp swords, each representing a wound inflicted upon the spirit.

The Ten of Swords symbolizes the ultimate culmination of pain, betrayal, and the crushing weight of defeat. It speaks of endings, of finality, and the bitter sting of loss that cuts through the very soul like a dagger in the night.

As The Fool approaches, they feel the heavy burden of despair—a palpable sense of sorrow that threatens to engulf them in its icy embrace. The figure lying before them is a tragic testament to the harsh realities of life, a reminder that even the strongest among us are not immune to the ravages of fate.

With a heavy heart, The Fool listens as the figure recounts tales of betrayal and deceit, of dreams shattered and hopes dashed upon the rocks of despair. Each sword that pierces their flesh is a painful reminder of the trials they have endured, a testament to the scars that mark their journey through the darkness.

Yet, even in their moment of despair, there is a glimmer of light—a flicker of hope that refuses to be extinguished. The figure's eyes, though clouded with pain, hold a spark of resilience, a silent defiance against the forces that seek to break them.

For the Ten of Swords is not merely a card of endings, but also of new beginnings. It reminds us that even in our darkest hour, there is the promise of renewal, the possibility of rising from the ashes of defeat to embrace a brighter tomorrow.

As The Fool stands in silent vigil beside the fallen figure, the reminder of the fragility of life and the resilience of the human spirit becomes clear to them. They understand while pain and suffering may be inevitable, so too is the capacity for hope, for healing, and for the enduring power of the human heart to overcome even the greatest of trials.

And so, as the night gives way to the dawn, The Fool bids farewell to the figure lying before them, their spirit unbroken, their resolve unwavering. For in the face of adversity, they know that even the deepest wounds can heal, and that with each new day comes the promise of a brighter tomorrow.

magic spell: time renewal and release spell:

By the power of the ten swords,
I release what no longer serves.
With each cut, I let go of pain,
Sorrow, and hurt.
May the darkness be
Transformed into light,
And from these wounds,
I emerge renewed and bright.

ingredients:

- A black candle
- Ten dried rosemary sprigs
- A small piece of black fabric or cloth
- A sharp object (such as a needle or pin)
- A quiet, sacred space

instructions:

- Begin by preparing your sacred space. Clear any clutter and create a peaceful environment where you can focus without distractions.
- Place the black candle in the center of your space and arrange the ten dried rosemary sprigs around it in a circular pattern.
- Take a moment to ground yourself by taking a few deep breaths and centering your energy.

- Light the black candle, allowing its flame to flicker and cast shadows in the room. Visualize the light dispelling darkness and bringing clarity to your intentions.
- Hold the piece of black fabric or cloth in your hands, focusing on the symbolism of the Ten of Swords card and the concept of closure and release.
- With the sharp object, carefully make ten small incisions or cuts into the fabric, representing the wounds or challenges you wish to release and leave behind.
- As you make each cut, visualize the pain and burdens associated with these challenges being severed and dissolved into the universe's energy.
- Place the piece of fabric in front of the black candle, allowing the flame to gently illuminate the cuts you've made.
- Speak aloud or silently affirm your intention for renewal and release. You may use words such as:

"By the power of the ten swords, I release what no longer serves. With each cut, I let go of pain, sorrow, and hurt. May the darkness be transformed into light, And from these wounds, I emerge renewed and bright."

- Take each of the dried rosemary sprigs and place them one by one onto the fabric, allowing their aromatic scent to fill the space. Visualize the healing properties of rosemary cleansing and purifying your spirit.
- Allow the candle to burn down completely, or extinguish it if necessary, knowing that the energy of your intention has been set in motion.
- Fold the piece of fabric with the cuts and rosemary sprigs inside, sealing in the energy of release and renewal.
- Bury the fabric in the earth or dispose of it in a respectful manner, symbolizing the physical and spiritual release of the challenges you've addressed.
- Close the ritual with gratitude for the opportunity to let go and move forward with a renewed sense of purpose and clarity.
- Carry the energy of this spell with you as you continue your journey, knowing that you have the power to release the past and embrace the possibilities of the future.

The ten of swords portrays a figure lying face down with ten swords piercing their back. The card signifies the culmination of pain, betrayal, and difficult endings. It's the lowest point which means the only way to go is up. It's the potential for new beginnings and transformation after experiencing hardship.

questions to ask yourself

1. What endings or betrayals am I experiencing in my life right now?
2. How can I find closure and acceptance in the face of painful endings?
3. What lessons can I learn from experiences of loss or betrayal?
4. Am I allowing myself to grieve and process my emotions fully?
5. How can I release resentments and forgive those who have hurt me?
6. What support systems or resources can I turn to for healing?
7. How can I cultivate resilience and strength in times of adversity?
8. What new beginnings or opportunities are hidden within this ending?
9. How can I trust that this ending is making space for new growth and transformation?
10. What steps can I take to honor the past while embracing the future?

page of swords

. . .

"Curiosity is my compass, and knowledge my sword. With eyes wide open, I navigate the realms of intellect and discovery," Page of Swords

Answer: Maybe

Key Words and Phrases:
Changes
Insights
Travel
Curiosity
Defensiveness
Decisive
Exploration
Intellect
Seeing an overview
Innovative
Youthfulness
Protective
Commutation
Written communication
Education
Fairness

SYMBOLS:

- The page is a young person symbolizing their readiness to engage with the world intellectually. The page represents the youthful pursuit of knowledge and the courage to challenge conventional wisdom.
- The sword signifies the power of the mind, intellect, and communication. The sword points upward, indicating a quest for truth, clarity, and understanding.
- The windy landscape reflects the dynamic and ever-changing nature of the mind. It symbolizes the swift flow of thoughts, ideas, and information that the Page of Swords is eager to explore.

In the quiet corners of the mind where thoughts dance like shadows, The Fool encounters the Page of Swords, a figure poised on the precipice of discovery and exploration. As the wind whispers secrets through the trees, the Page gazes out into the horizon, eyes alight with the thrill of intellectual pursuit.

The Page of Swords symbolizes the eager pursuit of knowledge, the quest for truth, and the unquenchable thirst for understanding. With sword in hand, the Page stands ready to cut through the veil of ignorance and uncover the mysteries that lie beyond.

In the story of the Page of Swords, we meet a young seeker on a journey of self-discovery. Drawn to the path of learning and enlightenment, the Page sets out to explore the vast expanse of the mind, eager to unravel the secrets that lie hidden within.

With each step along the winding road, the Page encounters challenges and obstacles that test their resolve and sharpen their intellect. Through adversity and triumph alike, they press on, driven by an insatiable curiosity and a hunger for truth.

The Page of Swords encourages us to embrace the power of the mind, to question, to reason, and to seek knowledge wherever it may be found. Like a beacon in the darkness, the Page reminds us that the pursuit of wisdom is a noble endeavor, one that leads to growth, enlightenment, and understanding.

The Page serves as a warning against the pitfalls of arrogance and hubris. In their quest for knowledge, the Page must be mindful of the dangers of intellectual pride and the temptation to wield their newfound wisdom as a weapon against others.

As The Fool walks alongside the Page of Swords, they remember that humility and open-mindedness are important in the pursuit of truth. They understand that true wisdom lies not in the possession of knowledge, but in the willingness to listen, to learn, and to grow.

And so, with a sword in hand and heart aflame with curiosity, the Page of Swords sets forth into the unknown, a beacon of intellect and insight in a world shrouded in shadow and mystery. As The Fool watches them disappear into the distance, a sense of wonder and awe fills them at the boundless possibilities that lie ahead.

magical spell - enhancing mental clarity:

> By the light
> Of this crystal clear,
> May mental fog
> Now disappear.
> Grant me clarity,
> Sharp and bright,
> To see my path
> In guiding light.

materials needed:

- A clear quartz crystal
- A white candle
- A small dish of salt
- A sprig of rosemary or lavender (optional)
- A quiet, tranquil space

instructions:

- Begin by preparing your sacred space. Clear the area of any clutter and ensure that you can focus without interruptions.
- Place the white candle in the center of your space and light it, allowing its pure flame to fill the room with gentle illumination.
- Sit or stand comfortably in front of the candle, holding the clear quartz crystal in your hands. Close your eyes and take several deep breaths, allowing yourself to relax and center your thoughts.
- Envision a bright, radiant light emanating from the clear quartz crystal, illuminating your mind and spirit with clarity and purpose.
- With focused intent, speak the following words aloud or silently:

"By the light of this crystal clear, May mental fog now disappear. Grant me clarity, sharp and bright, To see my path in guiding light."

- Visualize the radiant energy from the crystal infusing your being, dispelling any mental fog or confusion that clouds your thoughts.

- Take a pinch of salt from the dish and sprinkle it around the candle, symbolizing purification, and clarity of mind.
- If you have a sprig of rosemary or lavender, hold it to your nose and inhale deeply, allowing the soothing scent to calm your mind and enhance your focus.
- Focus your attention on the flame of the candle, allowing its gentle flicker to draw you into a state of deep inner peace and clarity.
- As you bask in the glow of the candlelight, visualize any mental clutter or distractions dissolving away, leaving behind a clear and tranquil state of mind.
- Hold the intention of mental clarity firmly in your heart, knowing that you possess the inner strength and wisdom to navigate life's challenges with ease and grace.
- Spend a few moments in silent meditation, allowing the energy of the spell to integrate and permeate every aspect of your being.
- When you feel ready, extinguish the candle, symbolizing the completion of the spell. Feel the energy of clarity and purpose continue to resonate within you.
- Express gratitude to the universe for the gift of mental clarity and reaffirm your commitment to embracing clarity in your thoughts and actions.
- Carry the clear quartz crystal with you as a talisman of clarity, serving as a constant reminder of your ability to see through the veils of confusion and uncertainty, and to embrace the brilliance of your own inner light.

The Page of Swords represents intellectual curiosity, mental agility, and the pursuit of knowledge. In tarot, Pages often symbolize youthful energy and a willingness to explore new ideas and perspectives. The Page of Swords encourages you to embrace your curiosity, ask questions, and seek answers as they navigate the complexities of life.

questions to ask yourself

1. What new ideas or perspectives am I exploring at this time?
2. How can I express myself more clearly and authentically?
3. What messages or insights am I receiving from my intuition?
4. Am I open to learning and expanding my knowledge?
5. How can I embrace curiosity and intellectual growth?
6. What challenges or obstacles am I eager to tackle head-on?
7. How can I use my communication skills to advocate for myself and others?
8. What opportunities for creative expression am I exploring?
9. How can I cultivate a sense of mental agility and adaptability?
10. What steps can I take to embody the qualities of the Page of Swords in my life?

knight of swords

...

"Swift and resolute, I charge forth with clarity of purpose. In the winds of change, I find my strength, wielding courage as my noble steed," Knight of Swords.

Answer: Maybe

Key Words and Phrases:
Ambitious
Driven
Impulsive
Communication
Rushing
Clarity
Quick change
New experiences
Truth
Fearless
Assertive
Independence
Decisive
Strength
Focused
Wisdom
Impatience
Quick decisions

SYMBOLS:

- The knight is depicted charging forward on horseback, sword raised high. He symbolizes courage, ambition, and the willingness to face challenges head-on. His determined expression reflects his unwavering commitment to his mission.
- The sword represents the power of intellect, clarity, and truth. The sword is held high which signifies the knight's readiness to cut through confusion and falsehoods, seeking clarity and understanding in all endeavors.
- The Windy sky reflects the swift and dynamic nature of the knight's journey. The clouds and turbulent winds symbolize the obstacles and challenges he must overcome on his quest for truth and justice.

In the swirling winds of change and challenge, The Fool encounters the Knight of Swords, a figure of swift action and determined purpose. With a gleaming sword held high, the Knight charges forward, cutting through obstacles with fearless determination.

The Knight of Swords symbolizes courage, intellect, and the drive to pursue one's goals with unwavering focus. The Knight personifies ambition and the tireless pursuit of truth and justice.

Imagine a young knight, clad in shining armor, galloping across a vast battlefield. His heart beats with the rhythm of adventure, his mind sharp and keen as the edge of his sword. With every stride, he charges headlong into the fray, undaunted by the perils that lie ahead.

The story of the Knight of Swords is one of valor and determination, of daring deeds and noble quests. He is the champion of justice, the defender of truth, and the guardian of righteousness in a world fraught with darkness and deception.

As The Fool watches the Knight ride forth, a sense of awe and admiration fills him for the bravery and resolve that drives the Knight forward. He sees in the Knight a reflection of his own inner strength and courage, a reminder that in the face of adversity, anything is possible.

But the Knight of Swords also carries a warning, a reminder of the dangers of recklessness and impulsiveness. In his single-minded pursuit of victory, he may become blinded to the consequences of his actions, charging forward without thought or consideration for the well-being of others.

The Fool contemplates the lessons of the Knight. He understands that true courage lies not only in the willingness to fight, but also in the wisdom to choose his battles wisely. He learns that one's strength of character is not only measured by the might of one's sword but also by the compassion and integrity with which one wields it.

The Knight of Swords vanishes, leaving The Fool feeling inspired and amazed, aware of the immense potential within each of us. With bravery and persistence, any obstacle can be conquered.

magical spell - clearing mental blocks:

> By the sword's edge and the flame's light,
> I call upon the Knight of Swords,
> shining bright. Grant me courage,
> grant me might,
> To face challenges with clarity,
> day or night.
> With every step, with every word,
> I embody the valor of the Knight, undeterred.

materials needed:

- A sword (or a representation of a sword, such as a drawing or a small figurine)
- A blue candle
- A piece of paper and a pen
- A quiet, open space

instructions:

- Begin by finding a quiet and peaceful space where you can focus without distractions. Set up your materials in front of you.
- Light the blue candle, symbolizing the clarity and determination of the Knight of Swords.
- Take the sword or representation of a sword in your hand and close your eyes. Feel its weight and imagine the strength and purpose it embodies.
- With a steady hand, write down on the piece of paper the qualities you seek to embody from the Knight of Swords. This could include traits such as courage, decisiveness, clarity of thought, and determination.
- Place the paper in front of the candle, allowing the flame to gently illuminate your words.
- Hold the sword above the flame and visualize the energy of the candle infusing the sword with the qualities you desire.
- Repeat the following incantation:

"By the sword's edge and the flame's light, I call upon the Knight of Swords, shining bright. Grant me courage, grant me might, To face challenges with clarity, day or night. With every step, with every word, I embody the valor of the Knight, undeterred."

- Visualize yourself embodying the strength and determination of the Knight of Swords, fearlessly facing any challenges that come your way.
- Take a few moments to meditate quietly, allowing the energy of the spell to resonate within you.
- When you feel ready, extinguish the candle, knowing that the energy of the Knight of Swords is now within you, guiding you on your path.
- Keep the sword or representation of a sword in a prominent place as a reminder of the qualities you wish to embody.
- Carry the energy of this spell with you, trusting in your inner strength and clarity to overcome any obstacles that may arise.
- Express gratitude for the guidance and empowerment you have received through the spell.
- Close the ritual with a sense of confidence and determination, knowing that you are ready to face whatever challenges lie ahead, armed with the valor of the Knight of Swords.

The Knight of Swords embodies swift action, determination, and a quest for truth. In tarot, knights represent movement, energy, and the pursuit of goals with vigor and intensity. The Knight of Swords urges you to embrace your ambitions, pursue your dreams, and fearlessly overcome obstacles that stand in your way.

questions to ask yourself

1. What goals or ambitions am I pursuing with passion and determination?
2. How can I channel my energy and drive towards achieving my objectives?

3. What obstacles or challenges am I prepared to overcome on my quest for success?
4. Am I being mindful of the impact of my actions on others?
5. How can I balance assertiveness with consideration for the feelings of others?
6. What risks am I willing to take in order to pursue my goals?
7. How can I remain focused and disciplined in the face of distractions?
8. What strategies or plans am I implementing to achieve victory?
9. How can I cultivate resilience and perseverance in the pursuit of my dreams?
10. What lessons can I learn from experiences of triumph and setback?

queen of swords

. . .

"Speak your truth with grace and wisdom, for clarity paves the way to understanding," Queen of Swords

Answer: Yes

Key Words and Phrases:
Independence
Truth
Determined
Direct
Helpful guidance
Fair
Wisdom
Unbiased
Communication
Intelligent

SYMBOLS:

- The Queen portrays a woman seated on her throne, holding a sword upright in her hand. Her posture exudes confidence and authority, symbolizing her ability to make clear and rational decisions.
- The sword represents the power of intellect, discernment, and truth. The Queen wields her sword with purpose, cutting through deception and falsehoods to uncover the truth.
- The clouds surround the Queen, symbolizing her detached perspective and her ability to rise emotional turmoil. Despite life's challenges, she maintains clarity of thought and remains focused on her goals.

In the realm of intellect and discernment, The Fool encounters the Queen of Swords, a figure of sharp intellect, clear communication, and independence. Seated upon her throne, she holds her sword aloft, symbolizing her command over the realm of thought and truth.

The Queen of Swords embodies the qualities of mental acuity, perceptiveness, and astuteness. She is a master of analysis, able to see through illusions and discern the truth in any situation. Her words are direct and honest, and she values clarity and transparency in all her interactions.

Imagine a queen, regal and composed, her piercing gaze cutting through ambiguity to reveal the heart of the matter. She is unafraid to speak her mind, even when the truth may be uncomfortable or difficult to hear. Her strength lies in her ability to face reality head-on and make decisions based on reason rather than emotion.

The story of the Queen of Swords is one of independence and self-assurance, of embracing one's intellect and trusting in one's own judgment. She represents the archetype of the wise counselor, whose insights and advice are sought after by all who seek clarity and guidance.

When the Queen of Swords appears in a tarot reading, she encourages you to embrace your intellect and speak your truth with confidence. She reminds you to trust in your ability to discern fact from fiction and to rely on your own judgment while making decisions.

However, the Queen of Swords also serves as a reminder of the importance of compassion and empathy. While intellect and honesty are valuable traits, they must be tempered by kindness and understanding. The Queen of Swords encourages the querent to consider the impact of their words and to communicate with sensitivity and empathy.

In essence, the Queen of Swords challenges the querent to embody the qualities of independence and intellect, to trust in their ability to discern truth from falsehood, and to communicate their thoughts and feelings with clarity and honesty, tempered by compassion and understanding.

magical spell - enhancing mental clarity:

With clarity of mind
and wisdom of heart,
I seek truth and
understanding in all I do.

materials needed:

- Purple candle
- Lavender essential oil
- Piece of amethyst crystal
- Pen and paper

instructions:

- Begin by anointing the purple candle with lavender essential oil, infusing it with the energy of clarity and insight.
- Light the candle in a quiet, comfortable space, and sit in a relaxed position.
- Hold the piece of amethyst crystal in your non-dominant hand, allowing its soothing energy to calm your mind and enhance your intuition.
- Close your eyes and take several deep breaths, focusing on the flame of the candle and the energy of the crystal.
- With a clear intention in mind, write down any questions or concerns you have on the piece of paper, allowing yourself to express your thoughts and emotions freely.
- Hold the paper between your palms and visualize a beam of purple light surrounding you, filling you with clarity and insight.
- Recite the affirmation:

"With clarity of mind and wisdom of heart, I seek truth and understanding in all I do."

- Place the paper under the candle and allow it to burn, releasing your intentions into the universe.
- Sit quietly for a few moments, absorbing the energy of the spell and feeling a sense of clarity and peace wash over you.

The Queen of Swords embodies intellect, wisdom, and clarity of thought. She represents a woman of strong character who is independent, perceptive, and able to see through illusions. In tarot readings, the Queen of Swords urges you to embrace your intelligence, trust your intuition, and seek truth in all aspects of your life.

questions to ask yourself

1. How am I embodying the qualities of independence and self-reliance in my life?
2. What boundaries am I setting to protect my energy and well-being?
3. How can I communicate my thoughts and feelings with clarity and honesty?
4. Am I fostering an environment of open dialogue and mutual respect in my relationships?
5. How can I use my intellect and discernment to make wise decisions?
6. What challenges or conflicts am I addressing with courage and grace?
7. How can I nurture my inner strength and resilience in the face of adversity?
8. What insights or wisdom can I share with others based on my experiences?
9. How can I cultivate compassion and understanding without compromising my boundaries?
10. What steps can I take to embody the qualities of the Queen of Swords more fully in my life?

king of swords

. . .

"Decisions carved from truth," King of Swords.

Answer: Yes

Lorelai Hamilton

Key Words and Phrases
Authority
Rational
Intellectual rigor
Integrity
Truth
Power
Balanced
Judgment
Innovative
Cooperation
Leadership
Strength
Committed
Clarity

SYMBOLS:

- The King is a mature and dignified figure seated on his thrown, holding a sword upright in his hand. His regal posture and focused gaze convey a sense of authority and command.
- The sword symbolizes the power of intellect, discernment, and truth. The king holds the sword with confidence, ready to cut through confusion and deception to uncover the truth.
- The bird often depicted accompanying the King, symbolizes wisdom, intuition, and keen insight. The bird's presence suggests the King's ability to see beyond the surface and perceive the deeper truths of any situation.
- The mountains represent challenges and obstacles that the king has overcome through his intellect and determination. They symbolize the strength and resilience needed to maintain clarity and focus in the face of adversity.

In the kingdom of intellect and reason, The Fool encounters the King of

Swords, a figure of wisdom, logic, and authority. Seated upon his throne, he holds his sword with a firm grip, symbolizing his command over the realm of thought and communication.

The King of Swords embodies the qualities of a sharp mind, strategic thinking, and effective communication. He is a master of analysis, able to cut through confusion and see situations with clarity and precision. Logic guides his decisions rather than emotion, and he values truth above all else.

Imagine a king, dignified and composed, his piercing gaze penetrating through complexities to uncover solutions. He is unyielding in his pursuit of justice, always striving to uphold fairness and integrity in all matters.

The story of the King of Swords is one of leadership and responsibility, of using one's intellect and discernment to navigate life's challenges. He represents the archetype of the wise ruler, whose decisions are guided by reason and who leads with authority tempered by compassion.

When the King of Swords appears in a tarot reading, he encourages the querent to embrace their intellect and trust in their ability to make sound judgments. He reminds them to communicate clearly and assertively, to stand up for what they believe in, and to seek truth and justice in all endeavors.

However, the King of Swords also serves as a reminder of the importance of balance. While intellect and logic are valuable tools, they must be tempered by empathy and understanding. The King of Swords encourages you to consider the human aspect of situations and to approach challenges with both wisdom and compassion.

The King of Swords challenges you to embody the qualities of leadership and intellect, to trust in their ability to think critically and make decisions, and to always seek truth and justice in all aspects of life.

Magical Spell - Enhancing Mental Clarity and Confidence:
With clarity of mind
and wisdom of heart,
I seek truth and understanding

in all I do."

materials needed:

- Blue candle
- Frankincense incense
- Clear quartz crystal
- Pen and paper

instructions:

- Begin by lighting the blue candle and the frankincense incense in a quiet, comfortable space, creating a calming atmosphere conducive to clarity and focus.
- Hold the clear quartz crystal in your hand, allowing its energy to amplify your intentions and enhance mental clarity.
- Sit in a relaxed position and take several deep breaths, allowing yourself to center and ground your energy.
- With the pen and paper, write down any areas in your life where you seek clarity or where you need to assert your authority and communicate with conviction.
- Visualize a beam of blue light surrounding you, filling you with a sense of calm and confidence.
- Hold the paper between your palms and recite the affirmation:

"With clarity of mind and strength of spirit, I assert my authority and communicate with confidence."

- Place the paper under the candle and allow it to burn, releasing your intentions into the universe.
- Sit quietly for a few moments, feeling the energy of the spell infusing you with clarity, confidence, and inner strength.

The Queen of Swords embodies intellect, wisdom, and clarity of thought. She represents a woman of strong character who is independent, perceptive, and able to see through illusions. In tarot readings, the Queen of Swords urges you to embrace your intelligence, trust your intuition, and seek truth in all aspects of your life.

questions to ask yourself

1. How am I using my leadership and authority to promote fairness and justice?
2. What decisions or judgments am I making with wisdom and clarity?
3. How can I inspire others to think critically and act with integrity?
4. Am I fostering an environment of intellectual curiosity and open-mindedness?
5. How can I communicate my vision and ideas with confidence and conviction?
6. What challenges or conflicts am I addressing with logic and reason?
7. How can I balance compassion and empathy with a commitment to truth and honesty?
8. What strategies or plans am I implementing to achieve my goals effectively?
9. How can I use my influence and power to create positive change in my community?
10. What lessons can I learn from experiences of leadership and responsibility?

ace of wands

...

"Embrace the spark of inspiration, for within it lies the flame of endless potential," Ace of Wands

Answer: Yes

Key Words and Phrases:
Great news
New beginnings
Passion
Falling into place.
Potential
New ideas
Creativity
Ambition
Inspiration

SYMBOLS:

- The hand emerging from the cloud symbolizes divine inspiration and the gift of creative energy bestowed upon you from the universe.
- The wand represents the element of fire, symbolizing passion, energy, and the power to ignite change and transformation.
- The leaves sprouting from the wand represent growth, vitality, and the potential for new beginnings and opportunities.

In the enchanted woods of possibility, The Fool encounters the Ace of Wands, a symbol of raw energy, inspiration, and new beginnings. The Ace of Wands emerges from the heart of nature, its vibrant flames dancing with the promise of creativity and adventure.

With the essence of fire, The Ace of Wands ignites passion and potential in one's soul. Its presence heralds the dawn of exciting opportunities and the birth of bold ideas. Like the first rays of sunlight breaking through the darkness, the Ace of Wands invites the querent to embrace the power of inspiration and take the first steps toward manifesting their dreams.

Imagine a young adventurer stumbling upon a hidden treasure buried beneath the ancient roots of a towering oak tree. As they unearth the treasure, they discover a gleaming wand, pulsating with untapped energy and boundless possibilities. With trembling hands, they grasp the wand and feel a surge of vitality coursing through their veins.

The story of the Ace of Wands is one of inspiration and potential, of tapping into the wellspring of creativity that lies within each of us. It reminds the querent that they possess the power to create their own destiny and shape their reality according to their deepest desires.

When the Ace of Wands appears in a tarot reading, it serves as a catalyst for action and innovation. It encourages the querent to follow their passions fearlessly and pursue their goals with unwavering determination. The Ace of Wands reminds them that the universe is conspiring in their favor, urging them to seize the opportunities that lie before them.

However, the Ace of Wands also cautions against impulsivity and recklessness. While the flames of inspiration may burn brightly, they must be tempered by careful planning and thoughtful consideration. The querent is reminded to channel their creative energy wisely and to harness it in service of their highest good.

The Ace of Wands challenges the querent to embrace the power of inspiration and creativity, to trust in their intuition, and to take bold action in pursuit of their dreams. It reminds them that the universe is abundant with possibilities, waiting to be explored by those who dare to dream and dare to do.

magical spell: spark of inspiration ritual:

Ace of Wands,
Ignite my fire,
Passion and creativity,
Take me higher.

With inspiration as my guide,
I take flight,
Bringing my dreams into the light."

materials needed:

- A quiet and comfortable space
- A red or orange candle
- A small piece of paper
- A pen or marker
- Cinnamon or ginger essential oil (optional)

instructions:

- Find a peaceful space where you can sit comfortably without distractions.
- Light the red or orange candle and place it in front of you.
- If you have essential oil, dab a drop on your wrists or pulse points to invoke a sense of passion and creativity.
- Take a few deep breaths to center yourself and connect with the energy of inspiration and potential.
- On the piece of paper, write down a creative project or goal that you wish to pursue with passion and enthusiasm.
- Hold the paper in your hands and visualize yourself fully immersed in the creative process, feeling inspired and energized.
- Recite the following affirmation aloud:

"Ace of Wands, ignite my fire, Passion and creativity, take me higher. With inspiration as my guide, I take flight, Bringing my dreams into the light."

- Allow yourself to feel a sense of excitement and motivation as you affirm your intentions.
- Fold the paper and hold it over the flame of the candle, allowing it to safely burn.
- As the paper burns, visualize the flames carrying your intentions out into the universe, where they will be manifested into reality.
- Once the paper has turned to ash, extinguish the candle and trust in the power of the Ace of Wands to ignite your passion and creativity as you pursue your dreams.

The Ace of Wands reminds you to embrace your creative potential and pursue your passions with enthusiasm and determination. By harnessing the power of inspiration and taking bold action towards your goals, you can manifest your desires and bring your dreams to life. Let the Ace of Wands be your guiding light as you embark on the journey of self-discovery and creative expression.

questions to ask yourself

1. What new opportunities or beginnings am I currently experiencing or considering in my life?
2. What passions or creative interests am I feeling particularly drawn to at this time?
3. How can I harness the energy of inspiration and creativity that the Ace of Wands represents?
4. What projects or endeavors am I feeling inspired to pursue or initiate?
5. Am I feeling a surge of motivation or enthusiasm for a particular aspect of my life, and if so, how can I channel this energy effectively?
6. What beliefs or perspectives might be holding me back from fully embracing this new beginning or creative potential?
7. How can I cultivate a mindset of openness and receptivity to new ideas and opportunities?
8. What steps can I take to nurture and support the growth of my passions and creative pursuits?
9. Am I willing to take risks and step out of my comfort zone to pursue my goals and aspirations?
10. How can I maintain a balance between spontaneity and careful planning as I embark on this new journey?

two of wands

...

"I stand at the threshold of opportunity, surveying the vast expanse of possibilities before me," Two of Wands.

Answer: Yes

Lorelai Hamilton

Key Words and Phrases:
Waiting
Planning
Achievement
Ownership
Ambition
Growth
Success
Future
Exploration
Moving
Distance
Vision
Travel
Decision

SYMBOLS:

- The figure holding the globe symbolizes ambition, exploration, and the desire to expand one's horizons.
- The globe represents the world of possibilities and opportunities that lie ahead, waiting to be explored and discovered.
- The wand in the other hand signifies the creative energy and power to manifest one's vision into reality.

The Fool meets the Two of Wands, a card full of exploration, ambition, and decision-making energy in the realm of endless possibilities. As The Fool gazes upon the horizon, two wands stand firmly planted beside them, each representing a pathway into the unknown.

The Two of Wands serves as a beacon of opportunity, urging you to step boldly into the uncharted territories of your destiny. It symbolizes the crossroads of choice, where decisions must be made, and paths must be chosen. Like a captain surveying the vast seas, the querent stands poised to embark on a journey of self-discovery and adventure.

Picture a young traveler standing atop a windswept cliff, gazing out at the boundless ocean stretching before them. In one hand, they hold a sturdy staff, symbolizing their strength and determination. In the other, they grasp a globe, representing the vast array of possibilities that lie beyond the horizon.

The story of the Two of Wands is one of vision and potential, of embracing the unknown with courage and conviction. It reminds the querent that they hold the power to shape their destiny and chart their course toward greatness. The world is yours to explore, and the winds of fate are at your back.

When the Two of Wands appears in a tarot reading, it encourages you to trust in your instincts and follow your heart's desire. It invites you to consider your long-term goals and aspirations and to take decisive action in pursuit of your dreams. The Two of Wands reminds you that the only limits that exist are those you've placed upon yourself.

However, the Two of Wands also cautions against complacency and indecision. While the world may be ripe with opportunity, it is up to the querent to seize the moment and make the most of it. They must be willing to step outside of their comfort zone and embrace the challenges that lie ahead.

The Two of Wands challenges the you to embrace the spirit of adventure and embrace the unknown with open arms. It's a reminder to embrace the spirit of adventure and the unknown with open arms, as the journey of life is filled with twists and turns that can be conquered with courage and determination to achieve your wildest dreams. The world is yours for the taking, and the Two of Wands is your guiding light in the darkness.

magical spell: pathfinding ritual:

Two of Wands,
guide my way,
Choices and opportunities,

here to stay.
With clarity and vision,
I make my choice,
Trusting in my intuition,
I find my voice."

materials needed:

- A quiet and comfortable space
- A blue or green candle
- A small piece of paper
- A pen or marker
- Sage or rosemary herbs (dried or fresh)

instructions:

- Find a peaceful space where you can sit comfortably without distractions.
- Light the blue or green candle and place it in front of you.
- If you have sage or rosemary herbs, sprinkle a small amount around the candle to cleanse the space and invite clarity and wisdom.
- Take a few deep breaths to center yourself and connect with the energy of exploration and possibility.
- On the piece of paper, write down a choice or opportunity that you wish to explore further or make a decision about.
- Hold the paper in your hands and visualize yourself standing at a crossroads, feeling confident and empowered to choose the path that resonates with your heart and soul.
- Recite the following affirmation aloud:

"Two of Wands, guide my way, Choices and opportunities, here to stay. With clarity and vision, I make my choice, Trusting in my intuition, I find my voice."

- Allow yourself to feel a sense of empowerment and clarity as you affirm your intentions.
- Fold the paper and hold it over the flame of the candle, allowing it to safely burn.
- As the paper burns, visualize the flames illuminating your path and guiding you towards the right decision or opportunity.
- Once the paper has turned to ash, extinguish the candle and

trust in the power of the Two of Wands to lead you on your journey of exploration and growth.

The Two of Wands reminds you to embrace the power of choice and seize the opportunities that lie before you. By trusting in your intuition and taking bold steps towards your goals, you can navigate the uncertainties of life with courage and vision. Let the Two of Wands be your guiding light as you embark on the journey of self-discovery and fulfillment.

questions to ask yourself

1. What goals or aspirations am I currently envisioning for my future?
2. How can I expand my horizons and explore new possibilities?
3. What decisions or choices am I facing as I chart my course forward?
4. Am I willing to step out of my comfort zone in pursuit of my dreams?
5. How can I balance ambition with patience and practicality?
6. What resources or support systems do I need to bring my vision to life?
7. How can I cultivate confidence and self-assurance in my abilities?
8. What insights or guidance am I receiving as I contemplate my next steps?
9. How can I stay focused and committed to my long-term objectives?
10. What actions can I take to claim my power and assert my intentions?

three of wands

...

"With each passing moment, my dreams draw nearer, carried by the winds of opportunity," Three of Wands.

Answer: Yes

Key Words and Phrases:
New opportunities
Success
Progress
Exploration
Setting goals
New ideas
Expansion
New coming
Anticipation
Good Advice
Ships coming in
Travel
Hopeful
Enterprise
Visions
Expansion

SYMBOLS:

- The figure standing on the hill symbolizes leadership, vision, and the willingness to take charge of one's destiny.
- The wands planted in the ground represent the foundation of success and the groundwork that has been laid for future growth and expansion.
- The ocean in the background symbolizes vast possibilities, uncharted territories, and the sense of adventure that comes with exploring new horizons.

The Fool encounters the Three of Wands is a card brimming with the energy of exploration, expansion, and anticipation. As The Fool gazes upon the horizon, they behold a figure standing proudly upon a cliff, gazing out at the vast expanse of the sea.

The Three of Wands is a beacon of vision and foresight, urging you to cast your gaze towards the distant shores of possibility. The figure in the card stands with three wands planted firmly on the ground, symbolizing the foundation of their aspirations and the seeds of their dreams taking root.

Picture a young adventurer standing at the edge of the world, the salty breeze tousling their hair as they survey the endless ocean before them. In their heart burns the fire of ambition, driving them to seek out new horizons and chart uncharted territories.

The story of the Three of Wands is one of ambition, enterprise, and forward momentum. It speaks to your ability to envision a brighter future and take proactive steps towards its realization. Like the figure in the card, you stand at the threshold of possibility, poised to set sail on a journey of discovery and adventure.

When the Three of Wands appears in a tarot reading, it serves as a call to action, encouraging the querent to harness their creative energies and set their sights on their long-term goals. It prompts them to think expansively, to dare to dream big, and to have faith in their ability to manifest their desires.

However, the Three of Wands also reminds you that the path to success is not always smooth sailing. It may be fraught with challenges, setbacks, and unforeseen obstacles. Yet, it is through adversity that true growth and transformation occur, and it is through perseverance, that the greatest victories are won.

Ultimately, the Three of Wands is a card of promise and potential, symbolizing the boundless opportunities that await those who have the courage to chase their dreams. It reminds the querent that the world is theirs to explore, and that the journey itself is as important as the destination.

The Three of Wands is a testament to the power of vision, determination, and ambition. It calls for you to embrace the adventure of life wholeheartedly, knowing that with each step forward, you move closer to realizing your fullest potential and unlocking the treasures that lie beyond the horizon.

magical spell: manifesting adventure ritual:

Three of Wands,
Guide my way,
Dreams and visions,
Here to stay.
With courage and determination,
I take flight,
Embracing adventure,
With all my might.

materials needed:

- A quiet and comfortable space
- A yellow or gold candle
- A small piece of paper
- A pen or marker
- Patchouli or sandalwood incense (optional)

instructions:

- Find a peaceful space where you can sit comfortably without distractions.
- Light the yellow or gold candle and place it in front of you.
- If you have incense, light it to cleanse the space and invite positive energy and inspiration.

- Take a few deep breaths to center yourself and connect with the energy of adventure and expansion.
- On the piece of paper, write down a goal or dream that you wish to pursue with courage and determination.
- Hold the paper in your hands and visualize yourself standing on the hill, overlooking the vast expanse of possibilities before you.
- Recite the following affirmation aloud:

"Three of Wands, guide my way, Dreams and visions, here to stay. With courage and determination, I take flight, Embracing adventure, with all my might."

- Allow yourself to feel a sense of excitement and anticipation as you affirm your intentions.
- Fold the paper and hold it over the flame of the candle, allowing it to safely burn.
- As the paper burns, visualize the flames igniting your passion and determination to pursue your dreams.
- Once the paper has turned to ash, extinguish the candle and trust in the power of the Three of Wands to lead you on your journey of exploration and expansion.

The Three of Wands reminds you to embrace the spirit of adventure and seize the opportunities that lie before you. By trusting in your vision and taking bold steps towards your goals, you can expand your horizons and manifest your dreams into reality. Let the Three of Wands be your guiding light as you embark on the journey of self-discovery and fulfillment.

questions to ask yourself

1. What opportunities for growth and expansion are on the horizon for me?
2. How can I build upon my past achievements and successes?
3. What long-term goals or aspirations am I currently working towards?
4. Am I ready to step into a leadership role and take charge of my destiny?
5. How can I cultivate patience and trust in the unfolding of my journey?
6. What partnerships or collaborations can help me reach new heights of success?
7. How can I expand my perspective and consider alternative pathways to success?
8. What steps can I take to assert my authority and claim my place in the world?
9. How can I stay true to my vision and values amidst external pressures?
10. What actions can I take to seize the opportunities that are presenting themselves to me?

four of wands

. . .

"This is a time of celebration, where friends and family gather to honor the milestones, we have achieved together," Four of Wands.

Answer: Yes

Key Words and Phrases:
Celebration
Harmony
Peace
Rest
Joy
Community
Achievement
Security
Stability
Marriage
Comfort
Improvement
Reward

SYMBOLS:

- Depicted as a joyful scene with figures dancing beneath a canopy of wands, it represents a time of harmony, unity, and community.
- The card signifies a period of peace, prosperity, and the recognition of accomplishments and blessings.

In the bustling realm of the tarot, The Fool encounters the Four of Wands, a card pulsating with the essence of celebration, harmony, and joy. Amidst a verdant landscape, adorned with colorful flowers and lush foliage, stand four grand wands, crowned with garlands of flowers, forming a majestic gateway.

The Four of Wands is a symbol of unity, camaraderie, and communal spirit. Imagine a vibrant festival, where people from all walks of life come together to revel in the shared bonds of friendship and fellowship. In the card, we witness a scene of jubilation and merriment, as individuals gather under the canopy of the wands to celebrate life's blessings and achievements.

This card tells the story of coming home, both literally and figuratively. It speaks of finding a place of belonging, where one can bask in the warmth of community and feel a sense of connection with others. Similar to the figures in the card, loved ones and kindred spirits surround The Fool, reminding them of the importance of building supportive networks and nurturing meaningful relationships.

The Four of Wands also serves as a reminder to pause and appreciate life's simple pleasures. It urges the querent to take a moment to revel in the beauty of the present moment, to count their blessings, and to express gratitude for all that they have. In a world often filled with hustle and bustle, this card encourages The Fool to slow down, to savor the sweetness of life, and to cherish the bonds that bind us together.

When the Four of Wands appears in a tarot reading, it heralds a time of joyous celebrations, happy reunions, and auspicious beginnings. It suggests that the querent may soon find themselves surrounded by love, support, and goodwill, as they embark on a new chapter filled with promise and possibility.

However, the Four of Wands also reminds The Fool that true happiness comes from within. It encourages them to cultivate a sense of inner peace and contentment, regardless of external circumstances. For it is only when one is at peace with themselves that they can fully embrace the joy and abundance that life has to offer.

The Four of Wands is a testament to the power of love, connection, and shared experiences. It reminds The Fool that they are never alone, and that the bonds of friendship, family, and community infinitely support them. May you always find solace knowing that you are surrounded by love, and that you are an integral part of something greater than themselves.

magical spell: harmony and celebration ritual:

Four of Wands,
bring me cheer,

> Celebrating blessings,
> drawing near.
> With gratitude and joy,
> I raise my voice,
> Embracing harmony,
> I rejoice.

materials needed:

- A quiet and comfortable space
- Four candles in different colors (red, yellow, green, blue)
- A small piece of paper
- A pen or marker
- Lavender or jasmine essential oil (optional)

instructions:

- Find a peaceful space where you can sit comfortably without distractions.
- Arrange the four candles in a circle around you, representing the four corners of stability and harmony.
- If you have essential oil, dab a drop on your wrists or pulse points to invoke a sense of peace and celebration.
- Take a few deep breaths to center yourself and connect with the energy of joy and abundance.
- On the piece of paper, write down a recent achievement or milestone that you wish to celebrate and honor.
- Hold the paper in your hands and visualize yourself surrounded by friends and loved ones, dancing and rejoicing in your success.
- Recite the following affirmation aloud:

"Four of Wands, bring me cheer, Celebrating blessings, drawing near. With gratitude and joy, I raise my voice, Embracing harmony, I rejoice."

- Allow yourself to feel a sense of gratitude and joy as you affirm your intentions.
- Light each candle, one by one, starting from the north and moving clockwise, representing the stability and abundance that surrounds you.
- Sit quietly and bask in the warm glow of the candles, feeling the love and support of those around you.

- Once you feel ready, extinguish the candles, knowing that the energy of celebration and harmony remains with you always.

The Four of Wands reminds you to embrace moments of celebration and joy, and to recognize the stability and support that surrounds you. By honoring your achievements and blessings, you can cultivate a sense of harmony and abundance in your life. Let the Four of Wands be your guide as you dance through life's celebrations and cherish the bonds of love and friendship that sustain you.

questions to ask yourself

1. What achievements or milestones am I celebrating in my life right now?
2. How can I cultivate a sense of joy and gratitude for my blessings?
3. What aspects of my life are providing stability and security?
4. Am I nurturing my relationships and connections with loved ones?
5. How can I create a harmonious and supportive environment for myself and others?
6. What rituals or traditions can I establish to honor moments of significance?
7. How can I celebrate my progress and accomplishments with authenticity?
8. What new beginnings or opportunities are emerging from a place of stability?
9. How can I share my abundance and success with those around me?

10. What steps can I take to maintain a sense of balance and harmony in my life?

five of wands

...

"True strength lies not in domination, but in collaboration," Five of Wands

Answer: No

Key Words and Phrases:
Challenge
Proving yourself
Practice
Physical Strength
Obstacles
Playing Games
Success through hard work
Stress
Competition
Disagreements
Delays
Territorial
Setting Priorities
Quarrel

SYMBOLS:

- The figures wielding wands symbolize individuals engaged in conflict and competition, each asserting their own ideas and interests.
- The chaotic scene represents the clash of egos and the struggle for supremacy.
- The wands themselves symbolize creative energy and the potential for growth and transformation, even amid conflict.

The Fool encounters the Five of Wands, a card swirling with the frenetic energy of conflict, competition, and discord. Amidst a whirlwind of wooden staves, figures engage in a spirited bout, each vying for dominance and supremacy.

The Five of Wands is a symbol of tension, disagreement, and the clash of wills. Imagine a bustling marketplace, alive with the clamor of voices and the flurry of activity, as merchants jostle for attention and customers haggle over prices. In the card, we witness a scene of frenzied commotion, as individuals grapple for control and strive to assert their authority.

This card tells the story of conflict and contention, both external and internal. It speaks of the challenges and obstacles that arise when competing interests collide and differing perspectives clash. Like the figures in the card, locked in a spirited struggle for dominance, The Fool is reminded of the importance of perseverance and resilience in the face of adversity.

The Five of Wands also serves as a cautionary tale, warning against the dangers of unchecked aggression and unchecked ego. It warns against the dangers of unchecked aggression and ego, emphasizing the importance of approaching conflict with care and consideration to avoid escalating tensions and fostering more discord.

When the Five of Wands appears in a tarot reading, it heralds a time of upheaval, disagreement, and discord. It suggests that you may soon find yourselves embroiled in conflicts and power struggles, as you navigate the turbulent waters of interpersonal relationships and navigate the choppy seas of competing interests.

However, the Five of Wands also offers a glimmer of hope amidst the chaos. It reminds The Fool that conflict, while challenging, also presents an opportunity for growth and transformation. It encourages them to rise above the fray, to seek common ground amidst the discord, and to find strength in solidarity and collaboration.

The Five of Wands is a testament to the complexities of human interaction and the intricacies of the human experience. It reminds The Fool that conflict is a natural part of life, and that true wisdom lies not in avoiding conflict, but in confronting it with courage, compassion, and understanding. As they journey through the tumultuous terrain of the human condition, may they always remember that it is through adversity that we discover our true strength, and it is through conflict that we find our deepest humanity.

magical spell: harmony amidst conflict ritual:

Five of Wands,
guide my way,
Conflict and tension,
here to stay.
With wisdom and grace,
I find my peace,
Resolving conflicts,
I release.

materials needed:

- A quiet and comfortable space
- A white candle
- A small piece of paper
- A pen or marker
- Lavender or chamomile herbs (dried or fresh)

instructions:

- Find a peaceful space where you can sit comfortably without distractions.
- Light the white candle and place it in front of you.
- If you have herbs, sprinkle a small amount around the candle to invoke peace and harmony.
- Take a few deep breaths to center yourself and connect with the energy of tranquility and balance.
- On the piece of paper, write down a conflict or challenge that you wish to address and resolve.
- Hold the paper in your hands and visualize the conflict being diffused and transformed into a peaceful resolution.
- Recite the following affirmation aloud:

"Five of Wands, guide my way, Conflict and tension, here to stay. With wisdom and grace, I find my peace, Resolving conflicts, I release."

- Allow yourself to feel a sense of calm and serenity as you affirm your intentions.
- Fold the paper and hold it over the flame of the candle, allowing it to safely burn.

- As the paper burns, visualize the flames transmuting the conflict into harmony and understanding.
- Once the paper has turned to ash, extinguish the candle and trust in the power of the Five of Wands to help you navigate conflicts with grace and wisdom.

The Five of Wands reminds you to confront conflicts and challenges with courage and resilience. By seeking peaceful resolutions and finding common ground, you can transform discord into harmony and foster positive relationships with others. Let the Five of Wands be your guide as you navigate the complexities of interpersonal dynamics and assert your own truth with integrity and compassion.

questions to ask yourself

1. What conflicts or tensions am I currently experiencing in my life?
2. How can I navigate disagreements or competition with grace and integrity?
3. What underlying fears or insecurities might be fueling these conflicts?
4. Am I approaching challenges with an open mind and a willingness to listen?
5. How can I find common ground and work towards a resolution?
6. What lessons can I learn from experiences of conflict or rivalry?
7. How can I assert myself without resorting to aggression or hostility?
8. What role am I playing in perpetuating or diffusing tension in my environment?

9. How can I cultivate empathy and understanding towards those I perceive as opponents?
10. What boundaries do I need to set to protect myself from toxic dynamics?

six of wands

. . .

"Bask in the glory of this triumph, be filled with gratitude for those who supported you along the way," Six of Wands.

Answer: Yes

Key Words and Phrases:
Success
Forward momentum
Accomplishment
Progress
Victory
Promotion
Recognition
Reward
Good news
Pride
Achievement
Winning
Encouragement
Confidence

SYMBOLS:

- The figure riding on the horse symbolizes leadership, confidence, and the sense of pride that comes from overcoming obstacles and achieving success.
- The laurel wreaths represent victory and honor, bestowed upon the figure as a symbol of recognition and acclaim.
- The wand held high symbolizes the creative energy and determination that propelled the figure to victory.

The Fool encounters the illustrious Six of Wands, a card adorned with symbols of victory, recognition, and triumph. Against a backdrop of cheering crowds and fluttering banners, a triumphant figure rides forth on a noble steed, basking in the adulation of the masses.

The Six of Wands is a beacon of success and achievement, a testament to The Fool's perseverance, courage, and unwavering determination. It tells the story of a hard-fought battle won, of obstacles overcome, and of dreams realized against all odds.

Imagine standing atop a mountaintop, surveying the vast expanse below, as the world unfolds at your feet. In the card, we witness a moment of triumph and glory as the victorious rider parades through the streets, greeted by the joyful cries of the people. It is a scene of jubilation and celebration, a testament to the power of courage, resilience, and unwavering faith.

The Six of Wands speaks of recognition and validation, of being acknowledged for your efforts and accomplishments. It heralds a time of honor, acclaim, and public recognition, as all who bear witness, celebrate, and applaud The Fool's achievements.

But amidst the revelry and applause, the Six of Wands also serves as a reminder of the importance of humility and gratitude. It encourages The Fool to remain grounded in the face of success, to remember those who have supported them along the way, and to pay tribute to the countless souls who have contributed to their journey.

The appearance of the Six of Wands in a tarot reading signifies triumph and victory, suggesting that The Fool's efforts will soon be recognized and their dreams will be realized. It encourages them to embrace their successes with humility and grace, to share their blessings with those around them, and to continue striving for greatness in all that they do.

The Six of Wands is a testament to the indomitable spirit of the human heart, a reminder that no obstacle is too great to overcome, and no dream is too lofty to achieve. As The Fool journeys forth into the boundless expanse of the unknown, may they take heart knowing that victory is not merely a destination but a journey, and that genuine success lies not in the destination but in the courage to embark upon the path.

Magical Spell: Confidence and Recognition Ritual

Six of Wands,
hear my plea,
Recognition and victory,
come to me.

With confidence and grace,
I stand tall,
Celebrating success,
I answer the call."

materials needed:

- A quiet and comfortable space
- A yellow or gold candle
- A small piece of paper
- A pen or marker
- Basil or mint herbs (dried or fresh)

instructions:

1. Find a peaceful space where you can sit comfortably without distractions.
2. Light the yellow or gold candle and place it in front of you.
3. If you have herbs, sprinkle a small amount around the candle to invoke confidence and recognition.
4. Take a few deep breaths to center yourself and connect with the energy of success and validation.
5. On the piece of paper, write down an accomplishment or achievement that you wish to celebrate and be recognized for.
6. Hold the paper in your hands and visualize yourself standing tall and proud, basking in the glow of admiration and appreciation from others.
7. Recite the following affirmation aloud:

"Six of Wands, hear my plea, Recognition and victory, come to me. With confidence and grace, I stand tall, Celebrating success, I answer the call."

1. Allow yourself to feel a sense of pride and self-assurance as you affirm your intentions.
2. Fold the paper and hold it over the flame of the candle, allowing it to safely burn.
3. As the paper burns, visualize the flames igniting your confidence and attracting recognition and admiration from others.
4. Once the paper has turned to ash, extinguish the candle and trust in the power of the Six of Wands to bring you the acknowledgment and validation you deserve.

The Six of Wands reminds you to take pride in your accomplishments and to celebrate your successes with confidence and humility. By acknowledging your achievements and embracing recognition from others, you can cultivate a sense of self-worth and fulfillment. Let the Six of Wands be your guide as you journey towards greater heights of triumph and recognition in all aspects of your life.

questions to ask yourself

1. What achievements or victories am I celebrating in my life right now?
2. How can I acknowledge and honor my successes with humility?
3. What challenges or obstacles have I overcome to reach this point?
4. Am I receiving recognition and validation for my efforts and accomplishments?
5. How can I use my platform or influence to inspire and uplift others?
6. What lessons can I learn from experiences of triumph and achievement?
7. How can I maintain a sense of momentum and continue moving forward?
8. What support systems or resources have contributed to my success?
9. How can I cultivate gratitude and appreciation for the journey that has led me here?
10. What new opportunities or endeavors am I inspired to pursue in light of my achievements?

seven of wands

. . .

"I pave the way for victory and earn the respect of those around me," Seven of Wands.

Answer: Yes

Lorelai Hamilton

Key Words and Phrases:
Determined
Challenge
Resilience
Confident
Tenacity
Courage
Being on top
Taking a stand
Opposition
Advantage
Defense

SYMBOLS:

- The figure standing on the hill symbolizes the position of strength and advantage, asserting dominance over those below.
- The wand wielded by the figure represents the power to defend oneself and uphold one's principles in the face of adversity.
- The adversaries below symbolize the challenges and obstacles that one must confront to maintain their position and assert their authority.

As The Fool traverses the tarot, they come across the Seven of Wands, a card that kindles the spirit with its fiery resolve and resolute determination. Amidst the tumultuous landscape of challenges and obstacles, a lone figure stands atop a hill, courageously wielding a wand as a symbol of defiance and resilience.

The discovery of the Seven of Wands reveals a narrative of bravery against challenge. Picture yourself amid a battlefield, surrounded by adversaries seeking to undermine your efforts and thwart your progress. The Seven of Wands challenges The Fool to stand firm in their convictions, to defend their beliefs against all opposition, and to confront their fears with unwavering resolve.

Symbolically, the Seven of Wands represents the indomitable spirit of the human heart, urging The Fool to rise above the chaos and assert their truth with courage and determination. It serves as a powerful reminder that true strength lies not in the absence of fear, but in the courage to confront it head-on.

When the Seven of Wands appears in a tarot reading, it carries a potent message of empowerment and resilience. It encourages The Fool to trust in their abilities, to embrace their inner strength, and to confront challenges with unwavering resolve. It reminds them they possess the courage and fortitude to overcome any obstacle, no matter how daunting it may seem.

Yet, amidst the chaos of battle, the Seven of Wands also serves as a cautionary tale against succumbing to arrogance or hubris. It reminds The Fool to remain vigilant, to choose their battles wisely, and to temper their defiance with wisdom and discernment.

Ultimately, the Seven of Wands imparts a powerful lesson in courage, resilience, and self-belief. It reminds The Fool that they can achieve greatness, even in the face of overwhelming odds, and that their unwavering resolve will carry them through even the darkest of times.

As The Fool continues their journey, may they draw strength from the lessons of the Seven of Wands, and may they emerge victorious in the face of adversity, emboldened by the fire of their own courage and determination.

magical spell: strength and resilience ritual:

Seven of Wands,
hear my plea,
Strength and courage,
come to me.
With resilience and fortitude,
I stand tall,
Facing challenges,

Lorelai Hamilton

I never fall.

Materials Needed:

- A quiet and comfortable space
- A red candle
- A small piece of paper
- A pen or marker
- Rosemary or cinnamon herbs (dried or fresh)

Instructions:

1. Find a peaceful space where you can sit comfortably without distractions.
2. Light the red candle and place it in front of you.
3. If you have herbs, sprinkle a small amount around the candle to invoke strength and resilience.
4. Take a few deep breaths to center yourself and connect with your inner power and determination.
5. On the piece of paper, write down a challenge or obstacle that you are currently facing and wish to overcome.
6. Hold the paper in your hands and visualize yourself standing tall and confident, ready to confront the challenge head-on.
7. Recite the following affirmation aloud:

"Seven of Wands, hear my plea, Strength and courage, come to me. With resilience and fortitude, I stand tall, Facing challenges, I never fall."

1. Allow yourself to feel a sense of inner strength and determination as you affirm your intentions.
2. Fold the paper and hold it over the flame of the candle, allowing it to safely burn.
3. As the paper burns, visualize the flames igniting your courage and resilience, empowering you to overcome any obstacle.
4. Once the paper has turned to ash, extinguish the candle and trust in the power of the Seven of Wands to guide you through adversity and uphold your convictions.

The Seven of Wands reminds you to stand firm in your beliefs and values, and to confront challenges with courage and resilience. By asserting yourself and defending what is important to you, you can overcome obstacles and emerge victorious in the face of adversity. Let the Seven of Wands be your guiding light as you navigate the complexities of adolescence and assert your true self with confidence and conviction.

questions to ask yourself

1. What challenges or obstacles am I currently facing in my life?
2. How can I stand my ground and defend my beliefs and values?
3. What fears or doubts am I confronting as I assert my position?
4. Am I prepared to take a stand and advocate for what I believe in?
5. How can I assert myself with confidence and conviction?
6. What support systems or allies do I have in my corner?
7. How can I overcome feelings of overwhelm or intimidation?
8. What lessons can I learn from experiences of resistance and opposition?
9. How can I cultivate resilience and perseverance in the face of adversity?
10. What strategies or tactics can I employ to overcome challenges and obstacles?

eight of wands

. . .

"Now is the time to seize the moment and make your dreams a reality," Eight of Wands.

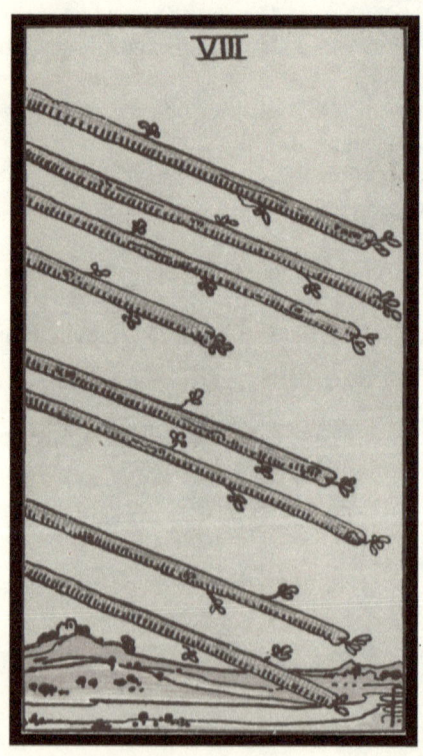

Answer: Yes

Key Words and Phrases:
Moving
Swiftness
Action
Communication
Momentum
Fast progress
Change
Travel
Vacations
Forward movement
Quick action
New ideas
Reaching goals

SYMBOLS:

- The eight wands in motion symbolize forward movement, speed, and the rapid progression of plans and ideas.
- The clear sky in the background signifies unobstructed paths and a lack of barriers, allowing the wands to move freely.
- The wands themselves represent creative energy, inspiration, and the potential for rapid manifestation.

The Fool encounters the Eight of Wands, a card that crackles with energy and propels them forward into the unknown. Amidst the chaos of swirling wands, The Fool finds themselves caught in a maelstrom of motion and momentum, urging them to embrace the swift currents of change and transformation.

The deeper The Fool goes, the more they unravel a narrative of quick advancement and unlimited promise within the Eight of Wands. Picture yourself standing at the edge of a vast expanse, watching as a flurry of wands streak across the sky like shooting stars, leaving trails of light in their wake. The Eight of Wands challenges The Fool to harness the power of movement and seize the fleeting opportunities that lie before them.

Symbolically, the Eight of Wands represents swift action, quick decisions, and the unstoppable force of change. It serves as a reminder to The Fool that life is in a constant state of motion, and that they must adapt and evolve in order to keep pace with the ever-shifting currents of existence.

When the Eight of Wands appears in a tarot reading, it carries a message of urgency and acceleration. It encourages The Fool to trust in the natural flow of events, to embrace the rapid pace of change, and to seize the moment with courage and conviction. It reminds them they possess the power to shape their own destiny and to propel themselves towards their goals with unwavering determination.

Yet, amidst the chaos of transformation, the Eight of Wands also serves as a cautionary tale against recklessness or impulsivity. It reminds The Fool to remain grounded amidst the storm, to weigh their options carefully, and to consider the potential consequences of their actions before forging ahead.

Ultimately, the Eight of Wands imparts a powerful lesson in agility, adaptability, and decisive action. It challenges The Fool to embrace the dynamic nature of life, to trust in their instincts, and to follow the path of their heart with unwavering courage and resolve.

The Fool finds strength in the teachings of the Eight of Wands as they navigate the tarot's labyrinth with grace, courage, and unwavering determination.

magical spell: manifestation momentum ritual:

Eight of Wands,
swift and true,
Manifest my wishes,
let them accrue.
With energy and focus,

I set the pace,
Rapid manifestation,
embrace.

materials needed:

- A quiet and comfortable space
- A purple or orange candle
- A small piece of paper
- A pen or marker
- Frankincense or cinnamon incense (optional)

instructions:

- Find a peaceful space where you can sit comfortably without distractions.
- Light the purple or orange candle and place it in front of you.
- If you have incense, light it to enhance the atmosphere and invoke an aura of manifestation.
- Take a few deep breaths to center yourself and connect with the dynamic energy of swift manifestation.
- On the piece of paper, write down a goal or desire that you wish to see manifest quickly in your life.
- Hold the paper in your hands and visualize the goal coming to fruition with speed and efficiency.
- Recite the following affirmation aloud:

"Eight of Wands, swift and true, Manifest my wishes, let them accrue. With energy and focus, I set the pace, Rapid manifestation, embrace."

- Allow yourself to feel the excitement and anticipation of your desire swiftly materializing.
- Fold the paper and hold it over the flame of the candle, allowing it to safely burn.
- As the paper burns, visualize the flames carrying your intentions into the universe, speeding up the manifestation process.
- Once the paper has turned to ash, extinguish the candle and trust in the power of the Eight of Wands to propel your desires into swift reality.

The Eight of Wands encourages you to harness the energy of swift momentum and seize the opportunities that come your way. By setting clear intentions and adapting to the rapid pace of life, you can manifest your desires with speed and efficiency. Let the Eight of Wands be your guide as you navigate the dynamic landscape of adolescence and bring your goals to fruition with enthusiasm and determination.

questions to ask yourself

1. What new opportunities or experiences are coming into my life with speed and momentum?
2. How can I harness the energy of change and transformation to my advantage?
3. What goals or aspirations am I eager to pursue with enthusiasm?
4. Am I open to unexpected developments and sudden shifts in direction?
5. How can I stay focused and organized amidst a flurry of activity?
6. What messages or insights am I receiving from my intuition?
7. How can I adapt to changing circumstances with agility and grace?
8. What obstacles or limitations am I leaving behind as I move forward?
9. How can I trust the process and embrace the journey with optimism?
10. What steps can I take to seize the opportunities that are presenting themselves to me?

nine of wands

. . .

"Victory may not be immediate, but with steadfast determination, it will be mine in the end," Nine of Wands.

Answer: Yes

Key Words and Phrases:
Persistence
Vigilance
Faith
Courage
Perseverance
Standing for your beliefs
Hard Work
Defense
Final challenge
Resilience
Strength
Determined
Wounded Warrior

SYMBOLS:

- The figure with a bandaged head symbolizes someone who has been through trials and tribulations but remains standing strong.
- The wands surrounding the figure represent the challenges and obstacles that the individual has faced and overcome.
- The defensive posture of the figure signifies the readiness to protect oneself and stand firm in the face of adversity.

The Fool stumbles upon the Nine of Wands, a card that exudes resilience, fortitude, and unwavering determination. The image of a lone figure standing amidst a field of wands captivates The Fool, pulling them into a tale of perseverance in the face of adversity.

Imagine a weary traveler, battered and bruised from the trials of their journey, yet unbroken in spirit. The figure depicted in the Nine of Wands stands tall, leaning on the final wand as a beacon of strength and resolve. Despite the obstacles that lie in their path, they refuse to yield to despair, standing firm in their defense of what they hold dear.

Symbolically, the Nine of Wands represents resilience, endurance, and the courage to keep fighting, even when the odds seem stacked against you. It serves as a reminder to The Fool that challenges and setbacks are an inevitable part of life's journey, but it is how they respond to adversity that defines their character.

When the Nine of Wands appears in a tarot reading, it carries a message of perseverance and tenacity. It urges The Fool to draw upon their inner reserves of strength and courage, to stand firm in the face of opposition, and to keep pushing forward, no matter how difficult the path may seem.

Yet, the Nine of Wands also serves as a cautionary tale against allowing fear or doubt to cloud one's judgment. It warns The Fool against becoming overly defensive or closed off to new possibilities, reminding them that true strength lies not in building walls, but in remaining open and vulnerable to the world around them.

Ultimately, the Nine of Wands imparts a powerful lesson in resilience and self-belief. It challenges The Fool to trust in their own abilities, to embrace the challenges that lie ahead, and to keep moving forward with unwavering determination, knowing that they have the strength to overcome whatever obstacles may come their way.

The Fool's journey is guided by the figure in the Nine of Wands, embodying the virtues of courage, resilience, and unwavering determination.

magical spell: strength and endurance ritual:

Nine of Wands,
strength I find,
Resilience and courage,
intertwined.
With endurance and fortitude,
I stand tall,

Lorelai Hamilton

Overcoming challenges,
I never fall.

materials needed:

- A quiet and comfortable space
- A white or green candle
- A small piece of paper
- A pen or marker
- Rosemary or sage herbs (dried or fresh)

instructions:

- Find a peaceful space where you can sit comfortably without distractions.
- Light the white or green candle and place it in front of you.
- If you have herbs, sprinkle a small amount around the candle to invoke strength and endurance.
- Take a few deep breaths to center yourself and connect with your inner resilience and determination.
- On the piece of paper, write down a challenge or obstacle that you are currently facing and wish to overcome.
- Hold the paper in your hands and visualize yourself standing tall and resilient, ready to face the challenge head-on.
- Recite the following affirmation aloud:

"Nine of Wands, strength I find, Resilience and courage, intertwined. With endurance and fortitude, I stand tall, Overcoming challenges, I never fall."

- Allow yourself to feel a sense of inner strength and determination as you affirm your intentions.
- Fold the paper and hold it over the flame of the candle, allowing it to safely burn.
- As the paper burns, visualize the flames igniting your courage and fortitude, empowering you to overcome any obstacle.
- Once the paper has turned to ash, extinguish the candle and trust in the power of the Nine of Wands to guide you through adversity and strengthen your resolve.

The Nine of Wands reminds you to tap into your inner strength and resilience as you face challenges and obstacles on your journey. By staying true to yourself and remaining steadfast in your beliefs and principles, you can overcome adversity and emerge stronger than before. Let the Nine of

Wands be your guiding light as you navigate the trials and tribulations of adolescence with courage and determination.

questions to ask yourself

1. What challenges or setbacks am I currently facing in my life?
2. How can I persevere in the face of adversity and keep moving forward?
3. What inner resources or reserves of strength can I draw upon for support?
4. Am I being cautious and protective of myself, or am I closing myself off to new experiences?
5. How can I overcome feelings of weariness or fatigue and regain my energy?
6. What lessons can I learn from experiences of resilience and endurance?
7. How can I trust myself and my abilities to overcome obstacles and achieve my goals?
8. What support systems or allies do I have to lean on during difficult times?
9. How can I cultivate a sense of determination and resolve in pursuit of my dreams?
10. What steps can I take to recharge and replenish my spirit?

ten of wands

...

"You don't have to do it all alone," 10 of Wands.

Answer: Yes

Key Words and Phrases:
Total effort
Hard Work
Release
Responsibility
Completion
Moving Forward
Burden
Overworking
Pressure
Overwhelm
Heavy Load
Struggle

SYMBOLS:

- The figure carrying a bundle of wands symbolizes someone who has taken on more than they can handle, burdened by the weight of responsibilities and obligations.
- The wands themselves represent the various tasks, commitments, and expectations that the individual is carrying.
- The strained posture of the figure reflects the physical and emotional toll of shouldering such a heavy burden.

The Fool encounters the Ten of Wands, a card that symbolizes heavy burdens and responsibility. As The Fool gazes upon the image of a figure laboriously carrying a heavy load of wands, they find themselves drawn into a story of struggle, perseverance, and the challenges of carrying life's burdens.

Picture a weary traveler trudging through the wilderness, each step weighed down by the bundle of wands they carry upon their back. The load is heavy, almost too much to bear, yet the figure presses onward, driven by a sense of duty and determination to reach their destination.

Symbolically, the Ten of Wands represents the burdens we carry, the responsibilities we shoulder, and the challenges we face as we navigate through life. The Ten of Wands serves as a reminder to The Fool that sometimes, we encounter obstacles and sacrifices on the path to fulfillment and success.

When the Ten of Wands appears in a tarot reading, it carries a message of hard work, perseverance, and the need to stay focused on long-term goals. It encourages The Fool to confront their responsibilities head-on, to tackle challenges with resilience and determination, and to keep pushing forward, even when the journey seems arduous and the road ahead feels uncertain.

The Ten of Wands also serves as a warning against taking on too much or shouldering burdens that are not theirs to bear. It reminds you that it's okay to seek help when needed, to delegate tasks, and to release the weight of unnecessary obligations in order to lighten your load and find balance in life.

Ultimately, the Ten of Wands imparts a powerful lesson in resilience, perseverance, and the importance of prioritizing self-care. It challenges The Fool to examine the burdens they carry, to discern which are worth bearing, and to release those that no longer serve their highest good.

The Fool gains strength from the unwavering determination of the figure in the Ten of Wands, facing life's challenges with courage and resilience, believing in their power to overcome obstacles.

magical spell: release and renewal ritual:

Ten of Wands,
burdens be gone,
Release and renewal,

I call upon.
With clarity and ease,
I let it all go,
Lightening my load,
I feel the flow."

materials needed:

- A quiet and comfortable space
- A blue or purple candle
- A small piece of paper
- A pen or marker
- Lavender or chamomile herbs (dried or fresh)

instructions:

- Find a peaceful space where you can sit comfortably without distractions.
- Light the blue or purple candle and place it in front of you.
- If you have herbs, sprinkle a small amount around the candle to invoke calmness and clarity.
- Take a few deep breaths to center yourself and connect with the energy of release and renewal.
- On the piece of paper, write down the burdens or responsibilities that are weighing you down.
- Hold the paper in your hands and visualize yourself releasing the heavy load, feeling lighter and freer.
- Recite the following affirmation aloud:

"Ten of Wands, burdens be gone, Release and renewal, I call upon. With clarity and ease, I let it all go, Lightening my load, I feel the flow."

- Allow yourself to feel a sense of relief and renewal as you affirm your intentions.
- Fold the paper and hold it over the flame of the candle, allowing it to safely burn.
- As the paper burns, visualize the flames carrying away your burdens, leaving you feeling refreshed and revitalized.
- Once the paper has turned to ash, extinguish the candle and trust in the power of the Ten of Wands to help you prioritize and lighten your load.

The Ten of Wands encourages you to reassess your responsibilities and seek support when feeling overwhelmed. By acknowledging your limits and prioritizing self-care, you can avoid burnout and find balance in your life. Let the Ten of Wands be your guide as you release burdens and embrace renewal, allowing space for joy and fulfillment to enter your life.

questions to ask yourself

1. What endings or betrayals am I experiencing in my life right now?
2. How can I find closure and acceptance in the face of painful endings?
3. What lessons can I learn from experiences of loss or betrayal?
4. Am I allowing myself to grieve and process my emotions fully?
5. How can I release resentments and forgive those who have hurt me?
6. What support systems or resources can I turn to for healing?
7. How can I cultivate resilience and strength in times of adversity?
8. What new beginnings or opportunities are hidden within this ending?
9. How can I trust that this ending is making space for new growth and transformation?
10. What steps can I take to honor the past while embracing the future?

page of wands

. . .

"This is a time of discovery and growth, where I am free to experiment, learn, and expand my horizons," Page of Wands.

Answer: Yes

Lorelai Hamilton

Key Words and Phrases:
Passion
Excitement
Enthusiasm
Enjoyment of life
Creativity
Good News
Courage
Exploration
Resourcefulness
Curiosity
New ideas
Potential
Growth

SYMBOLS:

- The young person holding the wand symbolizes youthfulness, curiosity, and the eagerness to explore the world.
- The wand itself represents creativity, passion, and the potential for growth and development.
- The desert landscape in the background symbolizes the vastness of possibilities and the sense of adventure that accompanies new beginnings.

The Page of Wands is a youthful figure standing at the threshold of adventure and discovery. As The Fool gazes upon the Page, they become immersed in a tale of enthusiasm, creativity, and the boundless potential of new beginnings.

Imagine a young traveler standing at the edge of a vast landscape, eyes alight with excitement and wonder. In one hand, they hold a wand, a symbol of potential and growth, while the other hand reaches out eagerly toward the horizon, ready to embark on a journey of exploration and self-discovery.

Symbolically, the Page of Wands represents the spirit of curiosity, enthusiasm, and creative inspiration. It is a herald of new opportunities and the spark of passion that ignites within us when we dare to dream and pursue our goals with unwavering determination.

When the Page of Wands appears in a tarot reading, it encourages The Fool to embrace their inner adventurer, to step boldly into the unknown, and to seize the opportunities that lie ahead with courage and enthusiasm. It reminds them that every journey begins with a single step, and that with perseverance and determination, they have the power to manifest their dreams into reality.

Yet, the Page of Wands also serves as a gentle reminder to remain open-minded and adaptable in the face of change. It urges The Fool to embrace spontaneity, to trust in their instincts, and to explore uncharted territories in search of new experiences and growth.

Ultimately, the Page of Wands imparts a powerful lesson in the importance of embracing our passions, pursuing our dreams, and cultivating a sense of adventure in our lives. It challenges The Fool to embrace the journey of self-discovery with an open heart and a willingness to embrace the magic that surrounds them.

May The Fool find inspiration in the limitless enthusiasm and creativity of the Page of Wands as they embark on their journey, filled with courage, curiosity, and an endless sense of wonder.

magical spell: ignite your creative flame:

Page of Wands,
ignite my flame,
Creativity and passion,
I reclaim.
With enthusiasm and joy,
I embrace,
My creative journey,

Lorelai Hamilton

I eagerly chase.

materials needed:

- A quiet and comfortable space
- A yellow or orange candle
- A small piece of paper
- A pen or marker
- Cinnamon or ginger herbs (dried or fresh)

instructions:

- Find a peaceful space where you can sit comfortably without distractions.
- Light the yellow or orange candle and place it in front of you.
- If you have herbs, sprinkle a small amount around the candle to invoke creativity and inspiration.
- Take a few deep breaths to center yourself and connect with your creative energy.
- On the piece of paper, write down a creative goal or project that you wish to pursue.
- Hold the paper in your hands and visualize yourself fully immersed in the creative process, feeling inspired and passionate.
- Recite the following affirmation aloud:

"Page of Wands, ignite my flame, Creativity and passion, I reclaim. With enthusiasm and joy, I embrace, My creative journey, I eagerly chase."

- Allow yourself to feel a surge of creative energy and excitement as you affirm your intentions.
- Fold the paper and hold it over the flame of the candle, allowing it to safely burn.
- As the paper burns, visualize the flames igniting your creative spark, fueling your passion and enthusiasm.
- Once the paper has turned to ash, extinguish the candle and trust in the power of the Page of Wands to guide you on your creative journey.

The Page of Wands encourages you to embrace your creativity, follow your passions, and embark on new adventures with enthusiasm and curiosity. By remaining open to new experiences and nurturing your creative spark, you can unlock your full potential and discover the joys of self-expression. Let the Page of Wands be your guide as you explore the vast landscape of your imagination and embrace the magic of creativity in your life.

questions to ask yourself

1. What new ideas or perspectives am I exploring at this time?
2. How can I express myself more clearly and authentically?
3. What messages or insights am I receiving from my intuition?
4. Am I open to learning and expanding my knowledge?
5. How can I embrace curiosity and intellectual growth?
6. What challenges or obstacles am I eager to tackle head-on?
7. How can I use my communication skills to advocate for myself and others?
8. What opportunities for creative expression am I exploring?
9. How can I cultivate a sense of mental agility and adaptability?
10. What steps can I take to embody the qualities of the Page of Swords in my life?

knight of wands

. . .

"This is a time of action and boldness, where I fearlessly pursue my goals and embrace the thrill of the unknown," Knight of Wands

Answer: Yes

Tarot Tales and Magic Spells

Key Words and Phrases:
Change
Creativity
Adventure
New experiences
Passion
New ideas
Travel
Relocation
Action
Athletic
Optimism
Courage
Adventure
Exploration
Enthusiastic

SYMBOLS:

- The knight on horseback symbolizes action, movement, and the pursuit of new horizons.
- The wand held by the knight represents creative energy, passion, and the desire for growth and expansion.
- The horse symbolizes strength, freedom, and the ability to overcome obstacles on the path to adventure and achievement.

The Knight of Wands is a bold and adventurous figure charging forth with unbridled energy and passion. As The Fool gazes upon the Knight, they are swept into a tale of daring exploration, untamed ambition, and the pursuit of excitement.

Imagine a knight astride a spirited steed, galloping across open plains with the wind at their back and the sun on their face. Their armor gleams in the sunlight, reflecting the fiery spirit that burns within them, while their wand, held aloft like a beacon of determination, points toward the endless horizon of possibility.

Symbolically, the Knight of Wands represents the essence of adventure, courage, and enthusiastic pursuit. They embody the spirit of spontaneity and the thrill of discovery, inspiring The Fool to embrace their own sense of daring and embark on new journeys with fearless determination.

When the Knight of Wands appears in a tarot reading, it signals a call to action, encouraging The Fool to seize the moment and pursue their passions with unwavering enthusiasm. It serves as a reminder that life is an adventure waiting to be explored, and that true fulfillment comes from embracing the unknown and embracing challenges with a sense of courage and resilience.

Yet, the Knight of Wands also carries a warning against recklessness and impulsive behavior. While their fiery spirit fuels their drive for success, it can also lead to hasty decisions and unexpected obstacles along the way. The Fool is reminded to temper their enthusiasm with patience and foresight, and to channel their energy into constructive pursuits that align with their long-term goals.

Ultimately, the Knight of Wands imparts a powerful lesson in the importance of embracing one's passions, taking bold risks, and pursuing dreams with unwavering determination. They remind The Fool that true greatness comes not from playing it safe, but from daring to venture into the unknown and embracing challenges with courage and conviction.

As The Fool continues their journey, they draw inspiration from the fearless spirit and unyielding determination of the Knight of Wands. They embark on their own adventures with courage, enthusiasm, and a sense of purpose that knows no bounds.

magical spell: courageous pursuit ritual:

Knight of Wands,
guide my way,

Courage and passion,
I display.
With determination and might,
I ride,
Fearlessly pursuing,
with passion as my guide.

materials needed:

- A quiet and comfortable space
- A red or gold candle
- A small piece of paper
- A pen or marker
- Ginger or cinnamon herbs (dried or fresh)

instructions:

- Find a peaceful space where you can sit comfortably without distractions.
- Light the red or gold candle and place it in front of you.
- If you have herbs, sprinkle a small amount around the candle to invoke courage and passion.
- Take a few deep breaths to center yourself and connect with your inner strength and determination.
- On the piece of paper, write down a goal or dream that you wish to pursue with courage and determination.
- Hold the paper in your hands and visualize yourself riding bravely into the unknown, fearlessly pursuing your dreams.
- Recite the following affirmation aloud:

"Knight of Wands, guide my way, Courage and passion, I display. With determination and might, I ride, Fearlessly pursuing, with passion as my guide."

- Allow yourself to feel a sense of courage and determination as you affirm your intentions.
- Fold the paper and hold it over the flame of the candle, allowing it to safely burn.
- As the paper burns, visualize the flames igniting your inner fire, propelling you forward on your courageous journey.
- Once the paper has turned to ash, extinguish the candle and trust in the power of the Knight of Wands to embolden you as you pursue your dreams.

The Knight of Wands inspires you to embrace adventure, take courageous action, and pursue your dreams with passion and determination. By harnessing your inner fire and riding bravely into the unknown, you can overcome obstacles and achieve your goals with confidence. Let the Knight of Wands be your guiding light as you journey forth with courage and enthusiasm, blazing new trails and embracing the thrill of the unknown.

questions to ask yourself

1. What goals or ambitions am I pursuing with passion and determination?
2. How can I channel my energy and drive towards achieving my objectives?
3. What obstacles or challenges am I prepared to overcome on my quest for success?
4. Am I being mindful of the impact of my actions on others?
5. How can I balance assertiveness with consideration for the feelings of others?
6. What risks am I willing to take in order to pursue my goals?
7. How can I remain focused and disciplined in the face of distractions?
8. What strategies or plans am I implementing to achieve victory?
9. How can I cultivate resilience and perseverance in the pursuit of my dreams?
10. What lessons can I learn from experiences of triumph and setback?

queen of wands

. . .

"Let my reign be one of inspiration and transformation, as I blaze a trail of success and fulfillment," Queen of Wands.

Answer: Yes

Lorelai Hamilton

Key Words and Phrases:
Courage
Ambitious
Creativity
Passion
Determined
Charisma
Confident
Leadership
Generous
Inspiration
Self-love
Organized

SYMBOLS:

- The queen seated on her throne represents authority, power, and a strong sense of self-confidence.
- The sunflowers symbolize vitality, growth, and the radiant energy that the queen embodies.
- The black cat at her feet represents intuition, independence, and the mysterious aspects of femininity.

The Fool encounters the Queen of Wands, a radiant and charismatic figure whose presence exudes warmth, creativity, and boundless energy. As The Fool looks upon the Queen, they are drawn into a story of passion, confidence, and the power of self-expression.

Picture a queen seated upon a throne adorned with the symbols of fire, her fiery mane cascading like waves of flame around her shoulders. Clutched in her hand is a wand, representing her energetic creativity and dynamic nature. Her eyes sparkle with determination, and her aura radiates with the vibrant hues of summer, echoing the warmth and vitality of the season.

Symbolically, the Queen of Wands embodies the essence of creativity, leadership, and self-assurance. She is a beacon of inspiration, encouraging The Fool to embrace their inner fire and pursue their dreams with unwavering confidence and passion. With her magnetic charm and unwavering optimism, she empowers The Fool to express themselves authentically and embrace their unique gifts and talents.

When the Queen of Wands appears in a tarot reading, she signals a time of bold self-expression, creative inspiration, and personal empowerment. She reminds The Fool to trust in their intuition, harness their creative energies, and pursue their goals with passion and enthusiasm. With her guidance, The Fool can overcome obstacles, conquer challenges, and emerge victorious in their endeavors.

Yet, the Queen of Wands also carries a message of balance and self-assurance. While her fiery spirit fuels her drive for success, she also understands the importance of patience, diplomacy, and inner strength. She encourages you to cultivate resilience in the face of adversity, to trust in your instincts, and to lead with grace and confidence.

Ultimately, the Queen of Wands serves as a powerful reminder of the transformative power of self-belief and the boundless potential that lives within each of us. She inspires The Fool to embrace their passions, follow their intuition, and fearlessly pursue their dreams, knowing that they possess the strength and courage to conquer any challenge that comes their way.

The Fool draws inspiration from the radiant spirit and unwavering confidence of the Queen of Wands. They fearlessly embrace their inner fire with courage, conviction, and limitless purpose.

magical spell: self-confidence elixir:

Queen of Wands,
empower me,
Confidence and grace,
I decree.

Lorelai Hamilton

With strength and poise,
I lead the way,
Embracing my power,
every day

materials needed:

- A quiet and comfortable space
- A yellow candle
- A small piece of paper
- A pen or marker
- Rosemary or cinnamon herbs (dried or fresh)

instructions:

- Find a peaceful space where you can sit comfortably without distractions.
- Light the yellow candle and place it in front of you.
- If you have herbs, sprinkle a small amount around the candle to invoke confidence and courage.
- Take a few deep breaths to center yourself and connect with your inner strength and self-assurance.
- On the piece of paper, write down a situation or area of your life where you wish to cultivate more confidence and leadership.
- Hold the paper in your hands and visualize yourself embodying the qualities of the Queen of Wands – confident, charismatic, and self-assured.
- Recite the following affirmation aloud:

"Queen of Wands, empower me, Confidence and grace, I decree. With strength and poise, I lead the way, Embracing my power, every day."

- Allow yourself to feel a sense of empowerment and self-assurance as you affirm your intentions.
- Fold the paper and hold it over the flame of the candle, allowing it to safely burn.
- As the paper burns, visualize the flames igniting your inner fire, filling you with confidence and vitality.
- Once the paper has turned to ash, extinguish the candle and carry the energy of the Queen of Wands with you as you navigate the world with confidence and grace.

The Queen of Wands inspires you to embrace your inner strength, exude confidence, and lead with authenticity and grace. By recognizing your unique qualities and standing tall in your convictions, you can inspire others and make a positive impact on the world around you. Let the Queen of Wands be your guiding light as you embrace your power, express yourself boldly, and lead with courage and charisma.

questions to ask yourself

1. How am I embodying the qualities of passion and creativity in my life?
2. What projects or endeavors am I currently nurturing and cultivating?
3. How can I inspire others to pursue their passions and dreams?
4. Am I leading with authenticity and integrity in all areas of my life?
5. How can I balance my fiery nature with sensitivity and compassion?
6. What challenges or obstacles am I addressing with courage and grace?
7. How can I empower others to embrace their unique gifts and talents?
8. What insights or wisdom can I share with others based on my experiences?
9. How can I cultivate confidence and self-assurance in my abilities?
10. What steps can I take to embody the qualities of the Queen of Wands more fully in my life?

king of wands

...

"My vision is clear, and my passion burns like a wildfire, inspiring others to follow in my footsteps" King of Wands.

Answer: Yes

Key Words and Phrases:
Courage
Ambitious
Leadership
Creativity
Passion
Charisma
Determined
Confident
Vision
Generous
Inspiration
Influence
Self-love
Organized

SYMBOLS:

- The king seated on his throne represents authority, power, and a strong sense of leadership.
- The wand he holds symbolizes creativity, passion, and the ability to manifest his vision into reality.
- The lion at his feet represents courage, strength, and the fearless pursuit of goals.

In the heart of the majestic kingdom, The Fool encounters the King of Wands, a figure of boundless energy and visionary leadership. Seated upon his throne, adorned with symbols of fire and vitality, the King exudes confidence and authority, commanding respect from all who behold him.

The King of Wands symbolizes the epitome of passion, creativity, and ambition. The magnetic force of his presence pulls The Fool into his realm of influence, motivating them to embrace their own potential for greatness.

As The Fool gazes upon him, they find themselves captivated by his story, a tale of triumph, innovation, and the relentless pursuit of one's dreams.

With his wand held high, the King of Wands embodies the essence of creative vision and entrepreneurial spirit. He is a trailblazer, unafraid to take risks and venture into the unknown, driven by an insatiable hunger for adventure and discovery. In his presence, The Fool feels a surge of excitement and possibility, knowing that they too possess the power to manifest their wildest dreams.

Symbolically, the King of Wands represents the power of inspired action and unwavering determination. He is a beacon of light in times of darkness, guiding The Fool along the path to success with courage and conviction. With his guidance, The Fool learns to harness the fire within them, channeling it into bold endeavors and daring feats of innovation.

When the King of Wands appears in a tarot reading, he heralds a time of great opportunity and potential. He encourages The Fool to embrace their inner leader and pursue their goals with passion and purpose. Thanks to his encouragement, The Fool develops self-assurance and faces upcoming difficulties, fully aware of their potential for greatness.

Yet, the King of Wands also carries a message of responsibility and integrity. While his fiery spirit drives him ever forward, he also understands the importance of patience, perseverance, and ethical leadership. He reminds The Fool to lead by example, inspiring others with their actions and staying true to their values and principles.

The indomitable spirit and visionary leadership of the King of Wands inspires The Fool as they continue their journey. May they embrace their own potential for greatness with courage, confidence, and a sense of purpose that knows no bounds, knowing that they possess the power to shape their own destiny and transform the world around them.

magical spell: manifesting your vision ritual:

King of Wands,

guide my way,
Vision and passion,
I display.
With courage and purpose,
I lead,
Manifesting my dreams,
I succeed.

materials needed:

- A quiet and comfortable space
- A red or gold candle
- A small piece of paper
- A pen or marker
- Basil or cinnamon herbs (dried or fresh)

instructions:

- Find a peaceful space where you can sit comfortably without distractions.
- Light the red or gold candle and place it in front of you.
- If you have herbs, sprinkle a small amount around the candle to invoke inspiration and manifestation.
- Take a few deep breaths to center yourself and connect with your inner strength and vision.
- On the piece of paper, write down a vision or goal that you wish to manifest with passion and determination.
- Hold the paper in your hands and visualize yourself achieving your vision, feeling empowered and inspired.
- Recite the following affirmation aloud:

"King of Wands, guide my way, Vision and passion, I display. With courage and purpose, I lead, Manifesting my dreams, I succeed."

- Allow yourself to feel a sense of empowerment and inspiration as you affirm your intentions.
- Fold the paper and hold it over the flame of the candle, allowing it to safely burn.
- As the paper burns, visualize the flames igniting your inner fire, fueling your determination to achieve your vision.
- Once the paper has turned to ash, extinguish the candle and trust in the power of the King of Wands to guide you as you manifest your dreams with confidence and purpose.

The King of Wands inspires you to embrace your vision, lead with passion, and manifest your dreams with confidence and determination. By trusting in your abilities, setting clear intentions, and taking inspired action, you can create a life filled with purpose and fulfillment. Let the King of Wands be your guiding light as you step into your power, inspire others with your vision, and lead with courage and conviction.

questions to ask yourself

1. How am I using my leadership and charisma to inspire others?
2. What projects or initiatives am I spearheading with passion and enthusiasm?
3. How can I channel my energy and drive towards achieving my goals?
4. Am I fostering an environment of creativity and innovation in my endeavors?
5. How can I lead with authenticity and integrity in all areas of my life?
6. What challenges or obstacles am I addressing with courage and determination?
7. How can I empower others to take charge of their own destinies?
8. What insights or wisdom can I share with others based on my experiences?
9. How can I cultivate confidence and self-assurance in my abilities?
10. What steps can I take to embody the qualities of the King of Wands more fully in my life.

ace of cups

. . .

"I am boundless love, overflowing emotions, and the potential for profound connections," Ace of Cups.

Answer: Yes

Key Words and Phrases:
Renewed emotions
Love
Happiness
Emotional
Sensitivity
Overflowing feelings
Beginnings
Creativity
Abundance
Compassion
Renewing love
Connection
Psychic
Intuition
Emotions

SYMBOLS:

- The hand emerging from the cloud symbolizes divine intervention and the offering of emotional blessings from the universe.
- The cup overflowing with water represents abundance, intuition, and the potential for deep emotional connection and fulfillment.
- The dove descending into the cup symbolizes peace, purity, and the spiritual nature of love.

In the garden of emotions, The Fool encounters the Ace of Cups, a vessel overflowing with the elixir of love, compassion, and deep spiritual connection. As The Fool approaches the shimmering waters of the cup, they feel a sense of peace and tranquility wash over them, like the gentle caress of a cool breeze on a warm summer's day.

The Ace of Cups symbolizes the beginning of a journey into the realm of the heart, where emotions flow freely and love knows no bounds. It represents a fresh start, a new chapter in The Fool's emotional landscape. The invitation is for them to explore the depths of their feelings and open themselves up to the transformative power of love.

As The Fool gazes into the depths of the cup, they see reflections of their own innermost desires and dreams, shimmering like jewels beneath the surface. The Ace of Cups beckons them to dive deep into the waters of their own soul, to embrace the full spectrum of human emotion and experience, from joy and ecstasy to sorrow and longing.

Symbolically, the Ace of Cups represents the purest essence of love and emotional fulfillment. It is a reminder that love is the greatest gift of all, a force that has the power to heal, to unite, and to transcend the boundaries of time and space. In the presence of the Ace of Cups, The Fool learns to open their heart fully to the world around them, to give and receive love without reservation or fear.

When the Ace of Cups appears in a tarot reading, it heralds a time of emotional renewal and spiritual awakening. It invites The Fool to be fully present in the moment, to embrace the beauty and wonder of life with an open heart and a receptive mind. It is a reminder that love is all around us, if only we have the courage to see it and the wisdom to embrace it.

Yet, the Ace of Cups also carries a message of balance and harmony. Like the delicate balance of the elements in nature, love requires care and attention to flourish. The Fool learns that true emotional fulfillment comes not from seeking love outside of themselves, but from cultivating a deep sense of self-love and acceptance from within.

As The Fool continues their journey through the mystical realms of the tarot, may they carry the wisdom and grace of the Ace of Cups in their heart, knowing that love is the guiding force that lights their path and illuminates their way forward. May they embrace the gift of love in all its forms, and may they be forever blessed by the boundless beauty and infinite possibilities that love has to offer.

Lorelai Hamilton

magical spell: heart's desire manifestation ritual:

Ace of Cups,
fill my heart,
With love and blessings,
I impart.
Renew my spirit,
heal my pain,
Let true love flow,
like gentle rain.

materials needed:

- A quiet and comfortable space
- A pink or blue candle
- A small piece of paper
- A pen or marker
- Rose petals or lavender herbs (dried or fresh)

instructions:

- Find a peaceful space where you can sit comfortably without distractions.
- Light the pink or blue candle and place it in front of you.
- If you have herbs, sprinkle a small amount around the candle to invoke love and emotional renewal.
- Take a few deep breaths to center yourself and connect with your heart's desires.
- On the piece of paper, write down a heartfelt wish or intention related to love, emotional healing, or authentic connections.
- Hold the paper in your hands and visualize your wish or intention coming to fruition, feeling the warmth and abundance of love surrounding you.
- Recite the following affirmation aloud:

"Ace of Cups, fill my heart, With love and blessings, I impart. Renew my spirit, heal my pain, Let true love flow, like gentle rain."

- Allow yourself to feel a sense of emotional renewal and openness as you affirm your intentions.
- Fold the paper and hold it over the flame of the candle, allowing it to safely burn.

- As the paper burns, visualize your wish or intention being released into the universe, manifesting with the power of love and intuition.
- Once the paper has turned to ash, extinguish the candle and trust in the magic of the Ace of Cups to guide you on your journey of emotional renewal and fulfillment.

The Ace of Cups invites you to embrace new beginnings, trust in the power of love, and open yourself up to deep emotional connections and experiences. By tapping into your intuition, honoring your emotions, and embracing vulnerability, you can cultivate profound emotional fulfillment and create meaningful connections in your life. Let the Ace of Cups be your guide as you embark on a journey of emotional renewal, self-discovery, and authentic connection.

questions to ask yourself

1. What new emotional experiences or connections am I feeling drawn to?
2. How can I open my heart to receive love and abundance?
3. What feelings of compassion and empathy am I cultivating within myself?
4. Am I honoring my emotional needs and nurturing my inner world?
5. How can I deepen my relationships and foster greater intimacy?
6. What opportunities for emotional healing and growth are presenting themselves to me?
7. How can I express my love and appreciation for those around me?

8. What creative outlets or practices bring me joy and emotional fulfillment?
9. How can I cultivate a sense of gratitude and appreciation for the blessings in my life?
10. In what ways can I connect more deeply with my own emotions and intuition?

two of cups

. . .

"I am the embodiment of partnership and shared emotions, inviting you to embrace the bonds of love and friendship," Two of Cups.

Answer: Yes

Key Words and Phrases:
Unity
Sharing
Harmony
Attraction
Connection
Soulmate Love
Partnership
Friendship
Love
Business Partnerships
Cooperation
Understanding
Commitment
Trusting

SYMBOLS:

- The two figures depicted on the card stand facing each other, holding their cups aloft in a gesture of unity and connection.
- The intertwined serpents on the caduceus above them represent healing, transformation, and the merging of energies.
- The caduceus is a symbol of harmony and balance, reflecting the harmonious nature of the relationship depicted on the card.

In the gentle embrace of unity and connection, The Fool encounters the Two of Cups, a card symbolizing the harmonious blending of two souls in perfect partnership and mutual understanding. As The Fool gazes upon the image of the intertwined cups, they feel a sense of warmth and companionship wash over them, like the comforting embrace of a dear friend.

The Two of Cups represents the profound bond that can form between individuals who share a deep emotional connection and mutual respect. It symbolizes the coming together of two hearts in a union of love, friendship, and shared purpose. In the presence of the Two of Cups, The Fool is reminded of the beauty and power of human relationships, and the transformative impact they can have on our lives.

As The Fool reflects on the symbolism of the Two of Cups, they recall a story from their own life—a story of two friends who met under unusual circumstances and formed an instant connection. Despite their differences in background and personality, they found common ground in their shared interests and values, and their friendship blossomed into something truly beautiful and profound.

The Two of Cups teaches The Fool that true partnership is not just about romantic love, but about the deep sense of understanding and acceptance that can exist between any two individuals who are willing to open their hearts to one another. It is a reminder that the most meaningful relationships are built on a foundation of trust, honesty, and genuine affection.

When the Two of Cups appears in a tarot reading, it serves as a powerful reminder to The Fool to nurture their relationships and cherish the connections they have with others. It encourages them to seek out meaningful connections in their lives and to cultivate a sense of empathy and compassion for those around them.

At its core, the Two of Cups represents the potential for profound emotional fulfillment and spiritual growth that comes from forming deep and meaningful connections with others. It is a testament to the transformative power of love and friendship, and a reminder that we are never truly alone as long as we have someone to share our journey with.

The Fool will carry with them the wisdom and insight of the Two of Cups, knowing that true happiness and fulfillment lie not in the pursuit of individual success, but in the bonds of love and connection that unite us all.

magical spell: friendship bonding ritual:

Two of Cups,
unite our hearts,
Friendship's bond,
it never parts.
With love and trust,
we stand as one,
Together always,
till our journey's done.

materials needed:

- A quiet and comfortable space
- Two small candles (one for each person)
- A small piece of paper for each person
- A pen or marker
- Rose petals or lavender herbs (dried or fresh)

instructions:

1. Find a peaceful space where you and your friend can sit comfortably facing each other.
2. Light the candles, placing one in front of each of you.
3. If you have herbs, sprinkle a small amount around the candles to invoke harmony and connection.
4. Take a few deep breaths together to center yourselves and create a sense of calm and presence.
5. Each person takes a piece of paper and writes down qualities they appreciate and cherish in their friendship, as well as any intentions they have for strengthening their bond.
6. Share your thoughts and feelings with each other, expressing gratitude and appreciation for your friendship.
7. Place the pieces of paper in a small bowl or container between the candles, symbolizing the shared intentions and connection between you.
8. Hold hands with your friend and recite the following affirmation together:

"Two of Cups, unite our hearts, Friendship's bond, it never parts. With love and trust, we stand as one, Together always, till our journey's done."

1. Allow yourselves to feel the warmth and connection between you, embracing the love and support of your friendship.
2. When ready, extinguish the candles, knowing that the bond you share will continue to grow and strengthen over time.

The Two of Cups reminds you of the importance of connection, harmony, and partnership in your relationships. By fostering mutual understanding, respect, and emotional authenticity, you can cultivate deep and meaningful connections with others. Let the Two of Cups be a guiding light as you navigate the intricacies of relationships, embracing the love, support, and companionship that enrich your life.

questions to ask yourself

1. What partnerships or relationships am I currently nurturing and cultivating?
2. How can I foster greater harmony and connection in my personal relationships?
3. What qualities am I seeking in a potential romantic partner or close friend?
4. Am I willing to be vulnerable and open my heart to love and intimacy?
5. How can I communicate my needs and desires effectively in my relationships?
6. What shared values or goals do I have with my partner or loved ones?
7. How can I cultivate empathy and understanding in my interactions with others?
8. What boundaries do I need to set to protect my emotional well-being?

9. How can I deepen my emotional connection and bond with my partner?
10. What steps can I take to resolve conflicts and strengthen my relationships?

three of cups

. . .

"Let us raise our cups high in celebration, as we dance in harmony and embrace the beauty of togetherness," Three of Cups.

Answer: Yes

Lorelai Hamilton

Key Words and Phrases:
Togetherness
Celebration
Thankful
Friendship
Togetherness
Abundance
Community
Achievement
Happiness
Playful
Fun
New Life
Joy
Trust

SYMBOLS:

- Three figures are depicted raising their cups in a toast, symbolizing unity, shared joy, and mutual support.
- The overflowing cups represent abundance, fulfillment, and the joy that comes from connecting with others.
- The circle formed by the figures represents the eternal cycle of friendship and celebration.

In the vibrant dance of celebration and camaraderie, The Fool encounters the Three of Cups, a card that speaks of joyous gatherings, deep friendships, and shared moments of happiness. As The Fool gazes upon the image of three figures raising their cups in a toast, they feel a sense of warmth and belonging wash over them, like the comforting embrace of kindred spirits.

The Three of Cups symbolizes the power of connection and the joy that comes from coming together with others in celebration and harmony. It represents the bonds of friendship, the support of community, and the shared experiences that enrich our lives and nourish our souls.

As The Fool reflects on the symbolism of the Three of Cups, they recall a story from their own life—a story of a spontaneous gathering with friends under the twinkling stars, where laughter flowed freely and hearts were light with the joy of being in each other's company. In that moment, they felt a profound sense of belonging and gratitude for the precious gift of friendship.

The Three of Cups reminds The Fool that life's veritable treasures are not found in material possessions or fleeting achievements, but in the moments we share with those we love. It encourages them to embrace the spirit of camaraderie and to celebrate the bonds of friendship that sustain us through life's joys and challenges.

When the Three of Cups appears in a tarot reading, it serves as a reminder to nurture relationships and to cherish the connections held with others. It encourages seeking opportunities for joy and celebration, and to share blessings with those around you.

At its core, the Three of Cups represents the abundance of love, laughter, and happiness that flows freely when we open our hearts to the beauty of human connection. It is a testament to the transformative power of friendship and community, and a reminder that we are never truly alone as long as we have others to share our journey with.

As The Fool continues on their journey through the world of tarot, may they carry with them the wisdom and insight of the Three of Cups, knowing that true happiness and fulfillment lie not in the pursuit of individual success, but in the bonds of love and connection that unite us all.

magical spell: friendship bond renewal ritual:

Three of Cups,
spirits bright,
Friendship's bond,

a guiding light.
With laughter, joy,
and love we share,
Our friendship grows,
beyond compare.

materials needed:

- A quiet and comfortable space
- Three small candles
- Paper and markers
- Dried lavender or rose petals

instructions:

1. Find a peaceful space where you can sit comfortably with your friends.
2. Place the three candles in a circle, symbolizing the bond between you and your friends.
3. Sprinkle the dried lavender or rose petals in the center of the circle to invoke love, friendship, and renewal.
4. Each person takes a piece of paper and writes down a cherished memory or quality about their friendship.
5. Share your thoughts and feelings with each other, expressing gratitude and appreciation for your friendship.
6. Take turns reading aloud what you've written and reflect on the importance of your friendship.
7. As a group, recite the following affirmation:

"Three of Cups, spirits bright, Friendship's bond, a guiding light. With laughter, joy, and love we share, Our friendship grows, beyond compare."

1. Allow yourselves to bask in the warmth and love of your friendship, embracing the bonds that unite you.
2. When ready, extinguish the candles, knowing that your friendship will continue to thrive and bring joy into your lives.

The Three of Cups reminds you of the importance of celebrating friendships and finding moments of joy in each other's company. By cherishing the bonds you share with your friends, embracing moments of celebration, and supporting each other through life's challenges, you can cultivate lasting connections that bring happiness and fulfillment. Let the Three of

Cups be a reminder to celebrate the gift of friendship and cherish the moments you share together.

questions to ask yourself

1. What reasons do I have to celebrate and express gratitude in my life right now?
2. How can I cultivate a sense of joy and camaraderie in my social circles?
3. What friendships or connections bring me a sense of belonging and support?
4. Am I taking time to nurture my relationships and create meaningful memories?
5. How can I prioritize fun and leisure activities to balance my responsibilities?
6. What shared interests or passions do I have with my friends or community?
7. How can I show appreciation for the people who bring positivity into my life?
8. What opportunities do I have to strengthen bonds and create lasting connections?
9. How can I let go of any jealousy or competitiveness in my social interactions?
10. In what ways can I contribute to a supportive and uplifting community atmosphere?

four of cups

. . .

"I am the reflection of inner longing and missed opportunities, urging you to pause and reassess your current path," Four of Cups.

Answer: Maybe

Key Words and Phrases:
Frustrated
Board
Dissatisfaction
Reevaluation
Looking within
Reflection
Depressed
Contemplation
Solitude
Withdrawn
Motivation
New opportunities

SYMBOLS:

- The figure sits with crossed arms, indicating a sense of withdrawal and introspection.
- The three cups in front of them represent opportunities or blessings that may be overlooked or underappreciated.
- The fourth cup, being offered by a hand emerging from a cloud, symbolizes a new opportunity or perspective that may not be immediately recognized.

In the quiet shade of a secluded grove, The Fool encounters the Four of Cups, a card that speaks of introspection, discontent, and the search for deeper meaning. As The Fool gazes upon the figure seated beneath the tree, their brow furrows in contemplation. The Fool feels a pang of recognition stirring within them—a sense of familiarity with the emotional landscape depicted in the card.

The Four of Cups symbolizes a period of emotional stagnation and disillusionment, where the world seems to lose its luster and even life's simplest pleasures fail to bring joy. The figure on the card sits with arms folded, seemingly oblivious to the cups offered to them by a mysterious hand emerging from a cloud. They fix their gaze upon the ground, lost in thought and disconnected from the world around them.

As The Fool reflects on the symbolism of the Four of Cups, they recall a time in their own life when they felt trapped in a cycle of apathy and indifference, unable to break free from the grip of their own discontent. They remember moments spent lost in daydreams, longing for something more but unsure of where to find it.

The Four of Cups serves as a gentle reminder to The Fool that while periods of introspection and self-reflection are important, they must guard against becoming too caught up in their own thoughts and emotions. It encourages them to open their eyes to the opportunities and blessings that surround them, even in moments of darkness and uncertainty.

When the Four of Cups appears in a tarot reading, it challenges The Fool to confront their feelings of discontent and to seek alternative sources of inspiration and fulfillment. It urges them to look beyond their current circumstances and to embrace the possibility of growth and transformation.

At its core, the Four of Cups represents the journey of the soul—the ebb and flow of emotions, desires, and experiences that shape our lives and define who we are. It is a reminder that even in our darkest moments, there is always hope and the promise of a brighter tomorrow.

The Fool will carry with them the wisdom and insight of the Four of Cups, knowing that true fulfillment comes not from the pursuit of external pleasures, but from the deep inner knowing that comes from embracing life's ever-changing tides.

magical spell: manifesting clarity ritual:

Four of Cups,
guide my way,
Through discontent,
I find my sway.
Illuminate my path with light,
Grant me clarity,
insight,
and sight.

materials needed:

- A quiet and comfortable space
- A white candle
- Paper and pen
- Lavender or chamomile herbs (dried or fresh)

instructions:

1. Find a peaceful space where you can sit comfortably and reflect.
2. Light the white candle, symbolizing clarity and illumination.
3. Take a few deep breaths to center yourself and calm your mind.
4. On the piece of paper, write down any feelings of discontent or confusion you may be experiencing.
5. Take a moment to reflect on what you truly desire and what brings you joy and fulfillment.
6. Visualize yourself releasing any negative emotions or doubts, allowing them to dissipate like smoke.
7. Sprinkle the lavender or chamomile herbs around the candle, invoking a sense of calm and clarity.
8. Recite the following affirmation aloud:

"Four of Cups, guide my way, Through discontent, I find my sway. Illuminate my path with light, Grant me clarity, insight, and sight."

1. Allow yourself to sit in quiet contemplation, opening yourself to receive insights and guidance.
2. When ready, extinguish the candle, knowing that clarity and understanding will come in their own time.

The Four of Cups reminds you to take time for introspection and self-reflection when feeling discontent or disconnected from your surroundings. By exploring your emotions, seeking clarity about your desires, and remaining open to new opportunities, you can navigate feelings of discontent and find a sense of purpose and fulfillment. Let the Four of Cups be a guiding light as you embark on a journey of self-discovery and inner growth.

questions to ask yourself

1. What feelings of dissatisfaction or discontent am I experiencing in my life?
2. How can I identify and address the root causes of my emotional stagnation?
3. What opportunities for growth and fulfillment am I overlooking?
4. Am I resisting or ignoring the blessings and opportunities that are available to me?
5. How can I cultivate gratitude and appreciation for the abundance in my life?
6. What changes or adjustments can I make to improve my emotional well-being?
7. How can I break free from complacency and embrace new experiences?
8. What creative outlets or activities bring me a sense of joy and fulfillment?
9. How can I practice mindfulness and presence to appreciate the beauty around me?
10. What steps can I take to reconnect with my emotions and reignite my passion for life?

five of cups

...

"Turn your gaze away from what has been lost and towards the glimmer of hope that remains," Five of Cups.

Answer: No

Lorelai Hamilton

Key Words and Phrases:
Sadness
Pessimism
Loss
New Phase
Waiting for resolutions
Grief
Disappointment
Transformation
Past Hurt
Healing
Regret
Reflection
Sorrow
Ending relationships
Failure
Blame

SYMBOLS:

- The spilled cups represent emotional pain and loss, while the figure's downward gaze reflects a focus on past sorrows rather than on the possibilities that lie ahead.
- The bridge in the background symbolizes the potential for moving beyond grief and finding a path to emotional healing and renewal.
- The two full cups behind the figure, symbolize the positive things in their life they're too blinded by loss to see.

The Five of Cups, is a card that speaks of loss, regret, and the painful process of letting go. As The Fool gazes upon the figure standing with head bowed before three spilled cups, they feel a wave of sorrow wash over them—a deep understanding of the emotional turmoil depicted in the scene.

The Five of Cups symbolizes a moment of profound disappointment and heartache, where the pain of past failures and missed opportunities threatens to overwhelm the spirit. Grief consumes the figure on the card, unable to see beyond the loss that looms large in their mind.

As The Fool reflects on the symbolism of the Five of Cups, they recall moments in their own life when they felt the sting of disappointment and the ache of shattered dreams. They remember the heaviness of sorrow, the weight of unshed tears, and the longing for what could have been.

The Five of Cups serves as a poignant reminder to The Fool that while loss and disappointment are an inevitable part of the human experience, they need not define us. It encourages them to acknowledge their pain, to honor their grief, and to find solace in the knowledge that healing is possible, even in the darkest of times.

When the Five of Cups appears in a tarot reading, it challenges The Fool to confront their feelings of loss and regret, and to embrace the transformative power of forgiveness and acceptance. It urges them to release the burdens of the past and to open their heart to the possibility of new beginnings and fresh starts.

At its core, the Five of Cups represents the delicate balance between sorrow and joy, loss and renewal. It is a testament to the resilience of the human spirit, and a reminder that even in our darkest moments, there is always the promise of hope and the potential for growth.

The Five of Cups has three spilt cups of wine at their feet. If they turn around and change their perspective, they will see two full cups of wine and a bridge to their destination. The Fool understands that changing their perspective is important for navigating through loss.

The Fool carries with them the wisdom and insight of the Five of Cups, knowing that while the road ahead may be fraught with challenges and hardships, it is also lined with moments of grace, redemption, and profound transformation.

Lorelai Hamilton

magical spell: healing heart ritual:

Five of Cups,
guide me through,
From loss and grief,
I find the new.
Heal my heart,
soothe my pain,
Renew my spirit,
let love reign.

Materials Needed:

- A quiet and comfortable space
- A black candle
- Paper and pen
- Rose petals or lavender herbs (dried or fresh)

Instructions:

- Find a peaceful space where you can sit comfortably and reflect.
- Light the black candle, symbolizing the acknowledgment of grief and loss.
- Take a few deep breaths to center yourself and connect with your emotions.
- On the piece of paper, write down any feelings of loss or disappointment you may be experiencing.
- Allow yourself to express your emotions freely, acknowledging the pain and sadness you feel.
- Sprinkle the rose petals or lavender herbs around the candle, invoking a sense of healing and comfort.

- Visualize a warm, healing light surrounding you, enveloping you in a blanket of love and support.
- Recite the following affirmation aloud:

"Five of Cups, guide me through, From loss and grief, I find the new. Heal my heart, soothe my pain, Renew my spirit, let love reign."

- Allow yourself to sit in quiet contemplation, embracing the healing energy that surrounds you.
- When ready, extinguish the candle, knowing that healing and renewal are within reach, and you are not alone in your journey.

The Five of Cups reminds you to acknowledge your feelings of loss and grief while also recognizing the potential for growth and renewal that lies ahead. By allowing yourself to mourn what has been lost and embracing the possibility of new beginnings, you can navigate through difficult times and find healing and emotional renewal. Let the Five of Cups be a guiding light as you journey toward healing and emotional well-being.

questions to ask yourself

1. What feelings of loss or disappointment am I currently grappling with?

2. How can I process my grief and honor my emotions in a healthy way?
3. What lessons can I learn from experiences of heartache and sadness?
4. Am I allowing myself to dwell on past regrets or mistakes, or am I ready to let go?
5. How can I shift my focus towards the blessings and opportunities still available to me?
6. What support systems or resources can I turn to for comfort and healing?
7. How can I cultivate resilience and strength in the face of adversity?
8. What new beginnings or silver linings can I find amidst moments of loss?
9. How can I practice self-compassion and kindness towards myself during times of sorrow?
10. What steps can I take to release the pain of the past and embrace a brighter future?

six of cups

. . .

"I am the vessel of fond recollections and heartfelt connections to the past," Six of Cups

Answer: Yes

Lorelai Hamilton

Key Words and Phrases:
Innocent
Happy Memories
Nostalgia
Joy
Old Friends
Soulmate Connection
Innocence
Celebration
Moving
Childhood
Playful

SYMBOLS:

- The children exchanging cups symbolize the sharing of kindness, love, and innocent joy.
- The flowers within the cups represent purity, innocence, and the beauty found in simple pleasures.
- The castle in the background signifies the safety and security of home and family, while the overarching theme is one of nostalgic reflection and innocence.

In the quiet corner of a sun-drenched garden, The Fool encounters the Six of Cups, a card that whispers of innocence, nostalgia, and the sweet memories of childhood. As The Fool gazes upon the scene, they feel a warm sense of familiarity wash over them—a gentle reminder of the joys of days gone by.

The Six of Cups symbolizes a return to simpler times, a reconnection with the purity and wonder of youth. In the card, two children stand face to face, exchanging cups filled with blooming flowers, their laughter echoing through the air like music.

As The Fool reflects on the symbolism of the Six of Cups, they are transported back to their own childhood, to days spent exploring hidden worlds, chasing dreams, and reveling in the magic of the everyday. They remember the taste of sunshine on their skin, the scent of freshly cut grass, and the feeling of endless possibility that seemed to linger in the air.

The Six of Cups serves as a gentle reminder to The Fool to embrace the innocence and wonder that still lives within their heart—to find joy in the simple pleasures of life and to cherish the memories that shape who they are. It encourages them to let go of the burdens of adulthood, if only for a moment, and to reconnect with the sense of wonder that once fueled their dreams.

When the Six of Cups appears in a tarot reading, it invites The Fool to explore their past with a sense of warmth and affection, to honor the experiences that have shaped them, and to find healing in the nostalgia of days gone by. It urges them to embrace the inner child that resides within us all, and to celebrate the magic of innocence, joy, and unbridled imagination.

At its core, the Six of Cups represents the beauty of nostalgia, the power of memory, and the enduring spirit of youth. It is a testament to the timeless nature of the human heart, and a reminder that no matter where life may lead us, the sweet memories of the past will always be a source of comfort, inspiration, and hope.

magical spell: remembering joy ritual:

Six of Cups,
guide me back,
To memories sweet,
no joy I lack.
In innocence and love,
I find,
The treasures of my youthful mind.

materials needed:

- A quiet and comfortable space
- A white candle
- Paper and pen
- Dried lavender or rose petals

instructions:

- Find a peaceful space where you can sit comfortably and reflect.
- Light the white candle, symbolizing purity, innocence, and joy.
- Take a few deep breaths to center yourself and connect with your inner sense of peace.
- On the piece of paper, write down a fond memory or joyful experience from your childhood.
- Allow yourself to fully immerse in the memory, recalling the sights, sounds, and feelings associated with it.
- Sprinkle the dried lavender or rose petals around the candle, invoking a sense of nostalgia and warmth.
- Visualize yourself surrounded by the love, joy, and innocence of childhood.
- Recite the following affirmation aloud:

"Six of Cups, guide me back, To memories sweet, no joy I lack. In innocence and love, I find, The treasures of my youthful mind."

- Allow yourself to bask in the warmth and comfort of cherished memories, knowing that they will always be a source of strength and inspiration.
- When ready, extinguish the candle, carrying the warmth and light of childhood memories with you as you journey through life.

The Six of Cups reminds you to embrace the innocence, joy, and nostalgia of childhood memories while also finding comfort and guidance in the present moment. By honoring the lessons and experiences of the past, you can find solace and inspiration as you navigate the complexities of adolescence and beyond. Let the Six of Cups be a reminder to cherish the innocence and beauty of childhood memories and find joy in the simple pleasures of life.

questions to ask yourself

1. What memories from the past am I revisiting or reminiscing about?
2. How can I reconnect with the innocence and joy of childhood?
3. What lessons or wisdom can I glean from my experiences growing up?
4. Am I holding onto nostalgia or sentimentality, or am I ready to embrace the present?
5. How can I use my past experiences to inform and enrich my present-day life?
6. What relationships from my past am I feeling drawn to revisit or reconcile with?
7. How can I honor and appreciate the people who have shaped me into who I am today?
8. What aspects of my childhood or upbringing continue to influence me as an adult?
9. How can I heal any wounds or traumas from my past in order to move forward?
10. In what ways can I integrate the lessons and experiences of my past into my present reality?

seven of cups

. . .

"By grounding yourself in reality, you can navigate the labyrinth of choices with wisdom and purpose," Seven of Cups.

Answer: Maybe

Key Words and Phrases:
Confusion
Spoiled for Choice
Lots of options
Imagination
Opportunities
Fantasy
Wishful
Fantasizing
Feeling lost
Illusion
Distractions
Indecisive
Visions
Dreams
Choices

SYMBOLS:

- The seven cups represent a plethora of options and possibilities, each enticing in its own way.
- The symbols within the cups range from riches and treasures to fantasies and dreams, highlighting the allure of illusions and the challenge of distinguishing between reality and fantasy.
- The figure's contemplative stance reflects the need for careful consideration and discernment amidst the array of choices.

In the misty realm of dreams and desires, The Fool encounters the Seven of Cups, a card that beckons with its array of fantastical visions and boundless possibilities. As The Fool gazes upon the swirling images depicted in the card, they feel a sense of both wonder and caution wash over them—a reminder of the power of imagination and the need for discernment in the face of temptation.

The Seven of Cups symbolizes a world of illusion, where dreams and fantasies mingle with reality, blurring the lines between what is possible and what is merely a trick of the mind. In the card, seven cups overflow with all manner of treasures and delights, from glittering jewels and shimmering crowns to ethereal beings and mythical creatures.

As The Fool contemplates the symbolism of the Seven of Cups, they are reminded of the importance of clarity and focus in the pursuit of their goals and aspirations. They understand while dreams can inspire and motivate, they can also deceive and distract, leading one down paths of delusion and disillusionment.

The Seven of Cups serves as a gentle warning to The Fool to beware of the lure of illusion and the seductive call of wishful thinking. It encourages them to approach their desires with a clear mind and an open heart, to discern between what is truly meaningful and what is merely a fleeting fancy.

When the Seven of Cups appears in a tarot reading, it invites The Fool to explore the depths of their imagination and to acknowledge the myriad possibilities that lie before them. It encourages them to dream big and to dare to envision a future filled with wonder and enchantment. However, it also cautions them to remain grounded in reality, to exercise caution in their choices, and to remember that not all that glitters is gold.

At its core, the Seven of Cups represents the power of choice and the need for discernment in the pursuit of one's dreams. It is a reminder that while the world may be filled with endless possibilities, not all paths lead to fulfillment, and not all dreams are meant to be pursued. It encourages The Fool to choose wisely, to follow the guidance of their heart, and to trust in the wisdom of their own intuition.

magical spell: clarity of vision ritual:

Seven of Cups,
reveal to me,
The truth within,

the clarity I seek.
Illuminate my path,
guide my way,
Help me discern,
each and every day.

materials needed:

- A quiet and comfortable space
- A blue candle
- Paper and pen
- Clear quartz crystal

instructions:

- Find a peaceful space where you can sit comfortably and reflect.
- Light the blue candle, symbolizing clarity, truth, and discernment.
- Take a few deep breaths to center yourself and quiet your mind.
- On the piece of paper, write down the choices or decisions you are currently facing.
- Reflect on each option, considering its alignment with your values, aspirations, and genuine desires.
- Hold the clear quartz crystal in your hand, allowing its energy to amplify your intentions for clarity and discernment.
- Visualize a bright, clear light surrounding you, illuminating the path ahead and guiding you toward wise and informed decisions.
- Recite the following affirmation aloud:

"Seven of Cups, reveal to me, The truth within, the clarity I seek. Illuminate my path, guide my way, Help me discern, each and every day."

- Allow yourself to sit in quiet contemplation, opening yourself to receive insights and guidance.
- When ready, extinguish the candle, knowing that clarity and discernment will illuminate your path and empower you to make wise decisions.

The Seven of Cups reminds you to approach choices and decisions with clarity, discernment, and a focus on authenticity. By distinguishing between genuine aspirations and fleeting fantasies, you can navigate through uncertainty and make decisions that align with your values and aspirations. Let the Seven of Cups be a guiding light as you journey toward clarity, truth, and empowered decision-making.

questions to ask yourself

1. What dreams or fantasies am I currently indulging in?
2. How can I discern between wishful thinking and realistic goals?
3. What desires or aspirations am I feeling pulled towards manifesting?
4. Am I feeling overwhelmed by too many options or possibilities?
5. How can I prioritize my goals and focus my energy on what truly matters?
6. What fears or insecurities are preventing me from taking action towards my dreams?
7. How can I cultivate clarity and discernment in my decision-making process?
8. What steps can I take to turn my dreams into achievable goals?
9. How can I stay grounded and anchored in reality while still dreaming big?
10. What support systems or resources can help me turn my dreams into reality?

eight of cups

. . .

"Walking away from what no longer serves your highest good," Eight of Cups.

Answer: No

Lorelai Hamilton

Key Words and Phrases:
Walking away
Transition
Uncertainty
Turning point
Abandonment
Leaving the Past
Seeking
Introspection
Searching
Renewal
Change

SYMBOLS:

- The figure's departure from the cups represents the act of moving on from stagnant or unfulfilling aspects of life.
- The moon in the background symbolizes intuition and the subconscious mind, guiding the figure's journey into the unknown.
- The mountainous landscape signifies the challenges and obstacles that may arise during periods of transition and change.

In the hushed stillness of twilight, The Fool encounters the Eight of Cups, a card that speaks of journeys embarked upon in search of deeper meaning and emotional fulfillment. As The Fool gazes upon the solitary figure turning away from a cluster of upright cups, they feel a sense of melancholy mingled with a stirring of courage—a reminder of the transformative power of letting go and moving on.

The Eight of Cups symbolizes the act of leaving behind that which no longer serves the soul, of bravely stepping into the unknown in pursuit of a higher truth and a more authentic existence. In the card, the figure walks away from the familiar comforts of the cups, their back turned to the past as they set out on a quest for deeper fulfillment and spiritual growth.

As The Fool contemplates the symbolism of the Eight of Cups, they are reminded of the importance of honoring one's inner truth and heeding the call of the soul. They understand that sometimes the path to true happiness requires letting go of attachments and patterns that no longer resonate with the essence of who they are, and embracing the uncertainty of the journey ahead.

The Eight of Cups serves as a gentle invitation to The Fool to explore the depths of their own emotional landscape, to acknowledge and release that which holds them back, and to embrace the transformative power of self-discovery and renewal. It encourages them to trust in their own inner guidance, even when the path forward seems uncertain or daunting.

When the Eight of Cups appears in a tarot reading, it invites you to reflect on areas of life where you are feeling unfulfilled or stagnant, and to consider what changes may be necessary in order to reclaim a sense of purpose and vitality. It encourages you to listen to the whispers of your heart and to follow the call of their intuition. Even if it leads you away from the safety of the familiar.

At its core, the Eight of Cups represents the courage to walk away from that which no longer nourishes the soul, and the faith to trust in the wisdom of one's own inner journey. It is a reminder that true fulfillment lies not in clinging to the past or the known, but in bravely venturing forth into the uncharted territory of the self, guided by the light of one's own truth.

magical spell: release and renewal ritual:

Eight of Cups,
guide my way,
As I release and renew today.
Let go of the old,
welcome the new,
Embracing change,

my spirit true.

materials needed:

- A quiet and comfortable space
- A black candle
- Paper and pen
- Lavender or sage bundle

instructions:

- Find a peaceful space where you can sit comfortably and reflect.
- Light the black candle, symbolizing release, transformation, and renewal.
- Take a few deep breaths to center yourself and connect with your inner wisdom.
- On the piece of paper, write down any emotions, attachments, or situations you are ready to release and leave behind.
- Reflect on each item, acknowledging its impact on your life and your readiness to let it go.
- Hold the lavender or sage bundle in your hand, infusing it with your intentions for release and renewal.
- Visualize yourself letting go of the emotional baggage and burdens that no longer serve your highest good.
- Recite the following affirmation aloud:

"Eight of Cups, guide my way, As I release and renew today. Let go of the old, welcome the new, Embracing change, my spirit true."

- Allow yourself to feel the weight lift off your shoulders as you surrender to the process of transformation.
- When ready, extinguish the candle, knowing that by releasing the past, you create space for new beginnings and opportunities for growth.

The Eight of Cups invites you to embrace change, let go of the past, and embark on a journey of self-discovery and renewal. By releasing emotional attachments and embracing new horizons, you create space for personal growth, transformation, and the pursuit of authentic fulfillment. Let the Eight of Cups be a guiding light as you navigate the currents of change and embrace the opportunities for renewal and transformation that lie ahead.

questions to ask yourself

1. What feelings of disillusionment or dissatisfaction am I experiencing in my life?
2. How can I identify and address the root causes of my emotional unrest?
3. What aspects of my current situation are no longer serving my highest good?
4. Am I willing to release attachments or relationships that no longer align with my growth?
5. How can I honor my emotions and make decisions that prioritize my well-being?
6. What opportunities for emotional renewal and healing are available to me?
7. How can I navigate the discomfort of uncertainty and embrace the journey of self-discovery?
8. What lessons can I learn from experiences of letting go and moving on?
9. How can I cultivate resilience and strength as I embark on a new chapter of my life?
10. What vision or dreams am I being called to pursue as I leave the past behind?

nine of cups

...

"You have reached a place of emotional fulfillment and personal satisfaction, where your heart's deepest wishes have been granted," Nine of Cups.

Answer: Yes

Key Words and Phrases:
Contentment
Wishes
Joy
Satisfaction
Happiness
Wishes coming true
See the good
Fulfillment
Looking forward
Abundance
Gratitude
Completion

SYMBOLS:

- The figure's relaxed posture and satisfied expression convey a sense of contentment and emotional well-being.
- The nine cups represent abundance, happiness, and the fulfillment of desires, suggesting a period of emotional satisfaction and harmony.
- The arc formed by the cups symbolizes completion and wholeness, reflecting the fulfillment of long-held dreams and aspirations.

The Fool encounters the radiant Nine of Cups, a beacon of fulfillment and emotional abundance that illuminates the path of contentment and satisfaction. As The Fool gazes upon the figure surrounded by nine shimmering cups, they feel a sense of warmth and joy—a reminder of the power of gratitude and the fulfillment found in embracing life's blessings.

The Nine of Cups symbolizes emotional fulfillment, contentment, and inner happiness. On the card, the figure sits with a satisfied smile, surrounded by the cups that represent their deepest desires and aspirations. It is a testament to the realization of dreams, the attainment of personal goals, and the joy that comes from living a life aligned with one's authentic self.

As The Fool contemplates the symbolism of the Nine of Cups, they are reminded of the importance of cultivating a mindset of abundance and gratitude. They understand that true fulfillment comes not from external possessions or achievements, but from within—from cherishing the richness of life's experiences and embracing the present moment with an open heart.

The Nine of Cups serves as a gentle reminder to The Fool to take stock of all that they have accomplished and to celebrate the blessings that surround them. It encourages them to revel in the joy of living and to appreciate the beauty and wonder of the world around them.

When the Nine of Cups appears in a tarot reading, it serves as a message of encouragement and affirmation. It suggests that you are on the right path and that you have much to be grateful for in life. It encourages trusting in the universe's abundance and to continue following your heart's desires with confidence and optimism.

The Nine of Cups represents the fulfillment of the soul's deepest longings and the joy that comes from living a life of authenticity and purpose.

magical spell: manifestation ritual:

Nine of Cups,
hear my plea,
Manifest my desires,
set me free.
Joy and fulfillment,
abundance I seek,
In gratitude and harmony,
my dreams I speak.

materials needed:

- A yellow candle
- Paper and pen
- Citrine crystal or yellow gemstone
- A small bowl of water

instructions:

- Find a quiet and comfortable space where you can focus and reflect.
- Light the yellow candle, symbolizing joy, abundance, and manifestation.
- Take a few deep breaths to center yourself and connect with your intentions.
- On the piece of paper, write down your heartfelt desires, dreams, and aspirations for fulfillment and happiness.
- Visualize yourself experiencing the sense of contentment and emotional satisfaction that you seek.
- Hold the citrine crystal or yellow gemstone in your hand, imbuing it with your intentions for manifestation and abundance.
- Place the paper with your written intentions in front of the candle and the crystal.
- Dip your fingers into the bowl of water and sprinkle a few drops over the paper, symbolizing the flow of abundance and fulfillment into your life.
- Recite the following affirmation aloud:

"Nine of Cups, hear my plea, Manifest my desires, set me free. Joy and fulfillment, abundance I seek, In gratitude and harmony, my dreams I speak."

- Allow the candle to burn down safely, knowing that your intentions for fulfillment and happiness are being set into motion.

The Nine of Cups reminds you to embrace moments of contentment, celebrate your achievements, and cultivate gratitude for the blessings in your life. By recognizing and appreciating the abundance and fulfillment that surrounds you, you can manifest greater joy, happiness, and emotional satisfaction in your journey through adolescence and beyond.

Let the Nine of Cups be a beacon of hope and fulfillment as you navigate the path toward a life filled with joy, abundance, and heartfelt fulfillment.

questions to ask yourself

1. What brings me true happiness and fulfillment in my life?
2. How can I cultivate a sense of contentment and gratitude for what I have?
3. What desires or wishes am I currently manifesting or working towards?
4. Am I allowing myself to experience joy and pleasure without guilt or hesitation?
5. How can I create a life that aligns with my deepest values and aspirations?
6. What steps can I take to prioritize self-care and nurture my emotional well-being?
7. How can I share my abundance and blessings with those around me?
8. What dreams or goals have I achieved that bring me a sense of satisfaction?
9. How can I maintain a sense of optimism and positivity even in challenging times?
10. What lessons can I learn from experiences of abundance and emotional fulfillment?

ten of cups

. . .

"I am the symbol of ultimate happiness and harmony in relationships, where love flows abundantly, and hearts are united in perfect alignment," Ten of Cups.

Answer: Yes

Key Words and Phrases:
Dreams coming true
Marriage
Family
Security
Harmony
Bliss
Togetherness
Happiness
Unity
Love
Relationships
Harmony
Trust
Celebration
Hopeful
Gratitude

SYMBOLS:

- The rainbow symbolizes hope, blessings, and the fulfillment of dreams, casting a radiant glow over the family's home.
- The family members' joyful expressions and loving embrace convey a sense of unity, connection, and emotional fulfillment.
- The idyllic setting represents the ideal of harmonious relationships and emotional satisfaction within the family.

In the serene landscape of emotional fulfillment, The Fool encounters the enchanting Ten of Cups, a symbol of harmony, joy, and familial bliss that radiates warmth and love. As The Fool gazes upon the scene of familial love and contentment, they feel a sense of wonder and appreciation—a reminder of the profound connections that bind us together and the beauty of shared love and happiness.

The Ten of Cups symbolizes ultimate emotional fulfillment and domestic happiness. On the card, a loving couple stands together, surrounded by their children, raising their cups in celebration of the abundance of love and joy that fills their lives. It is a depiction of the ideal family unit, where love, understanding, and support create a sanctuary of happiness and security.

As The Fool contemplates the symbolism of the Ten of Cups, they are reminded of the importance of nurturing and cherishing the bonds of family and community. They understand that true fulfillment comes not from material wealth or external achievements, but from the love and support of those closest to us—from the shared laughter, the heartfelt conversations, and the comforting embrace of loved ones.

The Ten of Cups serves as a gentle reminder to The Fool to prioritize their emotional well-being and cultivate meaningful connections with others. It encourages them to cherish the relationships that bring them joy and to invest time and energy in nurturing those bonds. It is a call to celebrate the love that surrounds them and to find solace and strength in the embrace of family and friends.

When the Ten of Cups appears in a tarot reading, it signifies a period of profound emotional fulfillment and harmony in your life. It suggests that love, support, and understanding surround you, and that relationships are flourishing and deeply fulfilling. It encourages embracing the joy and abundance that life offers and to cultivate a sense of gratitude for the blessings that surround you.

At its core, the Ten of Cups represents the culmination of emotional growth and the realization of our deepest desires for love and connection. It is a reminder that true happiness comes from within—from the bonds we share with others and the love that binds us together in moments of joy and sorrow alike.

magical spell: family harmony ritual:

Ten of Cups,
bring harmony near,
Love and joy,
let it appear.
Family bonds,
strong and true,
In love and harmony,
we renew.

materials needed:

- Pink candle
- Paper and pen
- Rose quartz crystal or pink gemstone
- A small bowl of water

instructions:

- Find a quiet and comfortable space where you can focus and reflect.
- Light the pink candle, symbolizing love, harmony, and emotional connection.
- Take a few deep breaths to center yourself and connect with your intentions.
- On the piece of paper, write down any conflicts, tensions, or issues within your family that you wish to resolve and transform into harmony and understanding.
- Visualize your family members surrounded by love, acceptance, and understanding, fostering a sense of unity and emotional fulfillment.
- Hold the rose quartz crystal or pink gemstone in your hand, imbuing it with your intentions for love and harmony within the family.
- Place the paper with your written intentions in front of the candle and the crystal.
- Dip your fingers into the bowl of water and sprinkle a few drops over the paper, symbolizing the flow of love and harmony into your family relationships.
- Recite the following affirmation aloud:

"Ten of Cups, bring harmony near, Love and joy, let it appear. Family bonds, strong and true, In love and harmony, we renew."

- Allow the candle to burn down safely, knowing that your intentions for family harmony and emotional fulfillment are being set into motion.

The Ten of Cups reminds you to cherish the bonds of family, cultivate loving relationships, and foster harmony and understanding within your home. By nurturing open communication, fostering love and acceptance, and appreciating the blessings of family and community, you can create a supportive and nurturing environment where emotional fulfillment and harmony thrive. Let the Ten of Cups be a beacon of love, unity, and emotional fulfillment as you navigate the journey of adolescence and the complexities of family relationships.

questions to ask yourself

1. What feelings of love and connection am I experiencing in my relationships?
2. How can I cultivate a sense of harmony and unity within my family or community?
3. What traditions or rituals bring me closer to my loved ones and create lasting memories?
4. Am I nurturing my relationships with authenticity and compassion?
5. How can I create a supportive and nurturing environment for my loved ones?
6. What shared values or goals do I have with my family or community members?

7. How can I express my love and appreciation for those closest to me?
8. What opportunities for deep emotional fulfillment and joy are present in my life?
9. How can I contribute to the well-being and happiness of those I care about?
10. What lessons can I learn from experiences of love, connection, and emotional abundance?

page of cups

. . .

"I stir the waters of your soul, encouraging you to listen to the whispers of your heart and trust in your inner guidance" Page of Cups.

Answer: Yes

Key Words and Phrases:
Insights
Messages
Creativity
Comfort
Sensitivity
Possibilities
Imagination
Intuition
Inspiration
Curious
Talents
Curiosity
Ideas
Emotional exploration
Plans
Opportunities

SYMBOLS:

- The young person's curious gaze into the cup suggests a sense of wonder and introspection, as they explore the depths of their emotions and imagination.
- fish popping out of the cup symbolizes intuition, creativity, and the emergence of new ideas and insights.
- The calm waters in the background represent the subconscious mind and the vast depths of the emotional landscape.

The Page of Cups is a youthful messenger of creativity, intuition, and emotional sensitivity. As The Fool observes the Page delicately holding a cup adorned with a fish, they are drawn into a realm of imagination and emotional depth, where dreams and intuition flow freely.

The Page of Cups symbolizes the emergence of emotional awareness and artistic expression. In the card, the Page stands at the edge of the sea, dressed in colorful attire and a fanciful hat adorned with a single feather. The fish emerging from the cup symbolizes the subconscious mind and the depths of emotional intuition. The Page's gaze is serene, reflecting a deep connection to the world of emotions and creativity.

The Fool contemplates the symbolism of the Page of Cups and realizes the importance of embracing their innermost feelings and allowing their intuition to guide them on their journey. They understand that true wisdom comes not only from the intellect but also from the heart—from the depths of emotion and the whispers of the subconscious mind.

The Page of Cups encourages you to explore your emotional landscape with curiosity and openness. It invites you to embrace artistic impulses, to listen to the gentle whispers of your intuition, and to allow yourself to be guided by the currents of emotion that flow within you. It is a call to trust in the wisdom of the heart and find inspiration and meaning in the world around you.

When the Page of Cups appears in a tarot reading, it signifies a time of emotional discovery and creative exploration for The Fool. It suggests that they may be on the brink of a new artistic endeavor or that they are exploring their feelings in a deeper and more meaningful way. It encourages them to embrace their emotional sensitivity and to allow themselves to be guided by their intuition as they navigate the waters of their inner world.

At its core, the Page of Cups represents the beauty of emotional expression and the richness of the inner life. It is a reminder that true wisdom lies not only in the mind but also in the heart, and that by embracing our emotions and intuition, we can tap into a wellspring of creativity, inspiration, and insight.

magical spell: creative inspiration ritual:

> Page of Cups,
> hear my plea,
> Creative inspiration
> flows through me.
> Ideas bloom
> and dreams take flight,
> In creativity's embrace,
> I find delight.

materials needed:

- Blue candle
- Paper and pen
- Moonstone crystal or clear quartz
- A small bowl of water

instructions:

- Find a quiet and comfortable space where you can focus and ignite your creativity.
- Light the blue candle, symbolizing inspiration, intuition, and emotional exploration.
- Take a few deep breaths to center yourself and connect with your creative energies.
- On the piece of paper, write down any creative projects, ideas, or aspirations that you wish to explore and manifest.
- Visualize yourself immersed in a sea of creative inspiration, surrounded by endless possibilities and artistic expression.
- Hold the moonstone crystal or clear quartz in your hand, inviting its energies of intuition and clarity to guide your creative endeavors.
- Place the paper with your written intentions in front of the candle and the crystal.
- Dip your fingers into the bowl of water and sprinkle a few drops over the paper, symbolizing the flow of creative energy and inspiration into your life.
- Recite the following affirmation aloud:

"Page of Cups, hear my plea, Creative inspiration flows through me. Ideas bloom and dreams take flight, In creativity's embrace, I find delight."

- Allow the candle to burn down safely, knowing that your intentions for creative exploration and artistic expression are being set into motion.

The Page of Cups reminds you to embrace your creativity, explore your emotions, and trust your intuition as you navigate the journey of self-discovery and artistic expression. By honoring your unique talents, following your creative impulses, and delving into the depths of your emotions, you can unleash your creative potential and cultivate a deeper connection with your inner world. Let the Page of Cups be a guide on your creative journey, inspiring you to explore new horizons, express your authentic self, and embrace the wonders of imagination and emotional exploration.

questions to ask yourself

1. What new emotions or creative inspirations am I exploring at this time?
2. How can I embrace my sensitivity and intuition as sources of guidance?
3. What messages or insights am I receiving from my dreams or subconscious mind?
4. Am I open to exploring my emotional depths and expressing my true feelings?

5. How can I cultivate a sense of wonder and curiosity about the world around me?
6. What artistic or imaginative pursuits bring me joy and fulfillment?
7. How can I connect with my inner child and embrace a sense of innocence and playfulness?
8. What opportunities for emotional growth and self-discovery are presenting themselves to me?
9. How can I trust my intuition and follow the guidance of my heart?
10. What steps can I take to nurture my creative spirit and explore my emotional landscape?

knight of cups

. . .

"I am the embodiment of chivalry and passion, riding forth on a quest for love and inspiration," Knight of Cups.

Answer: Yes

Lorelai Hamilton

Key Words and Phrases:
New experiences
An offering
Romance
Imagination
Idealism
Kindness
Intuition
Follow your dreams
Overly optimistic
Compassion
Going with the flow
Inspiration
Romantic
Emotional Depth
Charming

SYMBOLS:

- The knight, adorned in armor and riding gracefully, represents chivalry, romance, and the pursuit of emotional fulfillment.
- The cup he holds symbolizes emotional sensitivity, intuition, and the quest for love and connection.
- The flowing river in the background symbolizes the journey of emotions, reflecting the ebb and flow of romantic pursuits and emotional experiences.

The Knight of Cups is a gallant figure on a quest for love, creativity, and emotional fulfillment. As The Fool observes the Knight riding gracefully on his noble steed, they sense an aura of romance, imagination, and sensitivity that surrounds him like a shimmering cloak.

The Knight of Cups symbolizes the pursuit of emotional fulfillment and the quest for spiritual enlightenment. On the card, the Knight rides forth with a chalice in hand, a symbol of his deep connection to the realm of emotions and intuition. His armor is adorned with images of fish, representing the depths of the subconscious mind and the mysteries of the soul.

As The Fool contemplates the symbolism of the Knight of Cups, they are drawn into a tale of chivalry and romance, where the quest for love and emotional connection takes center stage. They understand that the Knight's journey is not merely one of physical adventure but also of inner exploration—a quest to uncover the depths of the heart and to embrace the power of love and creativity.

The Knight of Cups inspires The Fool to follow their heart and to pursue their dreams with courage and passion. It reminds them that true fulfillment comes not from external achievements but from the richness of the inner world—from the depths of emotion, imagination, and spiritual connection.

When the Knight of Cups appears in a tarot reading, it signifies a time of emotional exploration and creative inspiration for The Fool. It suggests that they may be on the brink of a new romantic adventure or that they are beginning to explore their feelings in a deeper and more meaningful way. It encourages them to embrace their emotional sensitivity and to allow themselves to be guided by their intuition as they navigate the twists and turns of the heart's journey.

The Knight of Cups represents the beauty of emotional connection and the power of love to transform and uplift the soul. It is a reminder that true fulfillment comes from following the stirrings of the heart and embracing the magic of love, creativity, and spiritual insight.

magical spell: love attraction ritual:

> Knight of Cups,
> hear my plea,
> Love and romance
> come to me.
> Hearts entwine
> and passions soar,
> True love finds me,
> forevermore.

materials needed:

- Pink candle
- Rose petals or rose essential oil
- Paper and pen
- Rose quartz crystal or pink gemstone

instructions:

- Find a quiet and comfortable space where you can focus and ignite the flames of love.
- Light the pink candle, symbolizing love, romance, and emotional connection.
- Surround yourself with the scent of roses by sprinkling rose petals or using rose essential oil.
- Take a few deep breaths to center yourself and connect with your heart's desires.
- On the piece of paper, write down the qualities and characteristics you wish to attract in a romantic partner or relationship.
- Visualize yourself surrounded by love and affection, experiencing deep emotional connection and fulfillment.
- Hold the rose quartz crystal or pink gemstone in your hand, imbuing it with your intentions for love and romance.
- Place the paper with your written intentions in front of the candle and the crystal.
- Recite the following affirmation aloud:

"Knight of Cups, hear my plea, Love and romance come to me. Hearts entwine and passions soar, True love finds me, forevermore."

- Allow the candle to burn down safely, knowing that your intentions for love and emotional connection are being set into motion.

The Knight of Cups reminds you to honor your romantic ideals, embrace your emotional sensitivity, and pursue authentic connections with integrity and compassion. By trusting your heart's desires, following your intuition, and cultivating love and emotional fulfillment in your life, you can embark on a journey of romance and emotional exploration. Let the Knight of Cups be a guide on your quest for love and connection, inspiring you to pursue your dreams with courage, passion, and an open heart.

questions to ask yourself

1. What romantic or creative pursuits am I currently passionate about?
2. How can I express my emotions and desires with sincerity and authenticity?
3. What opportunities for love and connection am I open to exploring?
4. Am I willing to take risks in pursuit of my heart's desires?
5. How can I balance idealism with practicality in my romantic endeavors?
6. What qualities am I seeking in a potential romantic partner or creative project?
7. How can I channel my emotional energy towards meaningful expression and creation?
8. What obstacles or challenges am I willing to overcome in the pursuit of love or creativity?

9. How can I stay true to my values and integrity in matters of the heart?
10. What lessons can I learn from experiences of love, romance, and creative inspiration?

queen of cups

. . .

"I am the embodiment of emotional wisdom and nurturing compassion, offering solace and support to those in need," Queen of Cups.

Answer: Yes

Key Words and Phrases:
Nurturing
Caring
Intuition
Feelings
Empathy
Compassion
Sensitive
Nurturing
Imaginative
Sensitive
Imaginative
Emotional Intelligence
Empathy
Counseling
Generous

SYMBOLS:

- She holds a cup, representing the realm of emotions, intuition, and psychic insight.
- The ocean behind her symbolizes the vast depths of the subconscious mind and the mysteries of the emotional landscape.
- The throne upon which she sits signifies her authority and wisdom in matters of the heart and emotional understanding.

The Fool encounters the Queen of Cups, a gentle guardian of intuition, empathy, and inner wisdom. As The Fool gazes upon her serene countenance, they feel a profound sense of tranquility and emotional depth emanating from her presence.

The Queen of Cups symbolizes the mastery of emotions and the power of intuition. She sits upon her throne, cradling a beautiful cup adorned with images of sea creatures and symbols of the subconscious mind. Her gaze is soft yet penetrating, reflecting her deep connection to the mysteries of the heart and the vast ocean of human emotion.

The Fool becomes engrossed in a tale of compassion, empathy, and spiritual insight. They see the Queen as a beacon of emotional stability and inner strength, navigating the turbulent waters of the heart with grace and wisdom.

The Queen of Cups inspires The Fool to embrace their emotional nature and to trust in the guidance of their intuition. She reminds them that true wisdom comes not from the intellect alone but from the depths of the soul —from the wellspring of emotion and intuition that lies within each of us.

When the Queen of Cups appears in a tarot reading, it signals a time of emotional healing and spiritual growth for The Fool. It suggests that they may be called upon to tap into their intuition and to explore the depths of their emotions with honesty and compassion. It encourages them to listen to the whispers of their heart and to trust in the guidance of their inner voice as they navigate the journey of self-discovery.

At its core, the Queen of Cups represents the beauty of emotional authenticity and the power of empathy to heal and transform. She is a reminder that true strength lies not in the suppression of emotion but in the willingness to embrace it fully—to dive deep into the waters of the soul and to emerge with a profound sense of love, compassion, and understanding for oneself and others.

As The Fool reflects on the wisdom of the Queen of Cups, they understand that the path to emotional fulfillment lies not in the pursuit of external validation but in the cultivation of inner peace and self-acceptance. They embrace the Queen's teachings with an open heart, knowing that in doing so, they will find the courage to navigate the waters of life with grace, compassion, and unwavering love.

magical spell:

Self-Love and Emotional Healing: Queen of Cups,
guide me with your wisdom,
Help me navigate
the depths of my emotions.
With love and compassion,
I embrace myself,
Healing my heart,
restoring my inner wealth.

materials needed:

- Pink candle
- Rose quartz crystal or any calming crystal
- Lavender essential oil or dried lavender
- Journal and pen

instructions:

- Find a quiet and comfortable space where you can focus on your emotional well-being.
- Light the pink candle, symbolizing love, compassion, and emotional healing.
- Hold the rose quartz crystal or calming crystal in your hand, connecting with its soothing energy.
- Inhale the calming scent of lavender essential oil or dried lavender to promote relaxation and emotional balance.
- Take a few deep breaths to center yourself and tune into your emotions.
- Open your journal and begin writing down any emotions or thoughts that come to mind, allowing yourself to express your feelings without judgment.
- Reflect on any challenging emotions or experiences you may be facing and acknowledge them with compassion and understanding.
- Visualize yourself surrounded by a warm, healing light, enveloping you in a cocoon of love and emotional support.
- Repeat the following affirmation aloud or silently to yourself:

"Queen of Cups, guide me with your wisdom, Help me navigate the depths of my emotions. With love and compassion, I embrace myself, Healing my heart, restoring my inner wealth."

- Allow the candle to burn down safely as you continue to journal and reflect on your emotions, knowing that you are worthy of love and compassion.

The Queen of Cups encourages you to embrace your emotional sensitivity, trust your intuition, and cultivate compassion for yourself and others. By honoring your emotions, nurturing your inner wisdom, and practicing self-love and emotional healing, you can navigate the complexities of adolescence with grace and resilience. Let the Queen of Cups be your guide on your journey to emotional well-being and inner peace, empowering you to embrace your true essence and shine your light brightly in the world.

questions to ask yourself

1. How am I embodying the qualities of compassion and nurturing in my life?
2. What emotional support am I providing to myself and others?
3. How can I cultivate a deeper connection with my intuition and inner wisdom?
4. Am I honoring my emotions and allowing myself to feel fully?
5. How can I create a safe and supportive space for emotional expression?
6. What boundaries do I need to set to protect my emotional well-being?
7. How can I use my intuition to guide my decisions and actions?

8. What insights or wisdom am I able to offer to those in need of emotional support?
9. How can I practice self-care and prioritize my own needs without guilt?
10. What steps can I take to deepen my connection with my emotional self and those around me?

king of cups

. . .

"I am the embodiment of strength and stability in the realm of emotions, navigating the depths of the human heart with grace and empathy," King of Cups.

Answer: Yes

Key Words and Phrases:
Emotional Mastery
Feelings
Compassion
Wisdom
Wealth of Knowledge
Empowerment
Serenity
Good advice
Listening
Confident
Integrity

SYMBOLS:

- He holds a cup, representing the realm of emotions and intuition, indicating his deep understanding of the human heart and psyche.
- The calm waters around him symbolize emotional stability and serenity, reflecting his ability to remain composed even in turbulent times.
- The fish jumping out of the water symbolizes intuitive insights and the subconscious mind, highlighting the king's connection to his inner wisdom.

The King of Cups, a wise and compassionate ruler of the heart's domain. The King sits upon his throne, a symbol of his authority over the realm of emotions, and gazes out at the vast expanse of the sea with a serene countenance.

The King of Cups embodies emotional maturity, empathy, and understanding. He is a master of his feelings, navigating the ebb and flow of emotion with grace and wisdom. As The Fool observes the King's calm demeanor, they sense a deep reservoir of compassion and inner strength emanating from his presence.

In the story of the King of Cups, The Fool learns the importance of emotional intelligence and self-awareness. They see the King as a beacon of stability in times of turmoil, a guiding light that illuminates the path toward inner peace and harmony.

The King of Cups encourages The Fool to embrace their emotions fully, to acknowledge and honor the depth of their feelings without judgment or fear. He teaches them that true strength lies not in the suppression of emotion but in the willingness to explore the depths of the heart with openness and compassion.

When the King of Cups appears in a tarot reading, it heralds a time of emotional balance and maturity for The Fool. It suggests that they may be called upon to tap into their inner wisdom and to trust in the guidance of their intuition as they navigate the complexities of the human experience.

The King of Cups reminds The Fool that vulnerability is not a weakness but a source of profound strength and connection. He teaches them that by embracing their emotions authentically, they can forge deeper connections with others and cultivate a greater sense of empathy and understanding in their relationships.

The King of Cups symbolizes the power of emotional authenticity and the transformative nature of compassion. He is a reminder that true leadership stems from the heart—from the ability to lead with kindness, empathy, and integrity, even in the face of adversity.

As The Fool reflects on the wisdom of the King of Cups, they understand that the path to emotional fulfillment lies in embracing the full spectrum of human experience—to love deeply, to feel passionately, and to navigate the ever-changing currents of emotion with courage, grace, and unwavering compassion.

magical spell: emotional harmony and self-reflection:

King of Cups,
grant me the wisdom

Lorelai Hamilton

of emotional balance,
Guide me through
the depths of my heart
with grace.
With clarity
and compassion,
I embrace my emotions,
Finding harmony within,
I honor my inner space.

materials needed:

- Blue candle
- Clear quartz crystal or any calming crystal
- Chamomile tea or dried chamomile flowers
- Journal and pen

instructions:

- Find a quiet and comfortable space where you can focus on your emotional well-being.
- Light the blue candle, symbolizing emotional healing, clarity, and balance.
- Hold the clear quartz crystal or calming crystal in your hand, connecting with its grounding energy.
- Brew a cup of chamomile tea or prepare a small pouch of dried chamomile flowers, known for their calming and soothing properties.
- Take a few sips of chamomile tea or inhale the calming scent of chamomile to promote relaxation and emotional balance.
- Close your eyes and visualize a peaceful ocean, its waves gently lapping against the shore, symbolizing emotional harmony and serenity.
- Reflect on your emotions and experiences, allowing yourself to explore any feelings of unease or imbalance with compassion and understanding.
- Open your journal and begin writing down your thoughts, emotions, and reflections, allowing yourself to express your innermost thoughts without judgment.
- Write a letter to yourself, offering words of encouragement, love, and support as you navigate through life's challenges and uncertainties.

- Hold the clear quartz crystal or calming crystal close to your heart, envisioning its healing energy enveloping you in a cocoon of love and emotional support.
- Repeat the following affirmation aloud or silently to yourself:

"King of Cups, grant me the wisdom of emotional balance, Guide me through the depths of my heart with grace. With clarity and compassion, I embrace my emotions, Finding harmony within, I honor my inner space."

- Allow the candle to burn down safely as you continue to journal and reflect on your emotions, knowing that you possess the inner strength and resilience to navigate life's emotional currents with grace and wisdom.

The King of Cups encourages you to cultivate emotional balance, inner strength, and compassion as you navigate the complexities of adolescence and beyond. By embracing your emotions, honoring your inner wisdom, and practicing self-reflection and emotional healing, you can find peace, clarity, and resilience amidst life's ever-changing tides. Let the King of Cups be your guide on your journey to emotional mastery and self-discovery, empowering you to embrace your true essence and live authentically from the heart.

questions to ask yourself

1. How am I using my emotional intelligence and empathy to support others?
2. What leadership role am I taking on in matters of the heart and emotions?

3. How can I balance compassion with objectivity in my interactions with others?
4. Am I providing a stable and nurturing environment for those under my care?
5. How can I use my intuition to guide my decisions and actions?
6. What emotional boundaries do I need to set to maintain my own well-being?
7. How can I express my feelings and desires with authenticity and sincerity?
8. What lessons can I learn from experiences of emotional mastery and resilience?
9. How can I cultivate a sense of emotional balance and equanimity in all aspects of my life?
10. What steps can I take to lead with compassion and wisdom in my relationships and interactions?

ace of pentacles

. . .

"This is a journey of prosperity and financial security, knowing that abundance awaits those who are willing to seize the opportunities that present themselves," Ace of Pentacles.

Answer: Yes

Lorelai Hamilton

Key Words and Phrases:
Gifts
Money
Abundance
Talents
Manifestation
Financial improvements
Prosperity
Opportunity
Achievement
Material Success
Promotion
Fertility
Good things
Manifesting
Good Investments

SYMBOLS:

- The hand emerging from the clouds symbolizes divine intervention and the offering of new opportunities from the universe. It represents the potential for abundance and prosperity that awaits those who are open to receiving it.
- The pentacle depicts a five-pointed star enclosed in a circle, representing the elements of earth, air, fire, water, and spirit. It symbolizes the material world, wealth, and the manifestation of goals and desires in the physical realm.
- The garden represents fertility, growth, and the abundance of nature. It symbolizes the potential for prosperity and the rewards that come from nurturing one's goals and ambitions.
- The Mountains signify the challenges and obstacles that must be overcome to achieve success. They represent the journey toward prosperity and the determination required to reach one's goals.

In the bustling marketplace of earthly abundance, The Fool encounters the Ace of Pentacles, a symbol of opportunity, prosperity, and material manifestation. As The Fool gazes upon the radiant pentacle, they feel a surge of excitement and possibility coursing through their veins.

The Ace of Pentacles represents the beginning of a new financial or material venture—a seed of potential waiting to be nurtured and cultivated into tangible success. It serves as a reminder that the universe is abundant and ripe with opportunities for those who are willing to seize them.

In the story of the Ace of Pentacles, The Fool learns the importance of grounding their dreams and aspirations in practical action and diligent effort. They see the ace as a gift from the universe—a divine offering of resources and support to help them realize their goals and ambitions.

The Fool's contemplation of the symbolism of the pentacle serves as a reminder of the power of intention and manifestation. They understand that by aligning their thoughts, beliefs, and actions with their highest aspirations, they can attract abundance and prosperity into their lives with effortless ease.

The Ace of Pentacles encourages The Fool to plant the seeds of their desires with unwavering faith and confidence, trusting that the universe will conspire in their favor to bring their dreams to fruition. It is a symbol of new beginnings and fresh starts—a promise of prosperity and abundance on the horizon.

When the Ace of Pentacles appears in a tarot reading, it serves as a powerful omen of opportunity and potential. It suggests that the universe is conspiring to bless The Fool with the resources, support, and abundance they need to manifest their dreams into reality.

The Ace of Pentacles invites The Fool to step boldly into the realm of possibility—to embrace the unknown with courage and conviction, knowing that they are supported by the infinite abundance of the universe. It is a call to action—a reminder to seize the moment and embark on a journey of growth, expansion, and fulfillment.

The Ace of Pentacles symbolizes the infinite potential that resides within each of us—the power to create, manifest, and transform our lives in profound and meaningful ways. It is a beacon of hope and inspiration—a reminder that the universe is always conspiring in our favor, ready to bless us with blessings beyond our wildest dreams.

Lorelai Hamilton

magical spell: manifesting abundance and opportunity:

I am open to receiving
abundance and opportunities.
I welcome prosperity
into my life
with gratitude and joy.

materials needed:

- Green candle
- Patchouli incense
- Citrine crystal
- Pen and paper

instructions:

- Begin by lighting the green candle and the patchouli incense, creating a sacred space for abundance and prosperity to flow.
- Hold the citrine crystal in your hand, allowing its energy to amplify your intentions and attract abundance into your life.
- Sit in a comfortable position and take several deep breaths, allowing yourself to connect with the energy of the earth and the universe.
- With the pen and paper, write down your goals and desires related to abundance and prosperity. Be specific and clear about what you wish to manifest.
- Visualize yourself surrounded by a radiant green light, symbolizing the energy of growth, abundance, and prosperity.
- Hold the paper between your palms and recite the affirmation:

"I am open to receiving abundance and opportunities. I welcome prosperity into my life with gratitude and joy."

- Place the paper under the candle and allow it to burn, releasing your intentions into the universe.
- Sit quietly for a few moments, feeling the energy of the spell infusing you with confidence, abundance, and the promise of new beginnings.

With roots reaching deep into the earth and branches stretching towards the heavens, it symbolizes the potential for material wealth and earthly fulfillment. The Ace of Pentacles invites us to sow the seeds of prosperity, embrace opportunities for growth, and cultivate abundance in all areas of our lives.

questions to ask yourself

1. What new opportunities for material or financial abundance am I being presented with?
2. How can I cultivate a sense of prosperity and security in my life?
3. What practical skills or resources do I possess that can help me achieve my goals?
4. Am I open to receiving blessings and opportunities for growth in the material realm?
5. How can I manifest my vision for success and stability in the physical world?
6. What investments of time, energy, or resources will yield the greatest returns?
7. How can I align my actions and intentions with my long-term financial goals?

8. What seeds of potential am I ready to plant in order to create a solid foundation for the future?
9. How can I prioritize my financial well-being while still honoring my values and principles?
10. What steps can I take to manifest abundance and prosperity in all areas of my life?

two of pentacles

. . .

"Together, we've learned that life's challenges are but a dance, and with balance, we can navigate them with grace," Two of Pentacles.

Answer: Maybe

Lorelai Hamilton

Key Words and Phrases:
Balance
Seas of Change
Possibilities
Juggling multiple things
Flexible
Feeling pulled in different directions
Ships coming in
Decisions
Stability

SYMBOLS:

- The figure juggling two pentacles symbolizes the balancing act of managing multiple responsibilities and priorities. The figure's ability to juggle reflects the need for adaptability and flexibility in navigating life's challenges.
- The infinity symbol represents the cyclical nature of life and the interconnectedness of all things. It symbolizes the eternal dance of balance and harmony.
- The sea depicts the turbulent waters of life's journey. It symbolizes the ever-changing nature of circumstances and the need to stay grounded amidst life's ups and downs.
- The ships signify the voyages of life and the opportunities and challenges that come with them. They represent the need to navigate through turbulent waters with grace and resilience.

The Two of Pentacles is a symbol of balance, adaptability, and juggling life's demands with finesse. The Fool gazes upon the figure. They see a juggler effortlessly managing two pentacles, representing the material and earthly aspects of existence.

The Two of Pentacles represents the delicate dance of balancing responsibilities, priorities, and obligations in the ever-changing landscape of life. It serves as a reminder that while life may throw challenges and opportunities in our path, we possess the inner strength and resilience to navigate them with grace and ease.

In the story of the Two of Pentacles, The Fool learns the art of flexibility and adaptability in the face of life's twists and turns. They see the figure in the card as a beacon of inspiration—a reminder that even amidst chaos and uncertainty, there exists a sense of harmony and equilibrium waiting to be found.

The Fool reflects on the meaning behind the pentacles. They realize that true mastery lies not in avoiding challenges, but in embracing them with an open heart and mind. They understand that by maintaining a sense of balance and perspective, they can weather any storm and emerge stronger and more resilient than ever before.

The Two of Pentacles encourages The Fool to trust in their ability to navigate life's ups and downs with grace and confidence. It is a reminder that while the road may be rocky at times, they possess the inner wisdom and fortitude to overcome any obstacle that stands in their way.

When the Two of Pentacles appears in a tarot reading, it serves as a gentle nudge to find balance and harmony in all areas of life. It suggests that The Fool may need to reassess their priorities and make adjustments to ensure that they are allocating their time, energy, and resources in a way that serves their highest good.

The Two of Pentacles invites The Fool to embrace the fluidity of life—to surrender to the natural rhythms of change and transformation, knowing that they are capable of riding the waves of uncertainty with poise and grace. It is a call to trust in the inherent wisdom of the universe and to have faith that all things will unfold exactly as they should.

At its core, the Two of Pentacles symbolizes the beauty of balance and the power of adaptability—a reminder that true strength lies not in resistance, but in surrender; not in control, but in flow. It is a testament to the resilience of the human spirit and the infinite capacity for growth and transformation that lives within each of us.

magical spell: manifesting abundance and opportunity:

I am flexible
and adaptable.
I embrace change
with ease
and maintain balance
in all aspects of my life.

materials needed:

- White candle
- Lavender essential oil
- Amethyst crystal
- Pen and paper

instructions:

- Begin by anointing the white candle with lavender essential oil, infusing it with the energy of balance and harmony.
- Light the candle and take several deep breaths, allowing yourself to relax and center your energy.
- Hold the amethyst crystal in your hand, connecting with its calming and balancing properties.
- Sit in a comfortable position and reflect on areas of your life where you need to find balance and harmony.
- With the pen and paper, write down the tasks, responsibilities, and commitments that are currently weighing on your mind.
- Visualize yourself juggling these responsibilities with ease and grace, maintaining balance and harmony in all areas of your life.
- Hold the paper between your palms and recite the affirmation:

"I am flexible and adaptable. I embrace change with ease and maintain balance in all aspects of my life."

- Place the paper under the candle and allow it to burn, releasing your intentions into the universe.
- Sit quietly for a few moments, feeling the energy of the spell surrounding you with a sense of peace, stability, and equilibrium.

The Two of Pentacles represents the need for balance, flexibility, and adaptability in the face of life's challenges. It signifies juggling multiple responsibilities, managing priorities, and finding harmony amidst change. In tarot readings, the 2 of Pentacles encourages you to embrace the ebbs and flows of life, prioritize your commitments, and maintain equilibrium in both your external and internal worlds.

questions to ask yourself

1. What areas of my life am I currently juggling or balancing?
2. How can I maintain harmony and equilibrium amidst competing priorities?
3. What adjustments or adaptations do I need to make to manage my responsibilities more effectively?
4. Am I staying flexible and adaptable in the face of change and uncertainty?
5. How can I find joy and fulfillment in the process of multitasking and managing my commitments?
6. What systems or routines can I implement to streamline my workflow and reduce stress?
7. How can I stay grounded and centered amidst the ebb and flow of life's demands?
8. What areas of my life require more attention or investment to maintain balance?
9. How can I trust my intuition to guide me in prioritizing my tasks and obligations?
10. What lessons can I learn from experiences of finding balance and navigating transitions?

three of pentacles

...

"I am the embodiment of teamwork and dedication, urging you to harness the power of collective effort to achieve success." Three of Pentacles.

Answer: Yes

Key Words and Phrases:
Success
Completing goals
Teamwork
Implementing
Skill
Cooperation
Learning
Study
Work
Growth
Following dreams
Collaboration
Craftsmanship
Unique talents
Reaching goals
Achievement
On the right path
Advice
Value yourself
Value others

SYMBOLS:

- The figure juggling two pentacles symbolizes the balancing act of managing multiple responsibilities and priorities. The figure's ability to juggle reflects the need for adaptability and flexibility in navigating life's challenges.
- The infinity symbol represents the cyclical nature of life and the interconnectedness of all things. It symbolizes the eternal dance of balance and harmony, you that change is inevitable, but equilibrium is achievable.
- The sea depicts the turbulent waters of life's journey. It symbolizes the ever-changing nature of circumstances and the need to stay grounded amidst life's ups and downs.
- The ships signify the voyages of life and the opportunities and challenges that come with them. They represent the need to navigate through turbulent waters with grace and resilience.

In the bustling workshop of life's endeavors, The Fool encounters the Three of Pentacles, a symbol of collaboration, craftsmanship, and the rewards of hard work. As The Fool gazes upon the scene depicted in the card, they witness three figures working together to build a magnificent structure—a testament to the power of teamwork and dedication.

The Three of Pentacles represents the importance of cooperation and synergy in achieving shared goals and aspirations. It serves as a reminder that by combining our talents, skills, and resources with others, we can accomplish far more than we ever could alone.

In the story of the Three of Pentacles, The Fool learns the value of working harmoniously with others towards a common purpose. They see the figures in the card as exemplars of dedication and commitment—individuals who understand that true success is not measured by personal achievements alone, but by the collective impact we make on the world around us.

Reflecting on the pentacles, The Fool understands that the ability to collaborate and communicate effectively is what distinguishes us. They understand that by fostering an environment of mutual respect and cooperation, we can harness the full potential of our collective creativity and ingenuity.

The Three of Pentacles encourages The Fool to seek opportunities for collaboration and partnership in their own life. It is a reminder that by pooling our talents and resources with others, we can overcome obstacles, solve problems, and achieve greatness beyond measure.

When the Three of Pentacles appears in a tarot reading, it serves as a gentle nudge to embrace the spirit of teamwork. It suggests that The Fool may need to look beyond their own interests and ego and consider how their actions impact those around them. It encourages them to be open to feedback, constructive criticism, and new ideas, knowing that true growth and innovation arise from a diversity of perspectives.

The Three of Pentacles invites The Fool to celebrate their achievements and successes, no matter how small or seemingly insignificant they may be. It is a reminder that every contribution matters, and that by working together towards a common goal, we can create something truly extraordinary that will stand the test of time.

At its core, the Three of Pentacles symbolizes the beauty of the power of collective effort—a reminder that when we come together with a shared sense of purpose and vision, there is nothing we cannot accomplish.

magical spell: cultivating skills and collaboration:

I embrace collaboration,
mastery,
and the pursuit of excellence.
I am open
to learning from others
and sharing my unique gifts
with the world.

materials needed:

- Green candle
- Patchouli incense
- Rosemary herb
- Pen and paper

instructions:

- Begin by lighting the green candle and the patchouli incense, creating a sacred space for focus, clarity, and collaboration.
- Sprinkle a pinch of rosemary herb on the burning incense, infusing the space with the energy of mastery and skillful collaboration.

- Sit in a comfortable position and take several deep breaths, allowing yourself to center and ground your energy.
- With the pen and paper, write down your goals and aspirations related to personal growth, mastery of skills, and collaborative endeavors.
- Visualize yourself surrounded by a radiant green light, symbolizing the energy of growth, abundance, and success.
- Hold the paper between your palms and recite the affirmation:

"I embrace collaboration, mastery, and the pursuit of excellence. I am open to learning from others and sharing my unique gifts with the world."

- Place the paper under the candle and allow it to burn, releasing your intentions into the universe.
- Sit quietly for a few moments, feeling the energy of the spell empowering you to cultivate your skills, forge meaningful connections, and achieve your goals with the support of others.

The 2 of Pentacles represents the need for balance, flexibility, and adaptability in the face of life's challenges. It signifies juggling multiple responsibilities, managing priorities, and finding harmony amidst change. In tarot readings, the 2 of Pentacles encourages you to embrace the ebbs and flows of life, prioritize your commitments, and maintain equilibrium in both your external and internal worlds.

questions to ask yourself

1. What collaborative projects or endeavors am I currently involved in?

2. How can I contribute my skills and expertise to the greater good of the team or community?
3. What opportunities for learning and growth are available to me through collaboration?
4. Am I open to receiving feedback and constructive criticism from others?
5. How can I cultivate a spirit of cooperation and mutual respect in my interactions?
6. What role am I playing in contributing to the success of the group or collective effort?
7. How can I harness the collective wisdom and talents of those around me to achieve our goals?
8. What systems or structures can we put in place to enhance productivity and efficiency?
9. How can I celebrate and acknowledge the contributions of others to our shared accomplishments?
10. What lessons can I learn from experiences of working collaboratively towards a common goal?

four of pentacles

. . .

"While it is important to safeguard your resources, be mindful not to cling too tightly to that which you possess." Four of Pentacles.

Answer: Yes

Key Words and Phrases:
Ownership
Solid finance
Attachment
Financial goals
Possessing
Overly cautious
Inheritance
True values
Scarcity
Get it in writing
Cautious
Saving Money
Controlling
Greed

SYMBOLS:

- The figure holding pentacles typically depicted with a figure holding onto four pentacles, tightly grasping them to their chest or head. This symbolizes a strong attachment to material possessions, a desire for control, and a fear of losing what one has acquired.
- The crown representing authority, power, and status. It signifies the desire for recognition, social standing, and the need to maintain one's position or reputation in society.
- The cityscape often shown in the background, symbolizing the external world and the structures of society. It represents stability, order, and the established norms and values that govern everyday life.
- The feet sometimes depicted with the figure standing on uneven ground, signifying the need for balance and stability in both the material and spiritual realms.

In the quiet chambers of material stability and possession, The Fool encounters the Four of Pentacles, a card that speaks of security, control, and the fear of loss. The Fool gazes upon the figure clutching tightly onto four pentacles, unwilling to let go or share their wealth with others.

The Four of Pentacles symbolizes a mindset of scarcity and a reluctance to change or take risks. It reflects a fear of losing what one has acquired and a tendency to hoard resources out of a sense of insecurity or distrust. The figure on the card embodies the desire for control and stability, even at the expense of personal growth or emotional fulfillment.

In the story of the Four of Pentacles, The Fool learns the dangers of clinging too tightly to material possessions and the limitations of a life governed by fear and greed. They see the figure in the card as a prisoner of their own making, trapped by their attachment to worldly wealth and unable to experience true abundance and freedom.

As The Fool contemplates the symbolism of the pentacles, they recognize that true prosperity is not measured by the quantity of possessions one accumulates, but by the richness of one's relationships, experiences, and connections with others. They understand that the more we try to control and possess, the more we become enslaved by our own desires and insecurities.

The Four of Pentacles challenges The Fool to examine their relationship with money, possessions, and material success. It encourages them to let go of their fear of loss and embrace a mindset of abundance and generosity. It reminds them that true wealth lies not in what we own, but in what we give and share with others.

When the Four of Pentacles appears in a tarot reading, it serves as a warning against the dangers of greed, possessiveness, and a scarcity mindset. It suggests that you may be holding on too tightly to your resources or clinging to outdated beliefs and patterns of behavior that no longer serve you.

The Four of Pentacles invites The Fool to release their grip on the past and open themselves up to new opportunities and experiences. It encourages them to trust in the universe's abundance and to embrace a mindset of gratitude, generosity, and faith in the future.

The Four of Pentacles is a reminder that true wealth is not found in the accumulation of possessions, but in the richness of life itself—the love, joy, and connection we share with others, and the freedom that comes from letting go of our attachments and embracing the flow of life's ever-changing currents.

magical spell: cultivating abundance and generosity: i release fear

I release fear
and attachment,
embracing the flow of abundance
and sharing with an open heart.

materials needed:

- Green candle
- Patchouli incense
- Rose quartz crystal
- Pen and paper

instructions:

- Begin by lighting the green candle and the patchouli incense, creating a sacred space for abundance, generosity, and balance.
- Hold the rose quartz crystal in your hand, allowing its gentle energy to fill you with love, compassion, and gratitude.
- Sit in a comfortable position and take several deep breaths, allowing yourself to connect with the energy of the earth and the universe.
- With the pen and paper, write down any fears, attachments, or feelings of lack related to material possessions or security.
- Visualize yourself surrounded by a radiant green light, symbolizing the energy of abundance, prosperity, and generosity.
- Hold the paper between your palms and recite the affirmation:

"I release fear and attachment, embracing the flow of abundance and sharing with an open heart."

- Place the paper under the candle and allow it to burn, releasing any limiting beliefs or attachments into the universe.
- Hold the rose quartz crystal to your heart and envision yourself surrounded by a bubble of love and abundance, attracting blessings and opportunities into your life.
- Sit quietly for a few moments, feeling the energy of the spell empowering you to cultivate a spirit of generosity, abundance, and harmony with the universe.

questions to ask yourself

1. What fears or insecurities are driving my desire for stability and security?
2. How can I find a healthy balance between saving and spending money?
3. What possessions or resources am I holding onto tightly out of fear of scarcity?
4. Am I allowing my attachment to material wealth to hinder my spiritual or emotional growth?
5. How can I cultivate a sense of abundance and generosity in my life?
6. What areas of my life am I neglecting in my pursuit of financial security?
7. How can I release my grip on control and trust in the flow of abundance?
8. What opportunities for growth and expansion am I blocking by holding onto the past?

9. How can I redefine my relationship with money and possessions in a more empowering way?
10. What steps can I take to cultivate a sense of inner wealth and abundance?

five of pentacles
...
"Remember that even in the darkest of times, there is light to be found." Five of Pentacles.

Answer: No

Key Words and Phrases
Lack
Loss
Being left out in the cold
Hardship
Difficulties
Worry
Poverty
Depression
Struggle
Isolation
No Faith
Health problems
Cold
Support
Alone

SYMBOLS:

- Two figures outside the church depict individuals who appear impoverished and isolated, symbolizing the experience of exclusion, hardship, and feeling marginalized. They represent the struggles faced in feeling disconnected peers, family, or community support networks.
- The church stands as a symbol of sanctuary, spiritual refuge, and potential assistance. It represents the support systems and resources that may be available to those in need.
- Snow represents the cold, harsh conditions of adversity and struggle. It symbolizes the challenges and obstacles that one may encounter on their journey, including financial difficulties, social isolation, or emotional turmoil.
- Broken stained glass window signifies the shattered hopes and dreams of the individuals depicted. It represents the loss, disappointment, and feelings of inadequacy.

In the desolate streets of hardship and adversity, The Fool encounters the Five of Pentacles, a card that speaks of challenges, scarcity, and the need for perseverance. As The Fool gazes upon the image depicted in the card, they see two figures walking through the cold and snowy night, seemingly destitute and in need of help.

The Five of Pentacles symbolizes a time of financial hardship, physical illness, or emotional struggle. It represents a period of feeling left out in the cold, abandoned, or neglected by others. The figures in the card embody the sense of isolation and despair that can accompany times of loss and difficulty.

In the story of the Five of Pentacles, The Fool learns the importance of resilience, resourcefulness, and reaching out for support during times of need. They see the figures in the card as survivors, bravely facing their challenges and refusing to give up hope, despite their circumstances.

As The Fool contemplates the symbolism of the pentacles, they recognize that adversity is a natural part of life and that even in the darkest of times, there is always light to be found. They understand that true wealth is not measured by material possessions alone but by the strength of one's spirit and the depth of one's relationships with others.

The Five of Pentacles challenges The Fool to confront their fears and insecurities and to seek help and guidance when needed. It reminds them that they are not alone in their struggles and that there are people who care about them and are willing to offer support and assistance.

When the Five of Pentacles appears in a tarot reading, it serves as a reminder to The Fool to stay strong and resilient in the face of adversity. It suggests that they may be going through a difficult period in their lives but that there is always hope for a brighter future.

The Five of Pentacles invites The Fool to focus on what they have rather than what they lack and to cultivate an attitude of gratitude and abundance. It encourages them to reach out to others for help and to remember that no matter how difficult things may seem, they have the inner strength and resilience to overcome any challenge.

At its core, the Five of Pentacles reminds The Fool that adversity is temporary. The lessons learned, and the strength gained from overcoming it are enduring. It encourages them to embrace their struggles as opportunities for growth and transformation and to trust in the power of resilience and perseverance to see them through even the darkest of times.

magical spell: manifesting abundance and support:

I release fear and scarcity,
embracing abundance
and support
in all areas of my life.
I am worthy of love,
prosperity, and connection.

materials needed:

- Green candle
- Cinnamon incense
- Basil herb
- Pen and paper

instructions:

- Begin by lighting the green candle and the cinnamon incense, creating a sacred space for manifestation and abundance.
- Sprinkle a pinch of basil herb on the burning incense, infusing the space with the energy of prosperity and growth.
- Sit in a comfortable position and take several deep breaths, allowing yourself to center and ground your energy.
- With the pen and paper, write down your financial concerns, emotional struggles, or areas where you feel unsupported or excluded.
- Visualize yourself surrounded by a warm, comforting light, symbolizing the abundance and support that you seek.
- Hold the paper between your palms and recite the affirmation:

"I release fear and scarcity, embracing abundance and support in all areas of my life. I am worthy of love, prosperity, and connection."

- Place the paper under the candle and allow it to burn, releasing your intentions into the universe.
- Sit quietly for a few moments, feeling the energy of the spell empowering you to overcome adversity, cultivate resilience, and attract the resources and support you need to thrive.

The Five of Pentacles represents financial hardship, scarcity, and feeling left out in the cold. It often signifies times of struggle, adversity, and feeling disconnected from material and emotional support systems. In tarot readings, the Five of Pentacles urges you to acknowledge your challenges, seek assistance when needed, and cultivate resilience in the face of adversity.

questions to ask yourself

1. What feelings of lack or scarcity am I experiencing in my life?
2. How can I shift my perspective from scarcity to abundance?
3. What support systems or resources am I neglecting to tap into?
4. Am I isolating myself or shutting out help from others due to pride or shame?
5. How can I reach out for assistance and support during challenging times?
6. What lessons can I learn from experiences of financial hardship or loss?
7. How can I cultivate resilience and resourcefulness in the face of adversity?

8. What opportunities for growth and transformation are hidden within my struggles?
9. How can I practice gratitude and appreciation for the blessings that are present in my life?
10. What steps can I take to rebuild my sense of security and stability?

six of pentacles

. . .

"I am the symbol of abundance shared with those in need, urging you to cultivate a spirit of generosity and compassion," Six of Pentacles.

Answer: Yes

Key Words and Phrases:
Helping others
Generosity
Sharing
Charity
Managing money
Sharing Talents
Gifts
Compassion
Getting paid
Fairness
Grateful
Prosperity
Adding Value
Promotion

SYMBOLS:

1. Figure with scales is the central figure in the card, representing balance and fairness in distributing resources. This symbolizes the importance of giving and receiving in equitable measures.
2. Coins the coins being handed out by the central figure symbolize material wealth, abundance, and generosity. They represent the resources and assistance that individuals may offer to others in need.
3. Beggar figures in some variations of the card, there may be one or more beggar figures receiving coins from the central figure. These figures represent those who are in need of assistance and support, highlighting the dynamic of charity and compassion.
4. The overall composition of the card suggests a balance between giving and receiving. It emphasizes the idea that generosity and kindness can lead to abundance and fulfillment for both the giver and the receiver.

In the bustling marketplace of generosity and reciprocity, The Fool encounters the Six of Pentacles, a card that speaks of balance, charity, and the importance of giving and receiving. The Fool observes, the figure distributing coins to those in need, symbolizing acts of kindness, compassion, and support.

The Six of Pentacles symbolizes a time of abundance and generosity, where resources are shared freely and equitably among all members of the community. It represents the principles of charity, philanthropy, and the belief that wealth should be used to uplift and empower others.

In the story of the Six of Pentacles, The Fool learns the importance of giving back to others and supporting those less fortunate than themselves. They see the figure in the card as a symbol of compassion and altruism, demonstrating the power of generosity to transform lives and build stronger, more resilient communities.

The Fool contemplates the symbolism of the pentacles. They recognize that true wealth is not solely measured by material possessions, but by the richness of one's relationships and the impact one makes on the lives of others. They understand that the act of giving is not only a selfless gesture but also a powerful expression of empathy, compassion, and solidarity with those in need.

The Six of Pentacles challenges The Fool to examine their own attitudes towards wealth, abundance, and generosity. It encourages them to cultivate a spirit of generosity and to seek opportunities to give back to their community in meaningful and impactful ways.

When the Six of Pentacles appears in a tarot reading, it serves as a reminder to The Fool to be mindful of the ways in which they share their resources with others. It suggests that they may be in a position of abundance and have the ability to make a positive difference in the lives of those around them.

The Six of Pentacles invites The Fool to consider how they can use their time, talents, and resources to support others and contribute to the greater good. It encourages them to look for opportunities to give back to their community and to find fulfillment and purpose in acts of kindness, compassion, and service.

At its core, the Six of Pentacles reminds The Fool that true wealth lies not in the accumulation of possessions but in the quality of one's relationships and the impact one has on the world. It encourages them to embrace the principles of generosity, compassion, and altruism and to strive to make a positive difference in the lives of others, one act of kindness at a time.

magical spell: cultivating generosity and abundance:

With this salt,
I bless my intentions.
May my actions
be guided by kindness
and generosity.

materials needed:

- Green candle
- Small bowl of salt
- Pen and paper

instructions:

- Light the green candle, focusing on its flame and envisioning a sense of abundance and generosity surrounding you.
- Take a piece of paper and write down one act of kindness or generosity that you would like to manifest in your life.
- Fold the paper and hold it in your hands, visualizing the positive impact of your actions spreading out into the world.
- Place the folded paper in the bowl of salt, symbolizing purification and grounding of your intentions.
- Sprinkle a pinch of salt over the paper while reciting the affirmation:

"With this salt, I bless my intentions. May my actions be guided by kindness and generosity."

- Allow the candle to burn down completely, anchoring your intentions into the universe.
- Dispose of the paper and salt remains in nature, acknowledging the cycle of giving and receiving.

The Six of Pentacles in the Tarot deck symbolizes generosity, charity, and the balance of giving and receiving. The card typically depicts a figure, often interpreted as a wealthy individual or benefactor, distributing coins to those in need. It signifies acts of kindness, compassion, and the importance of sharing resources with others, whether material or emotional.

questions to ask yourself

1. In what ways am I giving and receiving abundance in my life?
2. How can I cultivate a spirit of generosity and compassion towards others?
3. What opportunities do I have to share my wealth, time, or resources with those in need?
4. Am I giving from a place of genuine care and concern, or out of obligation?
5. How can I create a sense of balance and fairness in my exchanges with others?
6. What lessons can I learn from experiences of giving and receiving with an open heart?
7. How can I overcome feelings of guilt or unworthiness around receiving help or support?
8. What impact am I having on the lives of those I choose to help or support?

9. How can I cultivate a mindset of abundance and trust in the flow of prosperity?
10. What steps can I take to create a more equitable and compassionate world?

seven of pentacles

. . .

"With patience and persistence, you will reap the rewards of your hard work and dedication." Seven of Pentacles.

Answer: Yes

Key Words and Phrases:
Growth over time
Hard work
Patience
Hard work pays off
Investment
Harvest
Reflecting on growth
Growth
Progress
Diligence
Change
Waiting for results

SYMBOLS:

1. The central figure in the card is usually depicted tending to a garden or vineyard. This symbolizes the effort and investment put into a project or goal. The garden represents the seeds of potential and the work required for them to flourish.
2. The fruits or pentacles on the vine represent the tangible results of the efforts made. They symbolize abundance, prosperity, and the rewards that come from patience and perseverance.
3. The posture of the figure, often gazing thoughtfully at the garden, reflects the need for introspection and evaluation. It suggests taking stock of progress, reflecting on achievements, and considering future strategies.
4. The overall tone of the card conveys the importance of patience and allowing things to unfold naturally. It reminds us that growth and success take time and require nurturing and dedication.

In the quiet fields of patience and perseverance, The Fool encounters the Seven of Pentacles, a card that speaks of reflection, assessment, and the anticipation of growth. The Fool observes a farmer gazing thoughtfully at the pentacles hanging from the vine, symbolizing the fruits of his labor and the potential for future abundance.

The Seven of Pentacles symbolizes a period of waiting and evaluation, where one takes stock of their progress and considers the next steps on their journey toward their goals. It represents the importance of patience, diligence, and foresight in achieving long-term success and prosperity.

In the story of the Seven of Pentacles, The Fool learns the value of taking a step back and reflecting on their efforts and accomplishments. They see the farmer as a symbol of resilience and determination, tirelessly tending to his crops and trusting in the natural rhythms of growth and harvest.

As The Fool contemplates the symbolism of the pentacles, they come to the realization that they can achieve genuine success by putting in sustained effort and dedication over time. They understand that the journey toward their goals may be long and arduous, but it is ultimately rewarding and fulfilling.

The Seven of Pentacles challenges The Fool to assess their current situation honestly and objectively. It encourages them to ask themselves whether they are satisfied with their progress thus far and whether they are on the right path toward realizing their dreams and aspirations.

When the Seven of Pentacles appears in a tarot reading, it serves as a reminder to The Fool to be patient and trust in the process of growth and transformation. It suggests that they may be at a crossroads in their journey, where they need to pause and reflect on their priorities and objectives before moving forward.

The Seven of Pentacles invites The Fool to consider what sacrifices they are willing to make in order to achieve their goals and whether they are prepared to endure the inevitable setbacks and challenges along the way. It encourages them to remain focused and determined in the pursuit of their dreams, knowing that their efforts will eventually bear fruit.

At its core, the Seven of Pentacles reminds The Fool that success is not measured solely by external rewards or material wealth but by the personal growth and fulfillment that come from pursuing one's passions and aspirations with courage, determination, and perseverance. It encourages them to trust in the journey and to believe in the power of their own resilience and resilience.

Magical Spell: Spell for Cultivating Patience and Growth
As this plant grows,
so too shall my dreams manifest.
I trust in the process and embrace patience.

materials needed:

- Green candle
- Piece of paper
- Pen
- Small plant or seeds

instructions:

1. Light the green candle, focusing on its flame and centering your energy.
2. Take the piece of paper and write down one goal or aspiration that you are working towards but feeling impatient about.
3. Hold the paper in your hands and visualize the growth and progress you wish to see in this area of your life.
4. Place the paper under the small plant or seeds, symbolizing the nurturing of your goals.
5. Whisper your intentions to the plant or seeds, expressing your desire for patience and steady growth.
6. Water the plant or seeds while reciting the affirmation:

"As this plant grows, so too shall my dreams manifest. I trust in the process and embrace patience."

1. Keep the plant in a visible place as a reminder of your commitment to your goals and the power of patience.

The Seven of Pentacles in the Tarot deck represents patience, evaluation, and the anticipation of future growth. It depicts a figure, often a farmer, gazing upon a vineyard or garden where the fruits of labor are beginning to show. This card signifies the need to assess progress, make adjustments if necessary, and trust in the process of growth and development.

questions to ask yourself

1. What investments of time, energy, or resources am I currently evaluating?
2. How can I assess the progress and growth of my long-term endeavors?
3. What areas of my life require patience and perseverance as I wait for results?
4. Am I trusting in the process and staying committed to my goals despite setbacks?
5. How can I adjust my strategies or approaches to achieve greater success?
6. What lessons can I learn from experiences of delayed gratification and hard work?
7. How can I cultivate a sense of trust and faith in the unfolding of my journey?
8. What signs of progress or growth am I currently witnessing in my life?
9. How can I celebrate small victories and milestones along the way?
10. What steps can I take to ensure that my efforts continue to bear fruit in the future?

eight of pentacles

...

"I am the symbol of diligence and continuous improvement, urging you to hone your skills and strive for excellence in your endeavors." Eight of Pentacles.

Answer: Yes

Lorelai Hamilton

Key Words and Phrases:
Apprentice
Self-Reliance
Training
Abundance
Craftsmanship
Prosperity
Mastery
Studying
Skill
Self-improvement
Independence
Money management
Perfection
Abundance
Self-employment
Luxury
Concentration

SYMBOLS:

1. The central figure in the card is often depicted as a craftsman or apprentice, diligently focusing on their work. This symbolizes the commitment to learning, practicing, and perfecting one's craft or skills.
2. The pentacles surrounding the figure represent the tangible results of the person's labor. They symbolize material wealth, prosperity, and the rewards that come from dedicated effort and skillful execution.
3. The posture of the figure, typically immersed in their task with a focused expression, reflects the importance of concentration and attention to detail. It suggests that true mastery comes from diligent practice and unwavering focus.
4. The repetitive nature of the task being performed emphasizes the need for consistency and discipline in pursuing one's goals. It reminds us that mastery is achieved through dedication and perseverance over time.

In the rhythmic cadence of craft and diligence, The Fool encounters the Eight of Pentacles, a card resonating with dedication, skill mastery, and the commitment to craftsmanship. As The Fool peers into the card's imagery, they witness a figure engrossed in their work, meticulously honing their craft with precision and care.

The Eight of Pentacles symbolizes the relentless pursuit of excellence, the journey of refinement, and the satisfaction found in the pursuit of one's passions. The figure diligently hammers away at the pentacles, each stroke a testament to their unwavering focus and determination to perfect their skills.

In the story of the Eight of Pentacles, The Fool learns the importance of dedication and the fulfillment that arises from investing time and energy into one's craft. They observe the figure as a symbol of commitment and perseverance, embodying the idea that true mastery is achieved through consistent effort and continuous improvement.

By reflecting on the pentacles, The Fool learns that genuine satisfaction stems from embracing the journey, not just the end result. They acknowledge that while achieving success can bring satisfaction, the true delight comes from the path of growth and discovering oneself.

The Eight of Pentacles challenges The Fool to immerse themselves fully in their endeavors and to embrace the path of learning and refinement. It encourages them to set aside distractions and to focus wholeheartedly on cultivating their skills and talents.

When the Eight of Pentacles appears in a tarot reading, it serves as a reminder to The Fool to embrace their inner craftsman and to approach their tasks with diligence and dedication. It suggests that they may be at a stage where they need to devote themselves wholeheartedly to their goals and aspirations, trusting that their efforts will lead to mastery and success.

The Eight of Pentacles invites The Fool to adopt a mindset of continuous growth and improvement, knowing that each step they take brings them closer to excellence. It encourages them to take pride in their work and to find fulfillment in the process of creation, regardless of external recognition or reward.

The Eight of Pentacles is a reminder that true mastery is not achieved overnight, but is the result of persistent effort and unwavering commitment. It encourages you to embrace the journey of self-discovery and to revel in the satisfaction that comes from pursuing your passions with purpose and dedication.

Magical Spell: Spell for Enhancing Skills and Knowledge

materials needed:

- Yellow candle
- Piece of paper
- Pen
- Small object representing the skill or knowledge you wish to enhance (e.g., paintbrush, musical instrument, book)

instructions:

- Light the yellow candle, focusing on its warm glow and the energy it emits.
- Take the piece of paper and write down the skill or knowledge you wish to enhance or master.
- Hold the paper in your hands and visualize yourself excelling in this area, feeling confident and empowered.
- Place the small object representing your skill or knowledge on the piece of paper, symbolizing your commitment to its development.
- Close your eyes and envision yourself practicing and honing your abilities with passion and dedication.
- Whisper your intentions to the object, expressing your desire to grow and improve in this area.
- Meditate on the flame of the candle, visualizing it infusing you with the energy and motivation to pursue your goals.

- Keep the object in a special place where you can see it daily, serving as a reminder of your dedication and commitment to mastery.

The Eight of Pentacles in the Tarot deck represents dedication, craftsmanship, and the pursuit of mastery in one's skills or endeavors. It portrays a person diligently working on a task, honing their abilities, and striving for excellence. This card signifies the importance of hard work, attention to detail, and continuous improvement.

questions to ask yourself

1. What skills or talents am I honing and developing in my life?
2. How can I approach my work with diligence, focus, and dedication?
3. What opportunities for growth and improvement am I actively pursuing?
4. Am I committed to mastering my craft and striving for excellence?
5. How can I find joy and fulfillment in the process of learning and skill-building?
6. What resources or mentors can I seek out to support my growth and development?
7. How can I maintain a sense of discipline and consistency in my practice?
8. What projects or endeavors am I investing my time and energy into?
9. How can I overcome perfectionism and embrace the journey of lifelong learning?

10. What steps can I take to turn my passions and interests into tangible achievements?

nine of pentacles

. . .

"I am the symbol of financial independence and material well-being, inviting you to savor the fruits of your labor," Nine of Pentacles.

Answer: Yes

Lorelai Hamilton

Key Words and Phrases:
Abundant
Self Sufficient
Independence
Seeing your worth
Financial Independence
Mastery
Success
Prosperity
Enjoying your Success
Fortune
Security
Enjoying Nature

SYMBOLS:

1. The central figure in the card stands amidst a bountiful garden, adorned with ripe fruits and blooming flowers. This symbolizes the rewards of disciplined effort and the ability to create a comfortable and fulfilling life.
2. Often depicted in the card, birds symbolize freedom, grace, and the harmony between the human and natural worlds. They represent the sense of peace and contentment that comes from being in alignment with oneself and one's surroundings.
3. The opulent surroundings in the card convey a sense of luxury and leisure. It represents the ability to enjoy life's pleasures and indulge in the finer things without relying on others for support.
4. The figure in the card exudes confidence and self-assurance, reflecting a strong sense of autonomy and independence. It suggests that the individual has worked hard to create a life of stability and security on their own terms.

In the lush gardens of abundance and prosperity, The Fool encounters the Nine of Pentacles, a card that whispers of independence, self-reliance, and the rewards of hard work. As The Fool gazes upon the image depicted in the card, they see a woman standing amidst a bountiful vineyard, surrounded by ripe grapes and luscious foliage. She exudes an air of contentment and satisfaction, her demeanor reflecting the fruits of her labor and the success she has achieved through her efforts.

The Nine of Pentacles symbolizes financial stability, material well-being, and the enjoyment of life's luxuries. It represents the culmination of one's endeavors and the attainment of a comfortable and secure lifestyle. The woman in the card serves as a reminder to The Fool that through diligence, discipline, and determination, they too can create a life of abundance and fulfillment.

In the story of the Nine of Pentacles, The Fool learns the importance of self-reliance and the satisfaction that comes from achieving one's goals and aspirations through their own efforts. They see the woman as a symbol of independence and empowerment, embodying the idea that true wealth is not just about material possessions but also about the freedom to live life on one's own terms.

As The Fool reflects on the symbolism of the pentacles, they recognize that true prosperity comes from within, rooted in a sense of self-worth, confidence, and inner fulfillment. They understand that while external success and financial security are important, they are ultimately meaningless without a sense of purpose and contentment that comes from living a life aligned with one's values and aspirations.

The Nine of Pentacles challenges The Fool to take ownership of their life and to cultivate a sense of self-reliance and independence. It encourages them to set ambitious goals for themselves and to pursue their dreams with passion, perseverance, and determination. It reminds them they have the power to shape their own destiny and to create the life they desire through their thoughts, actions, and choices.

When the Nine of Pentacles appears in a tarot reading, it serves as a reminder to The Fool to take pride in their achievements and to savor the rewards of their labor. It suggests that they may be at a stage in their journey where they can enjoy the fruits of their efforts and indulge in the pleasures and luxuries that life has to offer.

The Nine of Pentacles invites The Fool to embrace a mindset of abundance and gratitude, knowing that they have everything they need to create a life of prosperity and fulfillment. It encourages them to trust in their abilities and to have faith in the universe to provide for their needs as they continue on their journey of self-discovery and personal growth.

At its core, the Nine of Pentacles reminds The Fool that true wealth is not measured by the size of one's bank account but by the richness of their experiences, the depth of their relationships, and the sense of joy and fulfillment that comes from living a life of purpose and passion. It encourages them to celebrate their successes and to embrace the abundance that surrounds them, knowing that they are worthy of all the blessings that life has to offer.

magical spell: spell for cultivating self-sufficiency:

I am capable,
I am strong,
I am self-sufficient.
I trust in my abilities
to create the life I desire.

materials needed:

- Green candle
- Piece of paper
- Pen
- A small mirror

instructions:

- Light the green candle, focusing on its flame and the energy it emits.
- Take the piece of paper and write down one aspect of your life where you wish to cultivate greater independence and self-sufficiency.
- Hold the paper in your hands and visualize yourself embodying the qualities of self-reliance and empowerment.
- Place the paper in front of the small mirror, symbolizing self-reflection and inner strength.
- Gaze into the mirror and affirm aloud:

"I am capable, I am strong, I am self-sufficient. I trust in my abilities to create the life I desire."

- Allow the candle to burn while you meditate on your intentions, visualizing yourself stepping into a life of abundance and autonomy.
- When ready, extinguish the candle, carrying the energy of your intentions with you as you move forward.

The Nine of Pentacles in the Tarot deck represents self-sufficiency, independence, and enjoying the fruits of one's labor. It depicts a figure in a lush garden surrounded by abundance and luxury. This card signifies personal achievement, financial security, and the satisfaction that comes from hard work and dedication.

questions to ask yourself

1. How am I enjoying the fruits of my labor and achievements?
2. What luxuries or comforts am I treating myself to as a reward for my hard work?
3. How can I cultivate a deeper appreciation for the abundance in my life?
4. Am I embracing a sense of independence and self-sufficiency in my endeavors?
5. How can I create a harmonious and nurturing environment for myself?
6. What boundaries do I need to set to protect my time, energy, and resources?
7. How can I use my financial stability to pursue my passions and interests?

8. What areas of my life am I ready to invest in for long-term growth and prosperity?
9. How can I maintain a healthy balance between work and leisure?
10. What steps can I take to continue cultivating a sense of abundance and security?

ten of pentacles

. . .

"As you enjoy the comforts of wealth and abundance, remember to preserve and protect your legacy for future generations," Ten of Pentacles.

Answer: Yes

Lorelai Hamilton

Key Words and Phrases:
Tradition
Success
Wealth
Family connection
Comfort
Stability
Safety
Ancestry
Financial security
Family
Financial gains
Inheritance
Community
Legacy
Goals reached

SYMBOLS:

1. The card often depicts a multigenerational family gathered together in a prosperous setting. This symbolizes the strength and stability that come from strong family ties and supportive relationships.
2. The grand buildings and structures in the card represent the material wealth and security that the family has built over time. They symbolize the tangible assets and resources that contribute to the family's prosperity and success.
3. The presence of pentacles and other symbols of wealth throughout the card signifies financial abundance and material well-being. It suggests that the family has worked hard to accumulate assets and establish a comfortable lifestyle for themselves and future generations.
4. The card exudes a sense of tradition and heritage, emphasizing the importance of honoring family values and passing down wisdom from one generation to the next. It encourages individuals to connect with their roots and uphold the traditions that have shaped their family history.

In the bustling streets of a prosperous city, The Fool encounters the Ten of Pentacles, a card that speaks of legacy, heritage, and the culmination of familial wealth and stability. As The Fool observes the scene depicted in the card, they see a family gathered together in front of a grand estate, surrounded by symbols of affluence and security. The elders of the family sit upon thrones, adorned with symbols of their status and accomplishments, while the younger generations play and frolic at their feet, basking in the warmth of familial bonds and tradition.

The Ten of Pentacles symbolizes the pinnacle of material success and the fulfillment of generational aspirations. It represents the establishment of a lasting legacy and the passing down of wealth, wisdom, and tradition from one generation to the next. The scene before The Fool evokes a sense of belonging, security, and continuity, highlighting the importance of family, heritage, and community in the journey of life.

In the story of the Ten of Pentacles, The Fool learns the value of roots, heritage, and the bonds that tie generations together. They witness the family in the card as a testament to the enduring power of tradition and the richness of shared history. They see how the wealth accumulated by past generations serves as a foundation upon which future aspirations can be built, providing a sense of security and stability in an ever-changing world.

As The Fool reflects on the symbolism of the pentacles, they recognize that true wealth extends beyond material possessions and encompasses the intangible treasures of love, connection, and shared experience. They understand that while financial prosperity is important, it is ultimately the relationships we cultivate and the memories we create that give meaning and purpose to our lives.

The Ten of Pentacles challenges The Fool to honor their roots, embrace their heritage, and celebrate the contributions of those who came before them. It encourages them to take pride in their family traditions and to cherish the bonds of kinship that connect them to their ancestors and descendants alike.

When the Ten of Pentacles appears in a tarot reading, it serves as a reminder to The Fool to appreciate the abundance that surrounds them and to recognize the wealth of blessings they have inherited from their familial lineage. It suggests that they may be at a stage in their journey where they can draw upon the wisdom and support of their family and community as they pursue their own dreams and aspirations.

The Ten of Pentacles invites The Fool to embrace a mindset of gratitude, knowing that they are part of a rich culmination of history and tradition that extends far beyond their individual experiences. It encourages them to honor the legacy of those who came before and to take responsibility for preserving and enriching the heritage they will one day pass on to future generations.

magical spell: family harmony and prosperity:

By the light of this candle,
may our family be blessed.
May love, harmony,
and prosperity fill our home and hearts.
As we stand together,
may our bonds grow stronger
with each passing day.

materials needed:

- White candle
- Bay leaves
- Pen
- Small bowl of salt

instructions:

- Light the white candle, symbolizing purity, harmony, and clarity.
- Take a bay leaf and write the name of each family member on a separate leaf using the pen.
- Place the bay leaves in a circle around the candle, forming a symbol of unity and protection.
- Sprinkle a small amount of salt in the bowl, representing purification and grounding energy.
- Close your eyes and visualize your family members surrounded by love, harmony, and abundance.
- Repeat the following incantation aloud:

"By the light of this candle, may our family be blessed. May love, harmony, and prosperity fill our home and hearts. As we stand together, may our bonds grow stronger with each passing day."

- Allow the candle to burn down completely, infusing the space with positive energy and intentions.

The Ten of Pentacles represents wealth, abundance, and the establishment of a solid foundation for future generations. It symbolizes family, tradition, and the fulfillment that comes from achieving long-term stability and security. This card encourages individuals to focus on building a legacy that will endure through time, encompassing both material and emotional wealth.

questions to ask yourself

1. What aspects of my life bring me a sense of stability and security?
2. How can I honor and preserve my family's legacy and traditions?
3. What responsibilities or obligations am I fulfilling within my family or community?
4. Am I creating a strong foundation for future generations to thrive upon?
5. How can I nurture and strengthen my familial and ancestral connections?
6. What wealth of knowledge and wisdom do I have access to through my lineage?
7. How can I create a sense of unity and cohesion within my family unit?
8. What long-term investments am I making to secure my financial future?
9. How can I share my abundance and blessings with those I care about?
10. What steps can I take to create a legacy of prosperity and abundance for generations to come?

page of pentacles

. . .

"Every experience is an opportunity for growth and understanding," Page of Pentacles.

Answer: Yes

Lorelai Hamilton

Key Words and Phrases:
Productive
Learning
New discoveries
Being careful
Exploration
Good financial news
Eager to learn
Educational opportunities
Curiosity
Thrifty
Determination
Patience
Diligence
Foundations
New business
Practicality
Financial income
Creating success

SYMBOLS:

1. The Page is often depicted as a young person, symbolizing youth, curiosity, and the eagerness to explore new possibilities. This represents a time of discovery, learning, and growth.
2. The Pentacle held by the Page represents the element of Earth and the material world. It symbolizes practicality, resources, and the tangible aspects of life. The Page holds the Pentacle with curiosity and interest, eager to explore its potential.
3. The background of the card often depicts fertile landscapes or fields, representing the potential for growth and abundance. It suggests that the Page is surrounded by opportunities and is ready to embark on a journey of discovery and practical learning.
4. In some depictions, the Page may be shown holding a book or scroll, symbolizing knowledge, education, and the pursuit of learning. This highlights the importance of education and the willingness to seek out new information and skills.

In the quiet corners of the earth where nature meets civilization, The Fool encounters the Page of Pentacles, a youthful figure surrounded by the verdant abundance of the natural world. As The Fool gazes upon the scene, they see the Page of Pentacles engrossed in study, eagerly absorbing the knowledge contained within the pages of a book, while the earth beneath them teems with the promise of growth and potential.

The Page of Pentacles symbolizes the beginning of a journey toward material and intellectual mastery. They represent curiosity, diligence, and a thirst for knowledge, embodying the spirit of a lifelong learner eager to explore the mysteries of the world around them. In the story of the Page of Pentacles, The Fool learns the value of patience, dedication, and the pursuit of excellence in all endeavors.

As The Fool observes the Page of Pentacles, they recognize the importance of education and the acquisition of practical skills in navigating the complexities of life. They understand that true wealth is not just measured in material possessions, but also in the wisdom and understanding gained through experience and study.

The Page of Pentacles serves as a reminder to The Fool to approach new challenges with a curious and open mind, embracing opportunities for growth and discovery along the way. They understand that the path to success is paved with diligence, perseverance, and a willingness to learn from both success and failure.

In the story of the Page of Pentacles, The Fool sees themselves reflected in the youthful figure, recognizing their own potential for growth and achievement. They feel inspired to embark on their own journey of self-discovery, eager to uncover the hidden truths that lie beneath the surface of their own existence.

When the Page of Pentacles appears in a tarot reading, it encourages The Fool to embrace their curiosity and explore new avenues of learning and self-improvement. It suggests that they may be at the beginning stages of a new endeavor or project, filled with excitement and anticipation for what lies ahead.

The Page of Pentacles invites The Fool to approach their goals with a sense of purpose and determination, knowing that with patience and perseverance, they can achieve greatness. It reminds them to stay grounded in the present moment, focusing on the practical steps they can take to turn their dreams into reality.

As The Fool contemplates the message of the Page of Pentacles, they feel a renewed sense of purpose and clarity, ready to embark on the next chapter of their journey with confidence and enthusiasm. With the spirit of the Page of Pentacles as their guide, they know that the possibilities are endless, and the future is theirs to shape and mold according to their desires.

magical spell: manifesting goals:

With this candle's light,
I manifest my dreams.
With focused intent
and unwavering determination,
I call forth the practicality
and abundance I seek.

materials needed:

- Green candle
- Piece of paper
- Pen
- Small bowl of salt

instructions:

- Light the green candle, symbolizing growth, abundance, and prosperity.

- Write down your goals and aspirations on the piece of paper, focusing on practical and achievable outcomes.
- Fold the paper and hold it in your hands, visualizing your goals coming to fruition with clarity and determination.
- Place the paper in the small bowl of salt, representing grounding energy and stability.
- Focus on the flame of the candle and repeat the following incantation aloud:

"With this candle's light, I manifest my dreams. With focused intent and unwavering determination, I call forth the practicality and abundance I seek."

- Allow the candle to burn down completely, infusing your intentions with positive energy and empowering your efforts to achieve your goals.

The Page of Pentacles symbolizes new opportunities, potential, and the beginning stages of practical endeavors. It represents the eager pursuit of knowledge, the willingness to learn, and the practical application of skills to achieve one's goals. This card encourages individuals, to approach new challenges with curiosity, dedication, and a willingness to learn from experiences.

questions to ask yourself

1. What new opportunities for growth and learning am I exploring?
2. How can I approach my studies or projects with curiosity and enthusiasm?

3. What practical skills or knowledge am I seeking to develop?
4. Am I open to new experiences and adventures that expand my horizons?
5. How can I stay disciplined and focused on my goals and aspirations?
6. What resources or mentors can I turn to for guidance and support?
7. How can I ground my lofty ambitions in practical action and planning?
8. What steps can I take to manifest my dreams and aspirations into reality?
9. How can I embrace a mindset of abundance and possibility in my endeavors?
10. What lessons can I learn from experiences of growth and exploration?

knight of pentacles

. . .

"By staying grounded and dedicated to your pursuits, you lay the groundwork for long-term prosperity and fulfillment," Knight of Pentacles.

Answer: Yes

Lorelai Hamilton

Key Words and Phrases:
Good things take time
Self value
Reliability
Progress
New experiences
Diligence
Security
Loyal
Perseverance
Hard work
Patience
Practicality
Perfectionist
Stability
Productive

SYMBOLS:

1. The Knight is depicted as a figure on horseback, symbolizing forward movement and progress. He represents the determination and commitment to achieving his goals, even if it requires slow and steady progress.
2. The Pentacle held by the Knight symbolizes the material aspects of life, including finances, resources, and practical matters. It reflects the Knight's focus on stability, security, and the tangible rewards of hard work and dedication.
3. In the background of the card, there may be fields or farmland, representing the fertile ground for growth and productivity. This symbolizes the Knight's connection to the earth element and his ability to cultivate abundance through diligent effort.
4. The Knight may be depicted wearing armor and carrying tools, indicating his readiness to face challenges and overcome obstacles on his path to success. His preparedness reflects the importance of planning, resilience, and adaptability in achieving goals.

In the quiet fields of the countryside, The Fool encounters the Knight of Pentacles, a steadfast and diligent figure embodying dedication, responsibility, and practicality. As The Fool observes the scene depicted in the card, they see the Knight astride a sturdy horse, traversing the land with purpose and determination. The Knight's gaze is fixed ahead, focused on the task at hand, while the fields around them flourish with abundant crops and fertile soil.

The Knight of Pentacles symbolizes the virtues of hard work, reliability, and attention to detail. It represents a disciplined approach to achieving goals, emphasizing the importance of patience, perseverance, and methodical progress. The scene before The Fool evokes a sense of stability, productivity, and groundedness, highlighting the rewards that come from diligent effort and conscientious planning.

In the story of the Knight of Pentacles, The Fool learns the value of commitment, integrity, and the satisfaction that comes from seeing tangible results of one's labor. They witness the Knight as a symbol of reliability and dependability, embodying the qualities of a trustworthy steward who takes pride in their responsibilities and honors their obligations with unwavering dedication.

Reflecting on the symbolism of the pentacles, The Fool grasps the idea that success is not instantaneous but rather the outcome of persistent effort and a resolute pursuit of excellence. They understand that while the journey may be long and arduous, the rewards of perseverance and determination far outweigh the challenges encountered along the way.

The Knight of Pentacles challenges The Fool to embrace a mindset of discipline, patience, and practicality as they pursue their ambitions and aspirations. It encourages them to take a methodical approach to their goals, breaking tasks down into manageable steps and staying focused on the path ahead, even in the face of adversity or setbacks.

When the Knight of Pentacles appears in a tarot reading, it serves as a reminder to The Fool to stay grounded, stay focused, and stay true to their values and principles. It suggests that they may be at a stage in their journey where they need to embody the qualities of the Knight—to be diligent, responsible, and conscientious in their actions and decisions.

The Knight of Pentacles invites The Fool to cultivate a sense of purpose and direction, knowing that with patience, persistence, and determination, they can overcome any obstacles that stand in their way and achieve their dreams. It encourages them to trust in their ability to navigate the challenges of life with resilience and grace, knowing that they have the strength and fortitude to succeed in their endeavors.

magical spell: grounding and stability

materials needed:

- Brown candle
- Patchouli oil (or any grounding essential oil)
- Small piece of paper
- Pen
- Salt or soil

instructions:

- Anoint the brown candle with patchouli oil, focusing on infusing it with grounding energy and stability.
- Light the candle, symbolizing the illumination of your intentions and the manifestation of stability and security.
- Write down your goals and aspirations on the small piece of paper, emphasizing practical and achievable outcomes.
- Sprinkle a small amount of salt or soil over the paper, representing grounding energy and connection to the earth.
- Hold the paper in your hands and visualize yourself achieving your goals with determination and steadfastness.
- Place the paper near the candle and let it burn down completely,

infusing your intentions with the energy of stability and perseverance.

The Knight of Pentacles represents responsibility, diligence, and a methodical approach to achieving goals. This card embodies the qualities of reliability, patience, and steadfastness in pursuing one's ambitions. It encourages you to embrace discipline, focus on long-term objectives, and take practical steps toward their aspirations.

questions to ask yourself

1. What goals or ambitions am I pursuing with patience and determination?
2. How can I approach my tasks and responsibilities with diligence and reliability?
3. What systems or routines can I implement to increase efficiency and productivity?
4. Am I staying committed to my long-term objectives despite obstacles or setbacks?
5. How can I maintain a sense of groundedness and stability in the face of change?
6. What practical steps am I taking to achieve financial security and stability?
7. How can I embody the qualities of dependability and trustworthiness in my actions?
8. What resources or tools do I need to support me on my journey towards success?
9. How can I find joy and satisfaction in the process of hard work and dedication?

10. What lessons can I learn from experiences of perseverance and steadfastness?

queen of pentacles

. . .

"Embrace the abundance that surrounds you and cultivate a deep connection to the natural world," Queen of Pentacles.

Answer: Yes

Lorelai Hamilton

Key Words and Phrases:
Organization
Fertile
Prosperous
Abundant
Ownership
Resourceful
Foundations
Nurturing
Common sense
Security
Good Things Coming

SYMBOLS:

1. The Queen is depicted as a nurturing and compassionate figure, often surrounded by symbols of abundance and fertility. She represents the qualities of generosity, practicality, and groundedness in both her actions and her relationships.
2. The Pentacle held by the Queen symbolizes material wealth, prosperity, and the abundance of resources. It reflects her ability to manage finances, create a secure home environment, and provide for the needs of herself and others.
3. The Queen may be depicted in a lush garden or natural setting, representing her connection to the earth element and her affinity for nurturing growth and fertility. This symbolizes the importance of grounding oneself in nature and finding solace in the abundance of the natural world.
4. The Queen may wear a crown or tiara, symbolizing her sovereignty and authority in matters of abundance and practicality. It signifies her confidence, self-assurance, and ability to take charge of her life and surroundings.

The Queen of Pentacles is a figure of nurturing abundance, earthly wisdom, and practicality. As The Fool observes the scene depicted in the card, they see the Queen seated amidst a lush landscape, surrounded by blooming flowers, fertile fields, and a gentle stream flowing nearby. Her presence exudes a sense of calm confidence and maternal warmth, inviting The Fool to take a moment of respite and reflection in her tranquil sanctuary.

The Queen of Pentacles symbolizes the qualities of nurturing care, material abundance, and groundedness in the physical world. She embodies the essence of motherhood, not only in the traditional sense, but also as a symbol of providing sustenance, stability, and security to those under her care. The garden around her flourishes under her tender touch, reflecting the bountiful blessings that come from her nurturing presence and practical wisdom.

In the story of the Queen of Pentacles, The Fool learns the importance of tending to the needs of oneself and others, cultivating a harmonious balance between the material and spiritual aspects of life. They witness the Queen as a symbol of generosity and hospitality, embodying the virtues of compassion, resourcefulness, and stewardship of the Earth's abundant gifts.

The Fool reflects on the symbolism of the pentacles. True wealth is not measured solely by material possessions but also by the richness of one's relationships, the depth of one's connection to nature, and the abundance of gratitude and contentment that fills the heart. They understand that the Queen's kingdom is not just one of tangible wealth but also one of emotional fulfillment and spiritual well-being.

The Queen of Pentacles challenges The Fool to embrace a mindset of practicality, resourcefulness, and responsible stewardship of their resources and talents. She encourages them to nurture their dreams and aspirations with care and diligence, knowing that with patience, perseverance, and prudent planning, they can manifest their desires into reality.

When the Queen of Pentacles appears in a tarot reading, it serves as a reminder to The Fool to cultivate a sense of abundance, gratitude, and generosity in their lives. It suggests that they may be at a stage in their journey where they need to embody the qualities of the Queen — to be nurturing, supportive, and grounded in their approach to achieving their goals and fulfilling their responsibilities.

The Queen of Pentacles invites The Fool to embrace the inherent wisdom of the natural world, to find solace and strength in the rhythms of the Earth, and to trust in the abundance of blessings that surround them. She assures them that by honoring the sacred balance of giving and receiving, they can create a life of lasting fulfillment, prosperity, and harmony.

Lorelai Hamilton

magical spell: nurturing self-care

materials needed:

- Green candle
- Lavender essential oil (or any calming oil)
- Small piece of paper
- Pen
- Dried lavender or rose petals

instructions:

1. Anoint the green candle with lavender oil, focusing on imbuing it with calming and nurturing energy.
2. Light the candle, symbolizing the illumination of self-care and abundance in your life.
3. Write down a list of self-care practices or affirmations on the small piece of paper, emphasizing nurturing and abundance.
4. Sprinkle dried lavender or rose petals around the candle, representing the soothing and nurturing qualities of nature.
5. Hold the paper in your hands and visualize yourself surrounded by abundance, security, and well-being.
6. Place the paper near the candle and let it burn down completely, infusing your intentions with the energy of nurturing self-care.

The Queen of Pentacles embodies nurturing, abundance, and practicality. She represents a nurturing and supportive figure who values security, stability, and the well-being of those around her. This card encourages you to embrace your nurturing qualities, take care of your physical and emotional needs, and cultivate a sense of abundance in your life.

questions to ask yourself

1. How am I nurturing and caring for myself on a physical, emotional, and spiritual level?
2. What practical steps am I taking to create a stable and supportive home environment?
3. How can I use my resources and abilities to provide for the needs of those I care about?
4. Am I balancing my responsibilities to others with self-care and personal fulfillment?
5. How can I cultivate a sense of abundance and gratitude in my daily life?
6. What practices or rituals nourish and replenish my mind, body, and spirit?
7. How can I use my intuition and wisdom to make grounded and practical decisions?
8. What investments am I making in my own well-being and long-term security?
9. How can I share my wealth and blessings with those in need or less fortunate?
10. What lessons can I learn from experiences of nurturing and caretaking?

king of pentacles

...

"Trust in your ability to manifest your goals and dreams into reality, and embrace the responsibilities that come with leadership and prosperity," King of Pentacles.

Answer: Yes

Key Words and Phrases:
Security
Mastery
Progress
Responsibility
Practical
Stability
Success
Satisfaction
Content
Wealth
Hard work
Achievement
Leadership

SYMBOLS:

1. The King is depicted as a mature and successful individual who exudes confidence, authority, and competence in his endeavors. He symbolizes mastery over the material realm and the ability to manifest abundance through hard work and perseverance.
2. The Pentacle held by the King represents material wealth, financial security, and the tangible rewards of diligent effort and wise investments. It symbolizes his practical approach to life and his ability to manage resources effectively.
3. The King may be seated on a throne or adorned with a crown, signifying his status, authority, and leadership in matters of finance and material success. It reflects his ability to make sound decisions and provide stability and security for himself and others.
4. The King may be surrounded by a lush landscape or garden, symbolizing the fruits of his labor and his connection to the earth element. It represents the abundance and prosperity that result from nurturing and cultivating one's resources.

In the majestic realm of prosperity and stability, The Fool encounters the King of Pentacles, a symbol of earthly power, abundance, and mastery over the material world. As The Fool gazes upon the card, they see the King seated upon his throne, adorned with regal robes, a crown upon his head, and a scepter in his hand. His posture exudes authority and confidence, commanding respect and admiration from all who behold him.

The King of Pentacles epitomizes the qualities of wealth, success, and practicality. He is the embodiment of financial security, entrepreneurship, and material achievement. The lush landscape depicted in the card reflects the fruits of his labor—fertile fields, thriving vineyards, and prosperous orchards—symbols of his ability to cultivate abundance and prosperity in all aspects of his life.

In the story of the King of Pentacles, The Fool learns the importance of ambition, diligence, and strategic planning in achieving their goals and aspirations. They witness the King as a symbol of resilience and resourcefulness, embodying the virtues of hard work, perseverance, and sound financial management.

The Fool reflects on the symbolism of the pentacles. One does not merely measure success by monetary wealth but also by the legacy of integrity, generosity, and wisdom that one leaves behind. They understand that the King's kingdom is not just one of material riches but also one of honor, respect, and influence in the world.

The King of Pentacles challenges The Fool to embrace a mindset of abundance, confidence, and self-assurance in their journey toward achieving their dreams. He encourages them to leverage their talents, skills, and resources to create a life of fulfillment, purpose, and impact in the world.

When the King of Pentacles appears in a tarot reading, it serves as a reminder to The Fool to embody the qualities of leadership, stability, and responsibility in their endeavors. It suggests that they may be at a stage in their journey where they need to take charge of their financial affairs, make prudent investments, and build a solid foundation for their future.

The King of Pentacles invites The Fool to tap into their innate potential for success and prosperity, to harness the power of their ambitions, and to manifest their visions into reality with unwavering determination and confidence. He assures them that by embracing the principles of abundance, integrity, and discipline, they can ascend to new heights of achievement and fulfillment in their lives.

magical spell: financial abundance

materials needed:

- Green candle
- Patchouli essential oil (or any money-drawing oil)
- Small piece of paper
- Pen
- Bay leaves (dried or fresh)

instructions:

1. Anoint the green candle with patchouli oil, focusing on drawing abundance and prosperity into your life.
2. Light the candle, symbolizing the illumination of financial success and stability.
3. Write down your financial goals or intentions on the small piece of paper, emphasizing prosperity and abundance.
4. Place the bay leaves around the candle, symbolizing growth, abundance, and protection.
5. Hold the paper in your hands and visualize yourself achieving your financial goals with ease and confidence.
6. Place the paper near the candle and let it burn down completely, infusing your intentions with the energy of financial abundance.

The King of Pentacles embodies qualities of prosperity, stability, and success. He represents a mature and responsible figure who is grounded in the material world and values practicality, security, and financial abundance. This card encourages you to embody traits of resilience, responsibility, and ambition.

questions to ask yourself

1. How am I embodying the qualities of abundance, stability, and mastery in my life?
2. What practical steps am I taking to achieve financial success and security?
3. How can I use my resources and influence to create a positive impact in the world?
4. Am I staying grounded and connected to the earth and its natural rhythms?
5. How can I lead with integrity and wisdom in my business and financial dealings?
6. What investments am I making in my own personal and professional growth?
7. How can I cultivate a sense of generosity and philanthropy in my actions?
8. What legacy do I wish to leave behind for future generations?
9. How can I balance my material wealth with spiritual and emotional fulfillment?
10. What lessons can I learn from experiences of leadership and prosperity?

quick reference guide

...

WELCOME to the Quick Reference Guide! Tarot is a powerful tool for self-discovery, guidance, and insight into life's mysteries. While in-depth knowledge of each card's symbolism and interpretation is invaluable, I understand that sometimes you need quick answers or insights on the go. That's where this guide comes in handy.

In the next few pages, you'll find concise interpretations for the traditional meanings of each tarot card, as well as interpretations tailored for romance, success, and career readings. Whether you're seeking guidance on matters of the heart, career decisions, or overall success, this guide provides a quick and easy reference to help you tap into the wisdom of the tarot.

While this guide offers a convenient overview, I encourage you to explore the deeper meanings and symbolism of each card by diving into the thick of this book. Tarot is a rich and complex system that rewards deep exploration and study. So, while this guide serves as a handy tool for quick insights, I encourage you to immerse yourself in the world of tarot to unlock its full potential.

I hope the Quick Reference Guide to Tarot serve as a helpful companion on your journey of self-discovery and enlightenment. Enjoy your tarot readings, and may they bring you clarity, inspiration, and guidance whenever you need it most.

traditional meanings

major arcana:

1. The Fool: New beginnings, innocence, spontaneity.
2. The Magician: Manifestation, power, resourcefulness.
3. The High Priestess: Intuition, mystery, inner knowing.
4. The Empress: Fertility, abundance, nurturing.
5. The Emperor: Authority, stability, leadership.
6. The Hierophant: Tradition, spirituality, guidance.
7. The Lovers: Love, relationships, choices.
8. The Chariot: Determination, willpower, victory.
9. Strength: Courage, inner strength, compassion.
10. The Hermit: Soul-searching, introspection, solitude.
11. Wheel of Fortune: Destiny, luck, cycles.
12. Justice: Balance, fairness, accountability.
13. The Hanged Man: Surrender, letting go, new perspectives.
14. Death: Endings, transformation, rebirth.
15. Temperance: Balance, harmony, moderation.
16. The Devil: Temptation, bondage, materialism.
17. The Tower: Upheaval, sudden change, revelation.
18. The Star: Hope, inspiration, guidance.
19. The Moon: Illusion, intuition, fear.
20. The Sun: Joy, success, vitality.
21. Judgment: Rebirth, awakening, clarity.
22. The World: Completion, fulfillment, wholeness.

minor arcana:

wands:

- Ace of Wands: Inspiration, new beginnings, potential.
- Two of Wands: Planning, vision, progress.
- Three of Wands: Expansion, foresight, exploration.
- Four of Wands: Celebration, harmony, homecoming.
- Five of Wands: Conflict, competition, diversity.
- Six of Wands: Victory, recognition, success.
- Seven of Wands: Courage, determination, perseverance.
- Eight of Wands: Speed, action, movement.
- Nine of Wands: Resilience, perseverance, boundaries.
- Ten of Wands: Burden, responsibility, overload.
- Page of Wands: Enthusiasm, exploration, new opportunities.
- Knight of Wands: Action, adventure, impulsiveness.
- Queen of Wands: Confidence, leadership, independence.
- King of Wands: Charisma, vision, entrepreneurial spirit.

cups:

- Ace of Cups: Love, emotional beginnings, intuition.
- Two of Cups: Partnership, connection, mutual attraction.
- Three of Cups: Celebration, friendship, community.
- Four of Cups: Discontent, apathy, introspection.
- Five of Cups: Loss, regret, disappointment.
- Six of Cups: Nostalgia, childhood memories, innocence.
- Seven of Cups: Fantasy, choices, illusion.
- Eight of Cups: Withdrawal, transition, moving on.
- Nine of Cups: Contentment, satisfaction, emotional fulfillment.
- Ten of Cups: Harmony, happiness, family.
- Page of Cups: Creativity, intuition, new beginnings.
- Knight of Cups: Romance, charm, emotional depth.
- Queen of Cups: Compassion, intuition, nurturing.
- King of Cups: Emotional balance, wisdom, diplomacy.

swords:

- Ace of Swords: Mental clarity, truth, breakthroughs.
- Two of Swords: Indecision, stalemate, difficult choices.
- Three of Swords: Heartache, sorrow, emotional pain.
- Four of Swords: Rest, recuperation, contemplation.

- Five of Swords: Conflict, defeat, disharmony.
- Six of Swords: Transition, moving on, mental peace.
- Seven of Swords: Deception, sneakiness, betrayal.
- Eight of Swords: Restriction, imprisonment, self-imposed limitations.
- Nine of Swords: Anxiety, fear, nightmares.
- Ten of Swords: Betrayal, rock bottom, collapse.
- Page of Swords: Curiosity, intellect, communication.
- Knight of Swords: Ambition, assertiveness, decisiveness.
- Queen of Swords: Clarity, independence, directness.
- King of Swords: Authority, intellect, logic.

pentacles (coins):

- Ace of Pentacles: Manifestation, prosperity, opportunity.
- Two of Pentacles: Balance, adaptability, juggling priorities.
- Three of Pentacles: Collaboration, teamwork, skill mastery.
- Four of Pentacles: Stability, security, conservatism.
- Five of Pentacles: Hardship, poverty, financial loss.
- Six of Pentacles: Generosity, charity, giving and receiving.
- Seven of Pentacles: Assessment, patience, long-term planning.
- Eight of Pentacles: Diligence, craftsmanship, skill development.
- Nine of Pentacles: Abundance, self-reliance, luxury.
- Ten of Pentacles: Legacy, inheritance, long-term success.
- Page of Pentacles: Study, diligence, new opportunities.
- Knight of Pentacles: Reliability, responsibility, stability.
- Queen of Pentacles: Nurturing, practicality, abundance.
- King of Pentacles: Security, prosperity, financial mastery.

on love

...

major arcana:

1. The Fool: Represents new beginnings, taking risks, and being open to love.
2. The Magician: Symbolizes manifestation and the power to create a romantic connection.
3. The High Priestess: Suggests intuition and the need to listen to one's inner voice in matters of love.
4. The Empress: Signifies nurturing, abundance, and fertility, often representing a deep and caring romantic relationship.
5. The Emperor: Stands for stability, structure, and authority in love relationships.
6. The Hierophant: Reflects tradition, commitment, and spiritual guidance in romantic endeavors.
7. The Lovers: Represents a significant romantic relationship, often indicating a choice or decision to be made.
8. The Chariot: Symbolizes determination and overcoming obstacles together in a romantic partnership.
9. Strength: Suggests inner strength, courage, and resilience in love.
10. The Hermit: Indicates introspection and seeking wisdom before committing to a romantic relationship.
11. Wheel of Fortune: Represents destiny and changes in romantic situations, emphasizing the ups and downs of love.

12. Justice: Signifies fairness, balance, and honesty in romantic dealings.
13. The Hanged Man: Suggests surrendering to love and viewing situations from a different perspective.
14. Death: Represents transformation and endings, often indicating the need to let go of the past to embrace new love.
15. Temperance: Reflects patience, balance, and harmony in romantic connections.
16. The Devil: Signifies temptation and unhealthy attachments in romantic relationships.
17. The Tower: Indicates sudden upheaval or revelations that can lead to significant changes in love.
18. The Star: Symbolizes hope, inspiration, and healing in romantic situations.
19. The Moon: Suggests illusions and hidden emotions in love, encouraging one to trust their intuition.
20. The Sun: Represents joy, happiness, and fulfillment in romantic partnerships.
21. Judgment: Indicates self-reflection and accountability in love, often representing second chances.
22. The World: Signifies completion and fulfillment in romantic endeavors, suggesting a union of souls.

minor arcana:

cups:

- Ace of Cups: Signifies new beginnings in love, emotional fulfillment, and the potential for deep connections.
- Two of Cups: Represents mutual love, partnership, and harmony in relationships.
- Three of Cups: Symbolizes celebration, joy, and friendship within romantic connections.
- Four of Cups: Suggests contemplation, dissatisfaction, or apathy in love relationships.
- Five of Cups: Indicates loss, regret, or disappointment in romantic matters, but also the opportunity for emotional healing.
- Six of Cups: Reflects nostalgia, innocence, and reconnecting with past loves or childhood memories.
- Seven of Cups: Signifies fantasy, illusion, and the need to discern between reality and wishful thinking in love.

- Eight of Cups: Represents walking away from a situation that no longer serves one's emotional needs, seeking deeper fulfillment in love.
- Nine of Cups: Symbolizes emotional satisfaction, contentment, and fulfillment of desires in love relationships.
- Ten of Cups: Reflects ultimate emotional fulfillment, harmony, and happiness in romantic partnerships, often representing family and domestic bliss.
- Page of Cups: Symbolizes emotional exploration, new experiences, and messages of love or affection in romance.
- Knight of Cups: Indicates romance, charm, and emotional maturity, often representing a romantic suitor or the pursuit of love with chivalry.
- Queen of Cups: Symbolizes intuition, empathy, and nurturing qualities in romantic partnerships, often embodying emotional support and understanding.
- King of Cups: Indicates emotional balance, wisdom, and maturity in love relationships, often embodying the role of the caring and supportive partner.

swords:

- Ace of Swords: Signifies mental clarity, truth, and breakthroughs in communication within relationships.
- Two of Swords: Represents indecision, stalemate, or avoidance of conflict in romantic situations.
- Three of Swords: Indicates heartache, sorrow, and emotional pain in love relationships.
- Four of Swords: Suggests rest, recuperation, and healing from emotional wounds in romance.
- Five of Swords: Symbolizes conflict, betrayal, and power struggles within relationships.
- Six of Swords: Reflects moving on from difficult times, finding peace, and seeking a calmer, more stable romantic future.
- Seven of Swords: Signifies deception, dishonesty, or avoiding confrontation in love connections.
- Eight of Swords: Represents feeling trapped, restricted, or unable to see solutions in romantic matters.
- Nine of Swords: Indicates anxiety, fear, and worry in love relationships, often related to overthinking or nightmares.
- Ten of Swords: Symbolizes betrayal, rock bottom, and painful endings in romance, but also the opportunity for renewal and starting anew.

- Page of Swords: Represents curiosity, intellectual pursuits, and open communication in romantic connections.
- Knight of Swords: Represents determination, directness, and assertiveness in romantic pursuits or conflicts.
- Queen of Swords: Represents clear communication, independence, and strength in overcoming challenges within relationships.
- King of Swords: Represents intellect, authority, and clear boundaries in romantic connections, often embodying leadership and problem-solving abilities.

pentacles:

- Ace of Pentacles: Signifies new beginnings in practical matters, stability, and potential long-term commitment in love.
- Two of Pentacles: Represents balancing priorities, adaptability, and flexibility in romantic relationships.
- Three of Pentacles: Reflects teamwork, collaboration, and building a solid foundation together in love.
- Four of Pentacles: Suggests holding onto security, stability, or possessions in romantic connections, sometimes indicating fear of loss.
- Five of Pentacles: Indicates financial hardship, isolation, or feeling left out in love relationships, but also the importance of support and overcoming challenges together.
- Six of Pentacles: Symbolizes generosity, sharing, and mutual support within romantic partnerships.
- Seven of Pentacles: Signifies patience, perseverance, and waiting for results or rewards in love endeavors.
- Eight of Pentacles: Represents dedication, craftsmanship, and putting effort into improving romantic connections.
- Nine of Pentacles: Reflects independence, self-sufficiency, and enjoying the fruits of one's labor in love relationships.
- Ten of Pentacles: Suggests wealth, abundance, and long-term security within family and romantic bonds.
- Page of Pentacles: Signifies practicality, diligence, and a focus on tangible aspects of relationships, such as stability and security.
- Knight of Pentacles: Signifies reliability, responsibility, and patience in building stable and long-lasting romantic connections.
- Queen of Pentacles: Signifies practicality, stability, and nurturing of home and family in romantic unions, often embodying the role of the provider.

- King of Pentacles: Signifies security, stability, and material abundance in romantic partnerships, often embodying the role of the provider and protector.

wands:

- Ace of Wands: Signifies new beginnings, inspiration, and passionate energy in love endeavors.
- Two of Wands: Represents planning, decision-making, and taking the initiative in romantic pursuits.
- Three of Wands: Indicates expansion, progress, and looking towards the future with optimism in love relationships.
- Four of Wands: Reflects celebration, harmony, and stability within romantic unions, often symbolizing marriage or commitment ceremonies.
- Five of Wands: Symbolizes competition, conflict, or differing opinions within relationships.
- Six of Wands: Signifies victory, recognition, and success in romantic endeavors, often representing mutual admiration and support.
- Seven of Wands: Represents standing one's ground, defending beliefs, and overcoming challenges in love relationships.
- Eight of Wands: Suggests swift progress, communication, and forward movement in romantic connections.
- Nine of Wands: Indicates resilience, perseverance, and overcoming obstacles in love, often after experiencing setbacks or challenges.
- Ten of Wands: Reflects burdens, responsibilities, or feeling overwhelmed in romantic situations, but also the need to delegate or lighten the load together.
- Page of Wands: Reflects enthusiasm, creativity, and new opportunities for passion and adventure in love affairs.
- Knight of Wands: Reflects passion, energy, and a desire for adventure or excitement in love relationships.
- Queen of Wands: Reflects confidence, charisma, and leadership in love relationships, often inspiring passion, and creativity in partners.
- King of Wands: Reflects passion, creativity, and a bold approach to love and romance, often embodying leadership, and adventurous spirit in relationships.

on work and career
. . .

major arcana:

1. The Fool: Signifies new beginnings, taking a leap of faith, and embarking on a new career path or venture.
2. The Magician: Represents skill, creativity, and manifestation of career goals or projects.
3. The High Priestess: Suggests intuition, hidden knowledge, and trusting one's instincts in career decisions.
4. The Empress: Symbolizes abundance, creativity, and nurturing energy in work endeavors.
5. The Emperor: Signifies structure, organization, and leadership in the workplace.
6. The Hierophant: Reflects tradition, mentorship, and seeking guidance from experienced professionals in one's field.
7. The Lovers: Represents choices, partnerships, and collaboration in career-related decisions.
8. The Chariot: Indicates determination, drive, and overcoming obstacles to achieve career success.
9. Strength: Symbolizes inner strength, courage, and resilience in facing challenges within the workplace.
10. The Hermit: Suggests introspection, seeking guidance, and taking time to reflect on career goals and aspirations.
11. Wheel of Fortune: Represents changes, opportunities, and shifts in career circumstances.

12. Justice: Signifies fairness, balance, and ethical considerations in work-related matters.
13. The Hanged Man: Reflects a new perspective, surrendering to change, and seeing challenges as opportunities for growth in one's career.
14. Death: Indicates transformation, endings, and letting go of old career paths or beliefs to embrace new opportunities.
15. Temperance: Symbolizes balance, harmony, and moderation in work-life balance and career pursuits.
16. The Devil: Suggests feeling trapped, limited, or controlled by career-related obligations or unhealthy work environments.
17. The Tower: Represents sudden change, upheaval, or unexpected events that can impact one's career trajectory.
18. The Star: Signifies hope, inspiration, and finding one's true calling or purpose in a career.
19. The Moon: Reflects uncertainty, illusion, and navigating through periods of confusion or insecurity in one's career path.
20. The Sun: Symbolizes success, fulfillment, and achieving career goals with confidence and optimism.
21. Judgment: Indicates self-reflection, accountability, and making important decisions regarding one's career direction.
22. The World: Represents fulfillment, completion, and reaching the pinnacle of success in one's career journey.

minor arcana:

cups:

- Ace of Cups: Indicates new emotional beginnings, creativity, and potential opportunities in work that resonate with one's passions and emotions.
- Two of Cups: Represents harmony, cooperation, and partnership in the workplace, often indicating successful collaborations or teamwork.
- Three of Cups: Symbolizes celebration, community, and social connections in work-related events or achievements.
- Four of Cups: Suggests apathy, discontentment, or feeling emotionally disconnected from one's work, prompting the need for introspection or seeking new opportunities.
- Five of Cups: Indicates disappointment, loss, or setbacks in work endeavors, but also the opportunity to learn from mistakes and find emotional healing.

- Six of Cups: Reflects nostalgia, memories, and reconnecting with past experiences or colleagues in the workplace.
- Seven of Cups: Signifies choices, options, and daydreaming about future career paths or possibilities, but also the need to focus and make decisions.
- Eight of Cups: Represents leaving behind old work situations or projects that no longer fulfill emotionally, and embarking on a quest for deeper meaning and satisfaction in one's career.
- Nine of Cups: Symbolizes fulfillment, emotional satisfaction, and achieving personal or professional goals in the workplace.
- Ten of Cups: Indicates emotional fulfillment, harmony, and contentment in work-life balance, often reflecting a supportive and nurturing work environment.
- Page of Cups: Suggests creativity, intuition, and emotional sensitivity in work-related projects or endeavors, often representing a young or inexperienced colleague.
- Knight of Cups: Reflects charm, creativity, and pursuing work opportunities with passion and emotional depth, often representing a romantic or idealistic approach to career goals.
- Queen of Cups: Represents emotional intelligence, nurturing leadership, and creating a supportive work environment, often embodying empathy and understanding towards colleagues.
- King of Cups: Signifies emotional maturity, wisdom, and calm leadership in the workplace, often embodying empathy and compassion in managerial roles.

swords:

- Ace of Swords: Indicates mental clarity, breakthroughs, and new perspectives in work-related situations or projects.
- Two of Swords: Represents indecision, stalemate, or avoiding confrontation in work-related matters, prompting the need to make difficult decisions or seek compromise.
- Three of Swords: Symbolizes heartache, sorrow, or disappointment in work situations, but also the opportunity for healing and moving forward with clarity.
- Four of Swords: Suggests rest, recuperation, and taking a break from work-related stress or conflicts, emphasizing the importance of self-care and rejuvenation.
- Five of Swords: Indicates conflict, competition, or power struggles in the workplace, prompting the need for diplomacy and strategic thinking to resolve conflicts.

- Six of Swords: Reflects moving on from difficult situations or conflicts in work, seeking a calmer and more stable environment, and embracing positive changes or new opportunities.
- Seven of Swords: Signifies deception, betrayal, or dishonesty in work-related matters, urging caution and vigilance in trusting others or making decisions.
- Eight of Swords: Represents feeling trapped, restricted, or limited in work situations, often due to self-imposed limitations or negative thinking patterns, prompting the need for perspective and problem-solving.
- Nine of Swords: Symbolizes anxiety, worry, or stress related to work situations or responsibilities, prompting the need for self-care, support, and finding constructive solutions.
- Ten of Swords: Indicates betrayal, failure, or painful endings in work situations, but also the opportunity for renewal, letting go of the past, and starting fresh with valuable lessons learned.
- Page of Swords: Suggests curiosity, intellect, and communication skills in work-related projects or endeavors, often representing a young or inquisitive colleague.
- Knight of Swords: Reflects determination, ambition, and taking swift action to achieve work goals or overcome obstacles, often representing a competitive or assertive approach to career advancement.
- Queen of Swords: Represents clarity, independence, and objectivity in work-related matters, often embodying leadership and problem-solving abilities with a focus on fairness and honesty.
- King of Swords: Signifies authority, logic, and strategic thinking in the workplace, often embodying strong leadership and decision-making skills with a focus on integrity and accountability.

pentacles:

- Ace of Pentacles: Indicates new opportunities, financial prosperity, and the potential for career growth or stability in work endeavors.
- Two of Pentacles: Represents balance, adaptability, and juggling multiple responsibilities or projects in the workplace.
- Three of Pentacles: Symbolizes collaboration, teamwork, and recognition for one's skills or contributions in work-related projects or endeavors.

- Four of Pentacles: Suggests stability, security, and holding onto resources or material possessions in work-related matters, sometimes indicating a need to be more open to change or sharing.
- Five of Pentacles: Indicates financial hardship, instability, or feeling left out in work-related situations, but also the importance of seeking support and finding creative solutions to challenges.
- Six of Pentacles: Reflects generosity, sharing, and financial assistance in work-related matters, often indicating success through giving or receiving support from others.
- Seven of Pentacles: Signifies patience, perseverance, and waiting for results or rewards in work-related projects or endeavors, often emphasizing the importance of long-term planning and investment.
- Eight of Pentacles: Represents dedication, craftsmanship, and putting effort into honing one's skills or expertise in the workplace, often indicating mastery and success through hard work.
- Nine of Pentacles: Symbolizes independence, self-sufficiency, and enjoying the fruits of one's labor in work-related achievements or financial success.
- Ten of Pentacles: Indicates wealth, abundance, and long-term security in work-related endeavors or family businesses, often reflecting a legacy or inheritance.
- Page of Pentacles: Suggests diligence, practicality, and a focus on learning or developing new skills in work-related projects or endeavors, often representing a young or ambitious colleague.
- Knight of Pentacles: Reflects reliability, responsibility, and a methodical approach to work goals or projects, often indicating slow but steady progress towards success.
- Queen of Pentacles: Represents practicality, nurturing, and creating a stable and supportive work environment, often embodying leadership with a focus on financial security and growth.
- King of Pentacles: Signifies success, wealth, and financial stability in the workplace, often embodying strong leadership and business acumen with a focus on long-term planning and growth.

wands:

- Ace of Wands: Indicates new beginnings, inspiration, and creative opportunities in work-related projects or endeavors.
- Two of Wands: Represents planning, ambition, and taking the initiative to pursue career goals or ventures.
- Three of Wands: Symbolizes expansion, progress, and looking towards the future with optimism in work-related endeavors or projects.
- Four of Wands: Suggests celebration, success, and achieving milestones or goals in work-related projects or endeavors, often representing a sense of achievement and recognition.
- Five of Wands: Indicates competition, conflict, or differing opinions in the workplace, prompting the need for collaboration and finding common ground to achieve shared goals.
- Six of Wands: Reflects victory, recognition, and success in work-related endeavors or projects, often indicating leadership and public acclaim for achievements.
- Seven of Wands: Signifies standing one's ground, defending beliefs, and overcoming challenges or opposition in the workplace.
- Eight of Wands: Represents swift progress, communication, and momentum in work-related projects or endeavors, often indicating rapid growth or development.
- Nine of Wands: Symbolizes resilience, perseverance, and overcoming obstacles in work-related challenges or projects, often indicating determination and strength in adversity.
- Ten of Wands: Indicates burdens, responsibilities, or feeling overwhelmed in work-related situations, but also the need to delegate or find support to manage workload effectively.
- Page of Wands: Suggests enthusiasm, creativity, and a desire for new opportunities or experiences in work-related projects or endeavors, often representing a young or energetic colleague.
- Knight of Wands: Reflects passion, adventure, and taking bold action to pursue career goals or opportunities, often indicating travel or exploring new paths in one's career.
- Queen of Wands: Represents confidence, charisma, and leadership in the workplace, often embodying creativity and inspiration in work-related projects or endeavors.
- King of Wands: Signifies vision, entrepreneurship, and taking charge of one's career path or ventures, often embodying leadership, and ambition in achieving success.

on success
. . .

major arcana:

1. The Fool: Signifies embarking on a new journey with optimism and enthusiasm, success through taking risks and embracing new opportunities.
2. The Magician: Represents mastery, skill, and harnessing one's talents to achieve success in endeavors.
3. The High Priestess - Suggests intuition, inner knowledge, and trusting one's instincts to navigate towards success.
4. The Empress: Symbolizes abundance, fertility, and the nurturing energy that fosters growth and prosperity.
5. The Emperor: Signifies authority, structure, and disciplined leadership leading to success and achievement of goals.
6. The Hierophant: Reflects guidance, tradition, and seeking wisdom from mentors or established principles to attain success.
7. The Lovers: Represents harmony, alignment, and making choices that lead to success in love and partnerships.
8. The Chariot: Indicates victory, determination, and overcoming obstacles to achieve success through sheer willpower and focus.
9. Strength: Symbolizes inner strength, courage, and resilience, leading to success even in the face of adversity.
10. The Hermit: Suggests introspection, seeking guidance, and finding success through self-discovery and inner wisdom.
11. Wheel of Fortune: Represents luck, fate, and the cyclical nature

of success, indicating a turn for the better and positive outcomes.
12. Justice: Signifies fairness, balance, and ethical decisions leading to success and positive outcomes.
13. The Hanged Man: Reflects surrender, letting go, and gaining a new perspective that leads to success through unconventional means.
14. Death: Indicates transformation, endings, and new beginnings that pave the way for success and personal growth.
15. Temperance: Symbolizes moderation, balance, and harmony, leading to success through finding the middle path.
16. The Devil: Suggests overcoming limitations, breaking free from bondage, and achieving success by releasing unhealthy attachments.
17. The Tower: Represents sudden change, upheaval, and breakthroughs that lead to success by clearing away what no longer serves.
18. The Star: Signifies hope, inspiration, and success achieved through faith, optimism, and staying true to one's aspirations.
19. The Moon: Reflects intuition, illusion, and navigating through uncertainty to find success by trusting one's inner guidance.
20. The Sun: Symbolizes success, joy, and fulfillment in all aspects of life, radiating positivity and abundance.
21. Judgment: Indicates self-reflection, rebirth, and awakening to one's true purpose, leading to success through embracing transformation.
22. The World: Represents completion, fulfillment, and achieving success on a grand scale, symbolizing mastery, and wholeness.

minor arcana:

cups:

- Ace of Cups: Success in emotional fulfillment and deep connections.
- Two of Cups: Success in harmonious relationships and partnerships.
- Three of Cups: Success in celebration, friendship, and community.
- Four of Cups: Success through introspection and seeking new perspectives.
- Five of Cups: Success in finding resilience and emotional healing after setbacks.

- Six of Cups: Success through nostalgia, reconnecting with the past, and finding joy in memories.
- Seven of Cups: Success in manifesting dreams and making choices that align with desires.
- Eight of Cups: Success in moving on from what no longer serves and seeking deeper fulfillment.
- Nine of Cups: Success in emotional satisfaction and fulfillment of desires.
- Ten of Cups: Success in achieving emotional harmony and domestic bliss.
- Page of Cups: Success in emotional exploration, creativity, and new opportunities that spark inspiration and imagination.
- Knight of Cups: Success in emotional maturity, romantic pursuits, and following one's heart to achieve fulfillment and happiness.
- Queen of Cups: Success in nurturing relationships, emotional intelligence, and creating a supportive environment for growth and healing.
- King of Cups: Success in emotional stability, compassion, and leading with empathy to foster harmonious relationships and personal growth.

swords:

- Ace of Swords: Success in mental clarity and breakthroughs in communication.
- Two of Swords: Success in making decisions and finding balance amidst conflict.
- Three of Swords: Success in healing emotional wounds and finding closure.
- Four of Swords: Success in rest and recuperation, leading to clarity and renewal.
- Five of Swords: Success in overcoming challenges and asserting boundaries.
- Six of Swords: Success in moving forward from difficulties towards calmer waters.
- Seven of Swords: Success in strategic planning and avoiding pitfalls.
- Eight of Swords: Success in breaking free from limiting beliefs and restrictions.
- Nine of Swords: Success in overcoming anxiety and finding peace of mind.

- Ten of Swords: Success in embracing endings and starting anew with wisdom.
- Page of Swords: Success in intellectual pursuits, curiosity, and new ideas that lead to breakthroughs and innovation.
- Knight of Swords: Success in swift action, determination, and overcoming obstacles with clear focus and decisiveness.
- Queen of Swords: Success in clear communication, rational decision-making, and maintaining integrity in all endeavors.
- King of Swords: Success in strategic thinking, intellectual prowess, and making wise decisions that lead to achievement and recognition.

pentacles:

- Ace of Pentacles: Success in new financial opportunities and material abundance.
- Two of Pentacles: Success in balancing priorities and adapting to change.
- Three of Pentacles: Success in collaboration and recognition for skills or craftsmanship.
- Four of Pentacles: Success in financial stability and prudent management.
- Five of Pentacles: Success in overcoming financial hardship and seeking support.
- Six of Pentacles: Success in generosity and sharing wealth with others.
- Seven of Pentacles: Success in patience and perseverance towards long-term goals.
- Eight of Pentacles: Success in dedication to honing skills and craftsmanship.
- Nine of Pentacles: Success in independence and enjoying the fruits of labor.
- Ten of Pentacles: Success in creating a legacy and achieving long-term security.
- Page of Pentacles: Success in practical endeavors, learning new skills, and laying the groundwork for future achievements.
- Knight of Pentacles: Success in reliability, hard work, and steady progress towards long-term goals and financial stability.
- Queen of Pentacles: Success in practicality, financial management, and providing stability and security for oneself and others.
- King of Pentacles: Success in financial management, wealth

accumulation, and building a solid foundation for long-term prosperity and security.

wands:

- Ace of Wands: Success in creative endeavors and new opportunities for growth.
- Two of Wands: Success in planning and taking the first steps towards ambitious goals.
- Three of Wands: Success in expansion and looking towards the future with confidence.
- Four of Wands: Success in celebrating achievements and reaching milestones.
- Five of Wands: Success in overcoming obstacles and competition through determination.
- Six of Wands: Success in recognition and victory, receiving acclaim for efforts.
- Seven of Wands: Success in standing firm and defending convictions amidst challenges.
- Eight of Wands: Success in swift progress and communication, leading to breakthroughs.
- Nine of Wands: Success in resilience and perseverance, overcoming setbacks.
- Ten of Wands: Success in shouldering responsibilities and achieving goals, despite challenges.
- Page of Wands: Success in pursuing passions, taking initiative, and embracing opportunities for growth and adventure.
- Knight of Wands: Success in boldness, enthusiasm, and taking risks to pursue creative endeavors and entrepreneurial ventures.
- Queen of Wands: Success in leadership, charisma, and inspiring others to achieve their goals with passion and enthusiasm.
- King of Wands: Success in vision, entrepreneurship, and taking bold action to manifest dreams and lead others towards success.

on spirituality

...

major arcana

1. The Fool: Represents new beginnings, innocence, and trusting the universe in spiritual journeys.
2. The Magician: Symbolizes manifestation, personal power, and the ability to channel divine energy.
3. The High Priestess: Suggests intuition, inner wisdom, and connecting with the subconscious mind and spiritual realms.
4. The Empress: Reflects nurturing energy, fertility, and the divine feminine aspect of creation and abundance.
5. The Emperor: Signifies structure, authority, and the manifestation of divine order and stability.
6. The Hierophant: Represents tradition, spiritual guidance, and connecting with higher wisdom or teachings.
7. The Lovers: Symbolizes union, balance, and the merging of opposites in spiritual partnerships and connections.
8. The Chariot: Reflects willpower, determination, and spiritual victory over obstacles or challenges.
9. Strength: Signifies inner strength, courage, and overcoming ego-driven desires to connect with spiritual truths.
10. The Hermit: Suggests introspection, solitude, and seeking inner guidance and enlightenment.
11. Wheel of Fortune: Represents destiny, cycles of life, and the continuous flow of spiritual evolution.

12. Justice: Symbolizes fairness, balance, and karmic justice in spiritual matters.
13. The Hanged Man: Reflects surrender, sacrifice, and seeing situations from a higher perspective in spiritual growth.
14. Death: Signifies transformation, endings, and spiritual rebirth or renewal.
15. Temperance: Represents harmony, balance, and integration of opposing forces on a spiritual level.
16. The Devil: Symbolizes bondage, materialism, and the illusion of separateness from the divine in spiritual paths.
17. The Tower: Reflects sudden change, upheaval, and the breaking down of false structures on a spiritual journey.
18. The Star: Suggests hope, inspiration, and spiritual renewal, guiding the way towards enlightenment and inner peace.
19. The Moon: Represents intuition, subconscious mind, and navigating through illusions on the spiritual path.
20. The Sun: Symbolizes enlightenment, joy, and spiritual fulfillment, radiating divine blessings and clarity.
21. Judgment: Reflects spiritual awakening, redemption, and embracing one's true purpose and calling.
22. The World: Signifies completion, integration, and spiritual fulfillment, representing unity and oneness with the cosmos.

minor arcana:

cups:

- Ace of Cups: Represents spiritual love, emotional fulfillment, and divine blessings overflowing.
- Two of Cups: Symbolizes spiritual union, harmony, and deep connections with others on a soul level.
- Three of Cups: Reflects celebration, joy, and spiritual unity with community and loved ones.
- Four of Cups: Suggests introspection, spiritual discontent, and the need to seek deeper meaning and fulfillment.
- Five of Cups: Signifies spiritual loss, grief, and the opportunity for inner healing and transformation.
- Six of Cups: Represents nostalgia, innocence, and reconnecting with spiritual roots and childhood memories.
- Seven of Cups: Reflects spiritual choices, dreams, and fantasies, urging discernment and focus on higher truths.
- Eight of Cups: Symbolizes spiritual journey, leaving behind what no longer serves, and seeking deeper spiritual fulfillment.

- Nine of Cups: Suggests spiritual contentment, inner joy, and the fulfillment of spiritual desires.
- Ten of Cups: Represents spiritual harmony, bliss, and divine blessings within relationships and family.
- Page of Cups: Represents the beginning of emotional understanding and intuitive insights on the spiritual journey. This card suggests receptivity to spiritual messages, dreams, and the exploration of inner realms of emotion and intuition.
- Knight of Cups: Represents the quest for emotional fulfillment, inner harmony, and spiritual connection. This card encourages following the heart's desires, seeking spiritual experiences, and embodying compassion and empathy.
- Queen of Cups: Represents emotional depth, intuition, and spiritual receptivity. This card encourages nurturing inner wisdom, cultivating compassion, and embracing the flow of emotions on the spiritual journey.
- King of Cups: Represents emotional balance, compassion, and spiritual wisdom. This card encourages leading with empathy, fostering harmony in relationships, and trusting intuition as a guide on the spiritual path.

swords:

- Ace of Swords: Signifies clarity of thought, truth, and spiritual breakthroughs in understanding.
- Two of Swords: Reflects spiritual balance, inner conflict, and the need for clarity and decision-making.
- Three of Swords: Represents spiritual pain, heartache, and the opportunity for spiritual healing and growth.
- Four of Swords: Symbolizes spiritual rest, meditation, and inner peace amidst life's challenges.
- Five of Swords: Suggests spiritual conflict, disharmony, and the need for spiritual understanding and forgiveness.
- Six of Swords: Represents spiritual transition, moving towards peace, and finding spiritual guidance amidst challenges.
- Seven of Swords: Reflects spiritual deception, dishonesty, and the need for spiritual integrity and honesty.
- Eight of Swords: Signifies spiritual bondage, feeling trapped, and the journey towards spiritual liberation and truth.
- Nine of Swords: Symbolizes spiritual anxiety, fear, and the need to surrender worries to higher guidance and trust.
- Ten of Swords: Represents spiritual endings, release, and the opportunity for spiritual renewal and transformation.

- Page of Swords: Signifies the pursuit of truth, knowledge, and mental clarity on the spiritual path. This card encourages questioning, seeking answers, and embracing intellectual curiosity as a means of spiritual growth and understanding.
- Knight of Swords: Signifies the pursuit of truth, mental clarity, and spiritual breakthroughs. This card encourages taking decisive action, seeking intellectual understanding, and cutting through illusions on the spiritual journey.
- Queen of Swords: Signifies clarity of thought, intellectual insight, and spiritual discernment. This card encourages honesty, authenticity, and clear communication in spiritual matters, cutting through confusion and illusion.
- King of Swords: Signifies intellectual clarity, authority, and spiritual truth. This card encourages embodying integrity, seeking knowledge and wisdom, and upholding principles of justice and fairness in spiritual pursuits.

pentacles:

- Ace of Pentacles: Signifies spiritual abundance, prosperity, and the manifestation of spiritual blessings in the material world.
- Two of Pentacles: Reflects spiritual balance, adaptability, and finding harmony between spiritual and material aspects of life.
- Three of Pentacles: Represents spiritual collaboration, craftsmanship, and the alignment of spiritual purpose with practical work.
- Four of Pentacles: Symbolizes spiritual stability, security, and the need to release attachment to material possessions on the spiritual path.
- Five of Pentacles: Suggests spiritual hardship, feeling disconnected from divine abundance, and the need for spiritual resilience and trust.
- Six of Pentacles: Reflects spiritual generosity, sharing blessings, and the alignment of material wealth with spiritual principles.
- Seven of Pentacles: Signifies spiritual patience, perseverance, and the need to trust in divine timing and the natural cycles of growth.
- Eight of Pentacles: Represents spiritual dedication, craftsmanship, and the pursuit of spiritual mastery through diligent practice.
- Nine of Pentacles: Symbolizes spiritual independence, self-sufficiency, and the cultivation of spiritual abundance and inner wealth.

- Ten of Pentacles: Reflects spiritual legacy, ancestral wisdom, and the fulfillment of spiritual purpose within the material world.
- Page of Pentacles: Reflects the practical application of spirituality, the willingness to learn, and the pursuit of mastery in the material world. This card suggests grounding spiritual insights into tangible actions and experiences, fostering growth and abundance.
- Knight of Pentacles: Reflects dedication, reliability, and the disciplined pursuit of spiritual goals. This card suggests embodying patience, perseverance, and practicality in spiritual endeavors, laying solid foundations for long-term growth.
- Queen of Pentacles: Reflects practical wisdom, abundance, and spiritual nurturing. This card suggests grounding spiritual insights into everyday life, nurturing growth and stability, and fostering a deep connection with the natural world.
- King of Pentacles: Reflects material abundance, practical wisdom, and spiritual mastery. This card suggests embodying stability, providing support and guidance to others on the spiritual journey, and manifesting spiritual goals into tangible reality.

wands:

- Ace of Wands: Signifies spiritual inspiration, passion, and the ignition of spiritual creativity and potential.
- Two of Wands: Reflects spiritual vision, planning, and the exploration of new spiritual horizons and possibilities.
- Three of Wands: Represents spiritual expansion, growth, and the manifestation of spiritual goals and aspirations.
- Four of Wands: Symbolizes spiritual celebration, harmony, and the alignment of spiritual energies in sacred union.
- Five of Wands: Suggests spiritual competition, conflict, and the need for spiritual cooperation and understanding.
- Six of Wands: Reflects spiritual victory, recognition, and the affirmation of spiritual purpose and achievement.
- Seven of Wands: Signifies spiritual courage, standing up for spiritual beliefs, and defending spiritual truths.
- Eight of Wands: Represents spiritual momentum, swift spiritual progress, and the flow of divine energy in action.
- Nine of Wands: Symbolizes spiritual resilience, perseverance, and the strength to overcome spiritual challenges and obstacles.
- Ten of Wands: Reflects spiritual responsibility, burdens, and the need to release spiritual burdens and trust in divine support.

- Page of Wands: Symbolizes passion, inspiration, and the pursuit of spiritual adventures and creative endeavors. This card encourages taking bold steps forward, embracing opportunities for growth, and igniting the flame of spiritual enthusiasm.
- Knight of Wands: Symbolizes passion, inspiration, and the pursuit of spiritual adventures. This card encourages embracing spontaneity, taking risks, and following one's intuition on the spiritual path.
- Queen of Wands: Symbolizes creativity, passion, and spiritual leadership. This card encourages embracing one's inner fire, inspiring others on the spiritual journey, and manifesting dreams with confidence and determination.
- King of Wands: Symbolizes passion, vision, and spiritual leadership. This card encourages taking bold action, inspiring others with enthusiasm, and pursuing spiritual goals with confidence and courage.

tarot timing

・・・

TAROT CARDS ARE a versatile tool for gaining insights into various aspects of life, including the timing of events. While traditional tarot readings focus on understanding situations, emotions, and guidance, using tarot for timing adds an extra layer of depth to your readings. By associating specific cards with timeframes, you can get a sense of when something is likely to happen.

major arcana and timing

The Major Arcana cards are often linked to significant life events and longer time periods. Each card can represent a specific astrological sign, season, or a more abstract concept of timing:

1. **The Fool** - Unexpectedly
2. **The Magician** - Quickly
3. **The High Priestess** - It's a secret, or it's unknown
4. **The Empress** - When components align
5. **The Emperor** - March 21 - April 20 (Aries)
6. **The Hierophant** - April 21 - May 21 (Taurus)
7. **The Lovers** - May 22 - June 21 (Gemini)
8. **The Chariot** - June 22 - July 22 (Cancer)
9. **Strength** - July 23 - August 23 (Leo)
10. **The Hermit** - August 24 - September 22 (Virgo)
11. **Wheel of Fortune** - It's a surprise
12. **Justice** - September 23 - October 23 (Libra)

13. **The Hanged Man** - Patience, delays, waiting
14. **Death** - October 24 - November 22 (Scorpio)
15. **Temperance** - November 23 - December 21 (Sagittarius)
16. **The Devil** - December 22 - January 20 (Capricorn)
17. **The Tower** - Abruptly
18. **The Star** - January 21 - February 18 (Aquarius)
19. **The Moon** - February 19 - March 20 (Pisces)
20. **The Sun** - Daytime, Summer
21. **Judgment** - Quick, Slow, Permanent
22. **The World** - Slow but successful

minor arcana and timing

The Minor Arcana cards are divided into four suits, each with its own pace and associated timeframes:

swords (fastest moving – measured in days)

1. **Ace of Swords** - Fall Season
2. **Two of Swords** - September 23 – October 2
3. **Three of Swords** - October 3 – October 12
4. **Four of Swords** - October 13 – October 22
5. **Five of Swords** - January 20 – January 29
6. **Six of Swords** - January 30 – February 8
7. **Seven of Swords** - February 9 – February 18
8. **Eight of Swords** - May 21 – May 31
9. **Nine of Swords** - June 1 – June 10
10. **Ten of Swords** - June 11 – June 20
11. **Page of Swords** - December 22 – March 20
12. **Knight of Swords** - May 11 – January 10
13. **Queen of Swords** - September 12 – October 12
14. **King of Swords** - January 10 – February 8

wands (fast moving – measured in weeks)

1. **Ace of Wands** - Spring Season
2. **Two of Wands** - March 21 – March 30
3. **Three of Wands** - March 31 – April 10
4. **Four of Wands** - April 11 – April 20
5. **Five of Wands** - July 22 – August 1
6. **Six of Wands** - August 2 – August 11
7. **Seven of Wands** - August 12 – August 22

8. **Eight of Wands** - November 23 – December 2
9. **Nine of Wands** - December 3 – December 12
10. **Ten of Wands** - December 13 – December 21
11. **Page of Wands** - January 21 – September 22
12. **Knight of Wands** - November 13 – December 12
13. **Queen of Wands** - March 11 – April 10
14. **King of Wands** - July 12 – August 11

cups (slow moving – measured in months)

1. **Ace of Cups** - Summer Season
2. **Two of Cups** - June 21 – July 1
3. **Three of Cups** - July 2 – July 11
4. **Four of Cups** - July 12 – July 21
5. **Five of Cups** - October 23 – November 1
6. **Six of Cups** - November 2 – November 12
7. **Seven of Cups** - November 13 – November 22
8. **Eight of Cups** - February 19 – February 29
9. **Nine of Cups** - March 1 – March 10
10. **Ten of Cups** - March 11 – March 20
11. **Page of Cups** - September 23 – December 21
12. **Knight of Cups** - February 9 – March 10
13. **Queen of Cups** - June 11 – July 11
14. **King of Cups** - October 13 – November 12

pentacles (slowest moving – measured in years)

1. **Ace of Pentacles** - Winter Season
2. **Two of Pentacles** - December 22 – December 30
3. **Three of Pentacles** - December 31 – January 9
4. **Four of Pentacles** - January 10 – January 19
5. **Five of Pentacles** - April 21 – April 30
6. **Six of Pentacles** - May 1 – May 10
7. **Seven of Pentacles** - May 11 – May 20
8. **Eight of Pentacles** - August 23 – September 1
9. **Nine of Pentacles** - September 2 – September 11
10. **Ten of Pentacles** - September 12 – September 22
11. **Page of Pentacles** - March 21 – June 20
12. **Knight of Pentacles** - August 12 – September 11
13. **Queen of Pentacles** - December 13 – January 9
14. **King of Pentacles** - April 11 – May 10

Lorelai Hamilton

Using tarot for timing can add precision to your readings and provide you with a better understanding of when events might unfold. Whether you're planning a new venture, anticipating changes, or seeking the right moment to act, let the cards guide you on your journey.

about the author

Lorelai Hamilton is a seasoned tarot reader with over 15 years of professional experience in the field. Based in the enchanting landscapes of the Pacific Northwest, Lorelai has honed her craft and established herself as a trusted guide in the realm of tarot.

Her passion for tarot led her to create the renowned Living Color Tarot Deck, a vibrant and illuminating tool for spiritual exploration and self-discovery.

Alongside her tarot practice, Lorelai shares her expertise with a global audience. Having conducted readings for individuals across 25 countries, she has cultivated a deep understanding of the universal human experience and the interconnectedness of souls around the world.

Despite her worldly reach, Lorelai remains dedicated to providing personal and insightful readings for clients, offering virtual consultations that resonate with authenticity and compassion. In her journey as a tarot reader, she has been accompanied by her familiar, Ham, whose quiet presence adds an element of magic to her practice.

With a profound commitment to her craft and a heart open to the mysteries of the universe, Lorelai Hamilton continues to illuminate the paths of those who seek guidance, insight, and spiritual clarity through the ancient art of tarot.

Unlock the secrets of the Tarot! Subscribe to Lorelai Hamilton's newsletter and get a free ebook. Whether you're a seasoned reader or just curious, this guide will enhance your journey. Plus, be the first to know about upcoming books, events, and more!

Lorelai Hamilton

acknowledgments

This book has been a labor of love over the past five years, fueled by my passion for teaching tarot, a practice I've devoted myself to for the past decade. Throughout this journey, numerous individuals have inspired and supported me, and their contributions deserve heartfelt recognition. Thank you to my husband for supporting all my endeavors with endless encouragement and love.

To Jackson, thank you for your unwavering encouragement and relentless commitment to excellence, which has consistently motivated me to improve as a tarot reader. Your willingness to learn and push the boundaries of understanding is one of my favorite things.

I am profoundly thankful to my students, whose enthusiasm and curiosity have fueled my desire to share the transformative power of tarot with the world. Special mention goes to Ryan for countless late-night readings, delving into the mysteries of the cards together. You've made me a better reader for it. I miss all night tarot readings more than words will ever convey.

To my old friends Natalie, Nhi, Deb, Sara, and countless others who have offered unwavering support over the years and reminded me of the essence of who I am and why I embarked on this journey. I am eternally grateful.

Finally, to you, dear reader, who now holds this book in your hands, embarking on your own tarot journey—I extend my sincerest congratulations. May the wisdom and insights contained within these pages serve as guiding lights along your path, empowering you to trust in the magic of tarot and the intuition that lies within you.

With boundless gratitude and love,

-Lorelai

Lorelai Hamilton

additional titles by lorelai hamilton

Additional Titles by Lorelai Hamilton

Additional Titles by Lorelai Hamilton

Additional Titles by Lorelai Hamilton

Additional Titles by Lorelai Hamilton

Additional Titles by Lorelai Hamilton

Additional Titles by Lorelai Hamilton

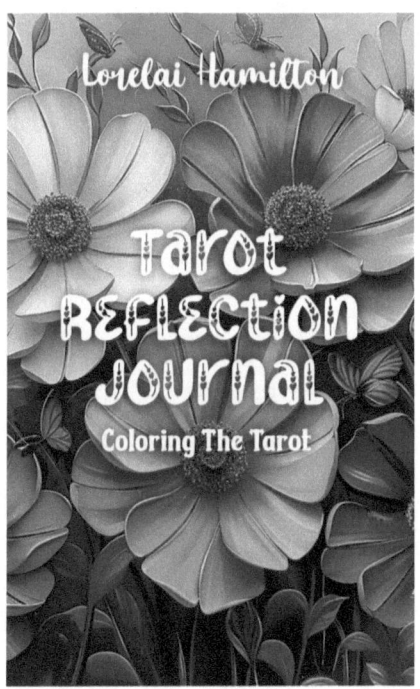

www.ingramcontent.com/pod-product-compliance
Lightning Source LLC
Chambersburg PA
CBHW030329240426
43661CB00052B/1572